T0400023

Writing, Speech and Flesh in Lacanian Psychoanalysis

This book explores the place of the flesh in the linguistically-inflected categories of Freudian and Lacanian psychoanalysis, drawing explicit attention to the organic as an inherent part of the linguistic categories that appear in the writings of Freud and Lacan.

Lacan's 'return to Freud' famously involves a 'linguistic turn' in psychoanalysis. The centering of language as a major operator in psychic life often leads to a dualistic or quasi-dualistic view in which language and the enjoyment of the body are polarized. Exploring the intricate connections of the linguistic and the organic in both Lacanian and Freudian psychoanalysis from its beginnings, Zisser shows that surprisingly, and not only in Lacan's late teaching, psycho-linguistic categories turn out to be suffused with organicity. After unfolding the remnant of the flesh in the signifier as a major component of Lacan's critique of Saussure, using visual artworks as objective correlatives as it does so, the book delineates two forms of psychic writing. These are aligned not only with two fundamental states of the psychic apparatus as described by Freud (pain and satisfaction), but with two ways of sculpting formulated by Alberti in the Renaissance but also referred to by Freud. Continuing in a Derridean vein, the book demonstrates the primacy of writing to speech in psychoanalysis, emphasizing how the relation between speech and writing is not binary but topological, as speech in its psychoanalytic conception is nothing but the folding inside-out of unconscious writing.

Innovatively placing the flesh at the core of its approach, the text also incorporates the seminal work of psychoanalyst Michèle Montrelay to articulate the precise relation between the linguistic and the organic. *Writing, Speech and Flesh in Lacanian Psychoanalysis* will be indispensable to psychoanalysts, literary theorists, rhetoricians, deconstructionists, and those studying at the intersection of psychoanalysis, language, and the visual arts.

Shirley Zisser practises Lacanian psychoanalysis in Tel Aviv, Israel. She is a member of the World Association of Psychoanalysis (AMP) and an associate professor of English at Tel Aviv University. Her work focuses on the interrelations between poetics, rhetorical and literary theory and psychoanalysis. Her publications include *The Risks of Simile in Renaissance Rhetoric* (2001), *Critical Essays on Shakespeare's 'A Lover's Complaint': Suffering Ecstasy* (2005, ed.), *Lacanian Interpretations of Shakespeare* (2009, ed.) and *Art, Death and Lacanian Psychoanalysis* (Routledge 2018, with Efrat Biberman).

Writing, Speech and Flesh in Lacanian Psychoanalysis

Of Unconscious Grammatology

Shirley Zisser

Routledge
Taylor & Francis Group

LONDON AND NEW YORK

First published 2022
by Routledge
2 Park Square, Milton Park, Abingdon, Oxon OX14 4RN

and by Routledge
605 Third Avenue, New York, NY 10158

Routledge is an imprint of the Taylor & Francis Group, an informa
business

British Library Cataloguing-in-Publication Data
A catalogue record for this book is available from the British Library

Library of Congress Cataloging-in-Publication Data
A catalog record has been requested for this book

ISBN: 978-0-367-48089-9 (hbk)
ISBN: 978-0-367-48088-2 (pbk)
ISBN: 978-1-003-03795-8 (ebk)

DOI: 10.4324/9781003037958

Typeset in Times New Roman
by SPi Technologies India Pvt Ltd (Straive)

Contents

Figures

Acknowledgments

Figure 0.1: Michal Na'aman, *The Man who Laughs with Cuts* (Crimson Joy) 2009. Oil and masking tape on canvas, 160 × 190 cm, private collection. Reproduced with the kind permission of the artist.

Figure 1.1: Bartolomé Esteban Murillo, *Self-Portrait*, c. 1670. Oil on canvas, 122 × 107 cm. © The National Gallery, London.

Figure 1.2: Annibale Carracci, *Self-Portrait on an Easel*, Italy, 1603–1604. Oil on panel. 42.5 × 30 cm. © State Hermitage Museum. Reproduced with the kind permission of the State Hermitage Museum, St. Petersburg.

Figure 1.3: Georg Friedrich Kersting, *Caspar David Friedrich in his Studio* (in the Dresden suburb Pirna, An der Elbe 26). Painting, c. 1812. Oil on canvas, 51 × 40 cm. Berlin, SMB, Alte Nationalgalerie. © akg-image.

Figure 1.4: Pompei, Villa of Mysteries, detail of salon decoration. Reproduced with the kind permission of the Ministero per i Beni e le Attività Culturali e per il Turismo – Parco Archeologico di Pompei.

Figure 1.5: Lucio Fontana, *Concetto Spaziale, Attese*, 1964. Water-based paint on canvas, 73 × 92 cm, catalogue no. 64 T 10. © Fondazione Lucio Fontana.

Figure 1.6: Lucio Fontana, *Taglio*, Milan, 1964. 567 × 787 cm. Photo Ugo Mulas © Ugo Mulas Heirs. All rights reserved.

Figure 2.1: Gian-Lorenzo Bernini, Apollo and Daphne, 1622–1625, Rome, Galleria Borghese, MiBACT – Borghese Gallery/photo: Luciano Romano. Reproduced courtesy of the Borghese Gallery, Rome.

Figure 2.2: Gian-Lorenzo Bernini, The Ecstasy of St. Teresa, 1647–1652, sculpture in marble, stucco, and gilt bronze, height 350 cm, Church of Santa Maria della Vittoria, Rome, photo © Bibliotheca Hertziana – Max-Planck-Institut für Kunstgeschichte, Rome.

Figure 4.1: Michal Na'aman, *Goulash*, 2005. Oil on canvas, 30 × 40 cm, artist's collection. Reproduced courtesy of the artist.

Epigraph featured at the start of Chapter 2 is taken from Jacques Lacan, 'Geneva Lecture on the Symptom', 1975, trans. Russell Grigg, Analysis 1, 1989, p. 24. Translation reproduced with the kind permission of Russell Grigg.

The first section in the third chapter of this book is a revised version of 'The Signifier in Motion: The Movement of Language in Psychoanalysis and in Aristotle's Linguistic Theory,' published in volume 28, number 3 (2016), of Fractal: Revista de Psicologia, available at: https://periodicos.uff.br/fractal/article/view/5140/4994.

Reprinted with kind permission of the editors.

Personal acknowledgments

This book is the product of a trajectory that has been long, at times excruciating, but always exciting. It was propelled by a desire to learn something more about the enigmas of language, spoken and written, in psychoanalysis, and their intrication with the flesh of the subject who speaks, but sometimes does not. The trajectory took me through the winding, often tortuous, but always impassioning route of a personal analysis. It is, in many ways, a product of this analysis and of the psychoanalytic formation and practice that ensued. My deepest and sincere thanks are due first of all to the man who for years and years has been silently listening and reading from behind the analytic couch, from the place of the cause, his attentive silences and precise punctuations helping me chisel out a route for my life and my desire in what sometimes seemed a momentous and opaque bloc of an undialectizable real that at first knew how to speak only in inhibitions, symptoms and anxieties.

The style of theorizing that informs what has finally become an art object in the world would not be as it is, were it not for the extraordinary brilliance of my fellow dreamer and *compagnon de route* of many years, Stephen Whitworth.

My thanks also to those few who were willing to read portions of this book while it was in the making: Michal Na'aman, Zafra Dan, Tamar Gerstenhaber and Keren Shafir. The rigour and medical knowledge of Atara Messinger helped me refine my reading of *Freud's Project for a Scientific Psychology* on many important points. Efrat Biberman has been a wise and faithful companion to this project as to many others, and her help with the graphic dimension of this book has been invaluable.

As this book makes its way to press, many parts of the world are under quarantine. Travel is all but impossible. Nevertheless, part of the desire this book speaks and speaks of is inseparable from the structure of displacement. To use the words of John Donne, many portions of this book were written in a breach that was at the same time an expansion – in London, Berlin, Rome – cities woven closely into my subjective texture. While contingency prevents the book's ending where it began, in the beautiful green of South East London, it is perhaps fitting that it should come to a close in my home in Tel Aviv. For it is here that I can appropriately inscribe my most profound thanks of all: to the man who has made my very life happily possible. Beyond anyone and anything else, the writing and completion of this book could not have been were it not for the quiet, solid, quotidian presence, support, and love of my very beloved husband, Eyal Zisser.

Tel Aviv, July 2020

Introduction

'The smile is a cut'

Israeli artist Michal Na'aman's 'The Man who Laughs,' is part of a series of works displaying what has become a stylistic dominant of her artistic endeavour since the mid-1990s: multi-layered masking-tape paintings which include a text. The paintings are produced by means of laborious technique. The artist divides the canvas into two unequal rectangles, one on top of the other, then divides each one of the rectangles into small squares she paints over in different colors. She then covers the outline of each one of the rectangles by means of strips of masking tape. The newly produced rectangle is again divided into squares which she paints over, covering the new rectangle again with strips of masking tape. This procedure is repeated again and again till the entire surface of the canvas is covered by a thick fabric of masking tape strips which create a pyramid of sorts. The painted squares remain covered, the dripping onto the surface of the painting their only trace. The painting's title is usually a phrase painted onto the canvas by means of a template or letter set.[1]

This particular painting involves another technique: the use of a razor blade or knife (such as had appeared in iconographic form in Na'aman's early collage works),[2] to carve into the three-dimensional surface obtained, exposing the color painted onto the otherwise hidden layers of squares. In 'The Man who Laughs,' the most prominent cut is a semi-circle in the middle upper part of the canvas, indexed by the self-referential text at the painting's bottom middle part: 'the smile is a cut.' The deep cut of the smile is supplemented by smaller and narrower cuts throughout the painting's middle section. Against the white background of much of this middle section, these cuts resemble bleeding cuts or scratches on skin (Figure 0.1).

Na'aman's work silently evokes a relation between pain-ting and pain. As some of the ensuing sections of this book will demonstrate, this relation, plastically animating much of Na'aman's work, has an intellectual antecedent in in the early work of Sigmund Freud, specifically the *Project for a Scientific Psychology* of 1895. The components of the nervous system, what Freud would later denominate the psychical apparatus, Freud writes there, are organic particles susceptible of being connected (in medical parlance, synapsing), and, more significantly, 'of being permanently altered by single

DOI: 10.4324/9781003037958-1

Figure 0.1 Michal Na'aman, *The Man Who Laughs with Cuts (Crimson Joy)* 2009.
Oil and masking tape on canvas 160 x 190 cm, private collection.
Source: Reproduced with the kind permission of the artist.

occurrences,' this propensity to alteration amounting to the potential production of a semiotic element: 'a possibility for representing memory.'[3] This alteration that terminates in a representation is predicated on the passage of a quantity of energy Freud labels 'Q' through the organic particles, on condition that these particles resist this passage.

In Letter 52 to Wilhelm Fliess, written a year later, Freud grants the product of the alteration of the organic particles by the energy that passes through them an even clearer semantic inflection: he calls them '*Zeichen*' [signs] a close homophone of '*Zeichnen*' [to draw], a verb that in German carries the same equivocation between 'to sketch' and 'to drag' as its English equivalent. The alteration of organic particles by the energy that passes through them, which, Freud says, amounts to representing memory, then, is, in Freudian terms, a drawing (of signs). In the same letter to Fliess, Freud gives the drawing or making of signs another name, the name of writing: underwriting [*Neiderschrift*] and repeated writing [*Weiderschrift*]. In the *Project*, Freud adds one other qualification to what is drawn/written in the particles of the psychic system. Since the particles are organic tissue, the passage of excitation through them gives rise to a *Reizbarkeit* [irritation].[4] What is written or drawn in organic substance, in other words, is an irritation resulting from a subtraction of that substance by what passes through it. The writing instituting memory, that is, is an irritation, a painful wound, in Na'aman's terms, a cut.

Na'aman's pain-ting offers an intriguing analogue to Freud's account of psychic writing. The masking tape blocks, varying in thickness, function as the organic particles, which are more or less dense, more or less filled with quantum, which makes them more or less permeable. The knife cuts made in the thick masking tape blocks are homologous with the irritation Freud speaks of, and the knowledge Na'aman offers psychoanalysis, especially in the blood-red color of the cuts, is perhaps an underscoring of pain as an inevitable price of psychic writing, even and perhaps especially when, as in the work above, it has the shape of a smile. If we follow the cue Freud gives us as he begins to discover psychoanalysis, a writing that is a cut in the flesh, that is what hurts in the smile, is at the very foundation of psychic life.

And yet when Lacan embarks on his return to Freud in the early 1950s, it is not the pain of painting, the cut of writing even when it is a smile that Na'aman's work accentuates, that he places at center stage. Indeed, it is only decades later that Lacan returns to the question of writing with full force. The aspect of language that the early seminars and *Écrits* foreground is not writing but speech, the medium in which the unconscious manifests itself in clinical work.

'Whether it wishes to be an agent of healing, training, or sounding the depths, psychoanalysis has but one medium: the patient's speech,' Lacan asserts in the programmatic 'Function and Field of Speech and Language'.[5] Desire, that elusive quality that Lacan insisted till quite late in his teaching is the essence of man, what makes the pain of existence possible to bear,[6] 'always becomes manifest at the joint of speech, where it makes its appearance, its sudden emergence. its surge forwards. Desire emerges just as it becomes embodied in speech.'[7]

What is more surprising is that as of *Seminar 18*, with the essay 'Lituraterre,' which includes a theorization of writing in terms of the pathways breached by water on land in the planes of Siberia as seen from an airplane,[8] Lacan's works manifest a growing interest in writing. Writing, for instance the writing on the wall in the Book of Daniel, reappears as a focus of interest in the text on the knowledge of the analyst, along with a meditation taking its cue from the notebooks of Leonardo da Vinci, in which painting, the layering of color upon a canvas, is distinguished from sculpture, an art that, Leonardo writes, proceeds by subtraction: the sculptor's chiseling at a slab of marble until a figure emerges from it.[9] The following year, in *Encore*, Lacan again devotes a lesson to writing, to which Jacques-Alain Miller gave the title 'The Function of the Written.'[10] In this lesson, Lacan returns to the theorization of writing as '*ravinement*,' the hollowing out of material from rocks by the waters that pass through them.[11] What is considered one of Lacan's major theoretical innovations in this seminar, the formulae of sexuation, is formalized not only in terms of Fregean predicate logic which tries to capture femininity or masculinity in relation to the phallus (signifier of castration) as quantifier, but in terms of a relation to writing. For instance, feminine, supplementary jouissance, such as the jouissance of the mystics who 'experience it but can say nothing about it,'[12] is formalized as 'what does not stop not being written,'[13] and a singular solution a woman invents to limit the often ravaging Other jouissance, Lacan's version of the '*Ablehnung der Weiblichkeit*' [repudiation of femininity][14] is formalized as what 'stops not being written.'[15] In the same seminar, Lacan introduces knot theory (specifically, the Borromean knot) as a more precise model of the psyche than the one which Saussurean linguistics had provided him. He divorces this structure from the signifier and signification, but not from writing: an alphabetical letter, Lacan says, is nothing but a flattened knot.[16]

From whence this shift from the emphasis on speech to an emphasis on writing and what does it have to do with the structure of the *parlêtre* Lacan advances in his late work? What, more specifically, might we learn from what one might call the scriptorial turn in Lacan's late teaching about the intrication of language, spoken and written, with the flesh?

The book before you is an attempt to answer this question. The answer it proposes results in an undoing of the binarism on which the question is based, namely the neat division between Lacan's late and early teaching. For this book finds the roots of Lacan's thinking of the intrication of language and flesh in instances of writing in seminal essays of what is commonly considered Lacan's structuralist period, emphasizing the signifier and the register of the symbolic, such as 'The Instance of the Letter in the Unconscious' and 'The Signification of the Phallus.' Most significantly, this book finds the roots of Lacan's scriptorial turn in some of the earliest work of the founder of psychoanalysis, Sigmund Freud, most importantly in the great roadmap that is the posthumously published *Project for a Scientific Psychology*, as well as the letter to Wilhelm Fliess of 6 December 1896, known as 'Letter 52.' The theory of language extractable from these early Freudian texts shakes neat binarisms between representation and quantum, or in Lacanian terms, between the signifier and jouissance. For in the *Project*, Freud theorizes representation as an unpleasurable irritation [*Reizbarkeit*][17] in organic neuronal matter, in effect, as a wound. This wound occurs in organic matter and is of the order of writing: Freud's term for it is

'*Neiderschrift*' [primal writing or under-writing].[18] Freud's thinking of the psychic apparatus in the *Project* and Letter 52, that is, grants logical precedence to writing over speech, an attribute ostensibly rare in Western thinking about language against which Jacques Derrida was to pitch his enterprise of deconstruction.

The question of the relation between writing and speech in which this book engages has obvious resonances with the grammatological project which Jacques Derrida unfolded from the late 1960s on in a series of groundbreaking studies, from *Of Grammatology* through *Writing and Difference*, not without explicitly engaging psychoanalysis.[19] Derrida's well-known claim is that Western thought about language, from Rousseau (and his antecedents) to Saussure is predicated on a hierarchical binarism, on the 'reduction of writing to the rank of an instrument enslaved to a full and originarily spoken language.'[20] Derrida's grand philosophical project, then, would be to 'liberate … the future of a general grammatology of which linguistics-phonology would be only a dependent and circumscribed area,'[21] to restore writing from the margins of philosophy[22] while pondering the stakes of its relegation to the margins.

It is a basic contention of this book, however, that the grammatology Derrida has in mind, and which involves the primacy of writing to speech, had already taken place, as he himself intuits in 'Freud and the Scene of Writing.' One of the sources of this grammatology is in the early and also foundational texts of Freudian metapsychology such as the *Project* and Letter 52. The locus of the grammatology at stake in this book is thus neither page nor brick wall but the fleshly walls of bodily orifices, real sources of the drive, for which the cavernous walls of the chapel of St. Anne are but an objective correlative.[23] Hence the book's subtitle: *Of Unconscious Grammatology*.

The book begins its mapping of unconscious grammatology wherein writing in the flesh logically precedes speech in the flesh with an exploration of the implication of the organic in some of Freud's psycho-semiotic categories. It also points to the organic ground of the unconscious signifier, theorized by Lacan as homologous with the hysterical symptom, which presents as a somatic lesion. Continuing to interrogate Freudian metapsychology in a Derridean vein but attending to the role of the flesh in the linguistic categories of metapsychology, the book emphasizes the logical primacy, for psychoanalysis, of psychic writing over speech, itself always an action of a body that lives.

This book, then, examines the place of the flesh in the linguistic components of the psyche from the vantage point of Lacanian psychoanalysis upon its Freudian roots. Although the question of the impact of speech on the body has been extensively discussed in Lacanian psychoanalysis, this book emphasizes that the linguistically-inflected categories of Freudian and Lacanian metapsychology not only affect the subject's flesh. They are themselves always already intricated with it.

The book is divided into three chapters, each interrogating the intrication of flesh in the semiotic components of the psyche from a different angle. Launching the investigation, the inaugural section of the book puts into question the conventional view of Lacan's early work as a 'return to Freud' informed by Saussurean linguistics. Revisiting Lacan's treatment of the Saussurean sign, I point out that Lacan's major critique of Saussure, strong enough to lead Lacan to state that psychoanalytic practice runs counter to Saussure's model of the linguistic sign as the conjunction of a slice of the nebula of thought and a portion of phonic material,[24] has to do with this model's blindness to the organic. What Saussure's account of the sign elides is the role played by a morsel of flesh as the ground and price for the signifier in which it nevertheless continues to resonate.

Taking its cue from Lacan's reference to visual art in his theorization, in *La relation d'objet*, of the phallus, precipitate of castration, as a special instance of self-portraiture, a veil on which absence paints itself,[25] the book shows, via a discussion of several self-portraits from the history of art, how Lacan himself ultimately lifts this veil, arriving in ...*Ou pire* at a conceptualization of castration as a ground for writing as lesions and incisions in the flesh whose objective correlative in visual art is the slashed canvases of Lucio Fontana.

The second chapter of the book, which consists of four sections, develops the consequences of the conceptualization of the unconscious signifier as, in Lacan's words in 'The Youth of Gide,' 'written in the sand of the flesh,'[26] mainly via a return to the foundational text of Freudian metapsychology, the *Project for a Scientific Psychology* of 1895. In this seminal work, Freud identifies two primal states of the psychic apparatus: the experience of pain (whose affective correlate is anxiety) and the experience of satisfaction (whose affective correlate is a 'wishful state' akin to what Lacan would conceptualize as desire).[27] Each of these primordial experiences serves as the ground for a particular form of psychic writing involving the flesh: a writ(h)ing. These two forms of psychic writ(h)ing developed in Freud's *Project for a Scientific Psychology* and subsequent works on metapsychology are correlative to two forms of sculpting theorized by Leon Battista Alberti in *De statua* (1464) and by Leonardo da Vinci in his *Treatise on Painting* (c. 1540)[28]: the *via di porre* (way of addition) and *via di levare* (way of subtraction). Intriguingly, Freud, in his essay 'On Psychotherapy' (1904) refers to these two forms of sculpting, aligning psychoanalysis with the way of subtraction in contradistinction to the psychotherapeutic practice of suggestion, which proceeds by an addition of sense.[29] Yet beyond its underpinning the distinction between psychoanalysis and psychotherapy, Freud's use of the analogy to the ancient distinction between two ways of sculpting indexes a tacit recognition of their operativity for metapsychological theorizing.

Forms of psychic writing proceeding by way of addition that can be located in Freud's work are the character trait, the unary trait, and the stereotype plate described by Freud as crucial to the operation of the transference, the mainspring of the analytic cure. All three categories are theorized by Freud in terms borrowed from the sphere of printing or embossing. All are characterized by a petrification of excess jouissance in the living organism affected by language. Bespeaking a subjective position with regard to jouissance, they resist analytic deciphering, appearing as the kernel of symptoms, the navel of dreams, or as the subject's erotic conditions. These forms of psychic writing by way of addition first theorized in the texts of Freud are instances where the flesh constitutes forms of inscription that are of an order more primal than that of the signifier. These forms, Lacan writes in 'The Youth of Gide,' register instances in the subject's early life where 'the fire of an encounter has etched his coat of arms.'[30]

The second section in this chapter of the book is devoted to the specification of the unconscious signifier and other psycho-semiotic categories as theorized by Freud and Lacan as at least in part constituted of material that is organic, as written not only on but with portions of the organism. The section also finds an antecedent to the Freudian theorization of the unconscious signifier in rhetorical theorizations of memory as a writing in wax that proceeds by way of subtraction, and especially in the myth of the invention of memory by the poet Simonides, resonating in the rhetorical tradition since Cicero.[31] In this myth, it is a poet who enables a catastrophic real of unidentified corpses to be encrusted with a symbolic lining, whose name is memory and whose essence is burial. The unconscious signifier, then, is also sepulchral, a finding resonant with the Freudian conceptualization of the unconscious memory trace as a repository of cannibalized ancestral memories, a point developed in the fourth section of this chapter of the book.

In order to specify the place of the flesh in several major metapsychological categories, I turn to Freud's well-known article 'A Note Upon the Mystic Writing Pad' (1925), but especially to his conceptualization of memory traces in the *Project for a Scientific Psychology* (1895). I show that Freud conceives of the unconscious memory trace as grounded in the passage of libidinal quantum in a portion of organic substance that resists.[32] The passage of libido through resisting neuronal substance hollows out portions of this substance. This hollowing out leaves behind furrows which serve as the ground for the unconscious signifier. But because the hollowing out of neuronal substance by the passage of libido through it also generates its excitation [*Reizbarkeit*],[33] the ground of signification as theorized by Freud seems paradoxical, involving at once a subtraction (of organic material) and an addition (of surplus excitation). It is precisely this seeming paradox, however, that makes the unconscious signifier isomorphic, as Lacan suggests in the *Logic of the Phantasm*, with the hysterical symptom, predicated on the coalescence of repressions (involving a subtraction of signifiers from conscious articulation) and *ragades* (organic lesions that do not heal easily, that remain as portions of the organism where quantum is high).[34] The unconscious signifier is thus an instance of hysteria *in minima*, a hypomnestic effigy of flesh in suffering ecstasy that also knows very well how to disappear.

Following Lacan's rereading of Freud's *Project*, especially in *Seminar 7*, the book proceeds, in its third section, to unfold the relation between writing and speech in psychoanalysis not as binary and hierarchical but as topological. Writing turns speech in a topological movement, which Lacan in *The Four Fundamental Concepts of Psychoanalysis* calls a 'syncopating pulsation,'[35] wherein the unconscious folds inside out to eject through the organic rim of the lips a memory trace coupled with what Freud calls a sound presentation [*Klangvorstellung*].[36] The first section in this chapter, based on a close reading of Freud's *Project* and of Lacan's reading of the *Project* in *The Ethics of Psychoanalysis*, consists in mapping the vicissitudes of psychic writ(h)ing, signifiers or memory traces pulsating in portions of flesh, as they percolate towards speech.

Speech as derived from its conceptualization in Freud's *Project* is grounded in the movements of writ(h)ings in the psychic apparatus, motion at its highest intensity, greater, Freud claims, than any intensity achievable by the motor apparatus or musculature.[37] This allows me to arrive at a definition of speech as grounded in unconscious writ(h)ing subjected to movement in the psychic apparatus. At times, this intensity of this movement is such that speech acquires real value. The second section in this chapter of the book offers a typology of spoken signifiers in the real, specifying their different inflections in different clinical structures. This section shows that speech acquires real value not only for the schizophrenic, but occasionally also for the obsessional neurotic who makes it an instrument of sadistic jouissance, or for the hysteric who registers it as a periodically inflamed *ragade* that in-forms her speech, at times so loaded with quantum it emerges as silence, a blank in the chain of signifiers she unfolds in the transference where it is not her lips but her silent body that speaks on the couch.

Beyond clinical structures, the book specifies a signifier of real value, a portion of what both Jacques-Alain Miller and Colette Soler have recently called the real unconscious. This portion of enjoying flesh turned word is an instance of an unprecedented signifier carved out from the ground of feminine jouissance, a ground which Freud describes as 'without signposts'[38] and Michèle Montrelay specifies as unexplorable, the 'ruin of representation.'[39] It is this portion of feminine flesh turned idiosyncratic word, I argue, which constitutes a woman's '*Ablehnung der Weiblichkeit*':[40] a subjective decision not to lean on a jouissance without words and without limits, but to use psychic material that is not deciphered from formations of the unconscious but chiseled from the opaque block of the real so as to forge a sinthomatic path, a woman's covenant with the word which can only be conjugated in the singular.

Notes

1 This description of Na'aman's work is based on the account given in Efrat Biberman's *Weaving a Painting: Israeli Art and Lacan's Late Teaching*, Jerusalem, Magnes (in Hebrew). In press, forthcoming.

2 Ibid.
3 Freud, S. (1895). *Project for a Scientific Psychology, The Standard Edition of the Complete Psychological Work of Sigmund Freud*, trans. J. Strachey et al., London, Vintage, 2001, 24 Vols, Vol. 1, p. 299, henceforth SE. References in German are to the German edition of Freud's complete works, *Gessamelte Werke*, ed. A. Freud, Frankfurt, Fischer Verlag, 1999, henceforth GW, save for references to Letter 52, cited from *Briefe an Wilhelm Fliess*, 1887–1904, Frankfurt, Fischer Verlag, 1962.
4 Ibid., p. 205; GW 18S, p. 389.
5 Lacan, J. (1953). 'The Function and Field of Speech and Language,' *Écrits: The First Complete Edition in English*, trans. B. Fink et al., New York, Norton, 2002, p. 206.
6 Lacan, J. (1958–1959). *The Seminar of Jacques Lacan Book 6: Desire and its Interpretation*, trans. B. Fink, Cambridge, Polity, 2019, p. 91.
7 Lacan, J. (1955–1956). *The Seminar of Jacques Lacan Book 2: The Ego in Freud's Theory and in the Technique of Psychoanalysis*, trans. S. Tomaselli, New York, Norton, 1988, p. 234.
8 Lacan, J. (1970–1971). *The Seminar of Jacques Lacan Book 18: On a Discourse that Might not be a Semblance*, trans. C. Gallagher from unedited typescripts, lesson of 12 May, 1971, unpublished. www.lacaninireland.com
9 Lacan, J. (1971–1972). *The Seminar of Jacques Lacan Book 19: … Or Worse*, trans, A.R. Price, Cambridge, Polity, 2019, pp. 59–60. This section of the seminar was originally a part of the series of lectures given by Lacan at the chapel of St. Anne hospital, where his first seminars took place. See Lacan (1971–1972). *Talking to Brick Walls*, trans. A. R. Price, Cambridge, Polity, 2019.
10 Lacan, J. (1972–1973). *The Seminar of Jacques Lacan Book 20: Encore*, trans. B. Fink, New York, Norton, 1998, pp. 26–38.
11 Ibid., p. 67.
12 Ibid., p. 76.
13 Ibid., p. 94.
14 Freud, S. (1937). 'Analysis Terminable and Interminable,' SE 23, p. 250; GW 16, p. 96.
15 Lacan, J. (1972–1973). *The Seminar of Jacques Lacan Book 20: Encore*, Op. cit., p. 94.
16 Ibid., p. 122.
17 Freud, S. (1895). *Project for a Scientific Psychology*, SE 1, p. 296; GW18S, p 389;
18 Freud, S. (1896). Letter to Wilhelm Fliess of 2 November, 1896 (Letter 52), SE 1, 233-234; *Briefe an Wilhelm Fliess*, 1887–1904, Op. cit., p. 151.
19 See Derrida, J. (1967). *Of Grammatology*, trans. G. Chakravorty Spivak, Baltimore, The Johns Hopkins University Press, 1974; Derrida, J. (1967). 'Freud and the Scene of Writing,' *Writing and Difference*, trans. A. Bass, Chicago, Chicago University Press, 1983, pp. 196–231; Derrida, J. (1969). 'Plato's Pharmacy,' *Dissemination*, trans. B. Johnson, Chicago, University of Chicago Press, 1981, pp. 61–171.
20 Derrida, J. (1967). *Of Grammatology*, Op. cit., p. 29.
21 Ibid.
22 Derrida, J. (1972). *Margins of Philosophy*, trans. A. Bass, Chicago, University of Chicago Press, 1984.
23 Lacan , J. (1970–1971). *Talking to Brick Walls*, Op. cit., pp. 82–83.
24 See de Saussure, F. (1916). *Course in General Linguistics*, trans. W. Baskin, New York, McGraw-Hill, 1976, p. 112; Lacan, J. (1953). 'The Instance of the Letter in the Unconscious or Reason Since Freud,' *Écrits*, Op. cit., p. 419.
25 Lacan, J. (1956–1957). *Le Séminaire de Jacques Lacan livre 4: La relation d'objet*, Paris, Seuil, 1994, p. 155, my translation.

26 Lacan, J. (1953). 'The Function and Field of Speech and Language in Psychoanalysis,' *Écrits*, Op. cit., p. 232.
27 Freud, S. (1895). *Project for a Scientific Psychology*, Op. cit., SE 1, pp. 317–333.
28 Alberti, L.B. (1464). *De statua*, trans. J. Arkles, Raleigh, NC, Lulu.com, p. 14; da Vinci (c. 1540). *A Treatise on Painting*, trans. J. F. Rigaud. London, J. Taylor, 1802, p. 656.
29 Freud, S. (1904). 'On Psychotherapy,' SE 7, p. 260.
30 Lacan, J. (1958). 'The Youth of Gide or the Letter and Desire,' *Écrits*, Op. cit., p. 649.
31 Cicero, M.T. *De Oratore*, trans. H. Rackham, Cambridge, MA, 1948, 2.68.
32 Freud, S. (1896). *Project for a Scientific Psychology*, Op. cit., SE 1, p. 300.
33 Ibid., p. 296, GW 18S, p. 389.
34 Lacan, J. (1966–1967). *The Seminar of Jacques Lacan Book 14: The Logic of Phantasy*, trans. C. Gallagher from unedited typescripts, lesson of 10 May, 1967, unpublished. www.lacaninireland.com
35 Lacan, J. (1964). *The Seminar of Jacques Lacan Book 11: The Four Fundamental Concepts of Psychoanalysis*, trans. A. Sheridan, New York, Norton, 1999, p. 32.
36 Freud, S. (1895). *Project for a Scientific Psychology*, Op. cit., SE 1, p. 365, GW 18S, p. 456.
37 Ibid., p. 300.
38 Freud, S. (1926). *Inhibitions, Symptoms and Anxiety*, SE 20, p. 212.
39 Montrelay, M. (1977). *L'ombre et le nom: sur la féminité*, Paris, Minuit, p. 66, my translation.
40 Freud, S. (1937). 'Analysis Terminable and Interminable,' SE 23, p. 250, GW 16, p. 96.

Chapter 1

Saussurean linguistics and its dis-contents

A Lacan's critique of Saussure

The Freudian unconscious is the province of the signifier in pure form, 'irreducible in its absolute nature of a signifier.'[1] It was to the signifier in this pure form that Freud 'immediately assigned' a 'constitutive role' when formulating the unconscious as the Other scene where subjective drama is determined and unfolds, and he did so 'in the most precise and explicit ways.'[2] In the 'experience [Freud] opened up for us,' the experience of the unconscious, then, it is the signifier that is the crucial term, 'necessary to any articulation of the analytic phenomenon,'[3] and operating as sole guarantor of this articulation's 'theoretical coherence.'[4] As for the signified, it has indubitable seductions for the neurotic, but misrecognizing it as a 'guiding thread' in the cure entails clinical perils. Not only, Lacan says, does such misrecognition throw the Freudian theorization of neurotic phenomena out of balance; it also precludes any apprehension of what is happening in the psychoses.[5] In effect, then, 'focusing attention back onto the signifier' is 'nothing other than returning to the starting point of the Freudian discovery.[6] The signifier is the decisive operator in psychic life, Lacan writes in the 'Seminar on "The Purloined Letter,"' strategically chosen to strike the opening chord of the *Écrits*. It 'essentially marks everything of the order of the unconscious,' he states in the third seminar, *The Psychoses*.[7] Towards the end of Lacan's teaching, where the focus is no longer the symbolic but the speaking body upon its mysteries of jouissance, he would still reiterate: 'the signifier is the foundation of the symbolic dimension that only analytic discourse allows us to isolate as such.'[8] For Lacan throughout his teaching, then, the signifier is at the core of what Freud 'discovered, and rediscovers ever more abruptly.' Its vicissitudes determine 'subjects' acts, destiny, refusals, blindnesses, success, and fate, regardless of their innate gifts and instruction, and irregardless of their character or sex.'[9] Such is the key note, note of the 'dominance of the signifier,'[10] Lacan reiterates and retains even in his late teaching, where the emphasis shifts to jouissance and the real unconscious. Lacan's repeated assertion of the primacy in the unconscious of the signifier in pure form, that is, the signifier in itself and not in conjunction with any other category linguistic or otherwise,

DOI: 10.4324/9781003037958-2

however, is not separate from his recognition of the signifier's 'utterly disconcerting' value for 'modern linguists,'[11] perhaps especially for the very inventor of the category of the signifier, Ferdinand de Saussure.

Alongside the work of Roman Jakobson, that of Saussure has, for Lacan, the status of the 'dawn and … culmination' of modern linguistics,'[12] because, Lacan says, 'it is thanks to [Saussure's] teaching that [the distinction between the signifier and the signified] is … included in the foundations of the human sciences.'[13] It is not that Saussure's work, which slightly postdates Freud's, in any way transforms Freud's findings or even makes it possible to read them in a new way. But although Freud, Lacan says, 'could not have taken into account modern linguistics,' in enunciating in detail the laws of the operation of the unconscious he discovered, he could not but anticipate its formulations.[14]

And yet Saussure's theorization of the sign, dawn of the category of the signifier that is a centrepiece of Lacan's early teaching is for Lacan cause of a discontent that pushes further where an admiring elation might have stopped. 'All our experience runs counter to this,' Lacan proclaims, pointing to one of Saussure's graphic renderings of the structure of the sign, the image resembling the wavy lines of the upper and lower Waters in miniatures from manuscripts of Genesis … a twofold flood in which the landmarks—fine streaks of rain traced by vertical dotted lines that supposedly delimit corresponding segments—seem insubstantial.[15]

It is the seeming 'insubstantial[ity]' of the delimiting marks, the dotted lines that, for Saussure, indicate at once the 'limit[ing]' and slicing of the otherwise amorphous registers of thought and phonematic material into 'segments' of irreducible difference, and the conjoining of two segments, one from each register, to form the linguistic sign as Saussure theorizes it, that is the object of Lacan's indignation, part of the 'limitations of [Saussure's] method' Lacan points out.[16] For the relation of a segment of language's phonematic mass, what Saussure calls the 'sound image' and aligns with the signifier, and a delimited segment of thought material Saussure aligns with the signified requires much more than 'fine streaks of rain' such as Lacan reads in the Saussurean diagram. Nor is this conjoining, for Lacan, the product of social convention, the 'social fact' Saussure speaks of as determining the bond between the signifier as sequence of phonemes and a delimited sequence of thought that is for him a signified,[17] for this conjoining is not to be sought anywhere but in the subject himself. 'Point de capiton' is the term Lacan uses in the 'The Instance of the Letter' and the seminar on the psychoses to denominate the element of conjoining, not so much in order to stress its relative substantiality as to indicate 'the dramatic transformation' it can 'effect in the subject.'[18] For without this point, so 'essential to human experience' and rooted in the father function on which Freud insisted to the point he was 'unable to abandon it in the slightest particular observation,' signifier and signified can present themselves in 'completely divided form,'[19] the signifier susceptible of being cathected to the point of acquiring real value and plaguing the subject as hallucination, the signified with its 'floating mass of meanings'[20] proliferating asymptotically till the point of the possible stabilization of a delusion.[21] With the father function which is but another name for the prohibition of incest as *sine qua non* of speech[22] in place for a subject, the subject's discourse can organize itself 'retroactively and prospectively' around particular signifiers,[23] homologues of the organizing element of a literary text Jakobson called its 'dominant,'[24] generating signifieds in ways determined by the particular script of the subject's phantasm.

Neither Saussure's ignorance of the substantiality of the paternal operator conjoining signifier and signified nor his mislocation of this conjoining outside the subject, however, is what grieves Lacan the most about Saussure's *Course*, marred 'dawn and culmination' of modern linguistics in which he nevertheless finds a precious resource for psychoanalysis. It is another of Saussure's graphic renderings of the relation between signifier and signified that is furthest, for Lacan, from what psychoanalytic experience continues to confirm concerning language in the wake of Freud's discovery. This is the graphic rendering of the sign as an oblong ellipse neatly sliced horizontally into two equal parts: the signified on top, and beneath it, the signifier.[25]

If this graphic inscription of the structure of the sign is precious for psychoanalysts, whom Lacan urges to familiarize themselves with Saussurean linguistics,[26] it is to the extent it brings into relief what Lacan affirms as the mainspring of the powers of language and as 'necessary to any articulation of the analytic phenomenon'[27]: 'the fundamental opposition between the signifier and the signified.'[28] And yet if Saussure's theory of the sign puts into circulation the categories of signifier and signified it so helpfully distinguishes to the point of opposition, it does not do so without first soldering the two 'as two sides of a sheet of paper,' that in Saussure's diagram are the two equal and symmetrical halves of the oblong in which they are 'intimately united.'[29]

It is not that psychoanalytic experience never encounters such intimate and harmonic unions of signifier and signified. It encounters them constantly as perennial perils of the practitioner: the joints of articulated discourse, Lacan says, 'onto which all resistance grabs hold and in which all suggestion finds its pivotal point.'[30] There is no dearth of moments in the cure, especially in the intellectualizing speech of the obsessional who, while speaking in the analysis, emits signifiers which masquerade as portions of the unconscious yet in effect are loaded with sense, part of formidable fortifications the obsessional does not cease to manufacture so as to plug up the split in the subject and resist the work of rectification, even in the dreams he recounts, replete with images of 'a fortified camp, or even a stadium.'[31]

As for the hysteric, from whose golden mouth Freud learnt much of what became his metapsychology,[32] her manoeuvres in the transference include ruses designed to get the analyst to supply her with signifiers which mean, hermetically sealed Saussurean signs. In her article on transference in hysteria, Michèle Montrelay describes moments in the cure when the hysteric falls into heavy silences in which nothing but the body seems present; reclining body of the analysand, body of the analyst thrown into unease. The temptation at such moments, writes Michèle Montrelay, is to speak at all costs, to inject sense where there is none, break the silence with signifiers whose signification is univocal (that is, seems bound to a single signified).[33] But the analyst who would yield to such temptations, Montrelay continues, would be doing no more than 'singing her own song,'[34] failing to generate any effects on the unconscious which her speech, locating itself on the imaginary, not symbolic register of psychic life, would plug up with signifiers neatly wed to signifieds. She would be doing no more, that is, than resorting to the practice of suggestion Freud abandoned precisely so as to heed the unconscious more closely, and hence manifesting the only form of resistance Lacan isolates in the analytic encounter: that of the analyst.[35]

Where psychoanalysis never encounters intimate, symmetrical and harmonic unions is not in speech, whose imaginary register, resting as it does on closed dyads of specular complementarity such as Saussure's diagram of the sign also suggests, is precisely where such unions can proliferate, but in the love life subjects complain about, whose vagaries their speech discloses without their knowing anything about this. The *rapport* or harmonic ratio between the sexes does not stop not being written, as Lacan famously says in *Encore*, each mode of sexuation, masculine or feminine, answering to a different logic with respect to castration and evincing a proclivity for a different mode of satisfaction (jouissance).[36] The hardships plaguing even the happiest love relations are precipitates of this disjunction of what are in essence subjective modes of relation to the cataclysmic event of the registration of castration traced as early as Freud's articles on the Oedipus complex, from 'The Infantile Genital Organization' to the lecture on 'Femininity.'[37] What this means, of course, is that myths of sexual and amatory complementarity such as Aristophanes offers in Plato's *Symposium* owe their lasting appeal precisely to their illusory nature. But what this also means is that it is when what is at stake in speech is sexual difference upon its consequences in the love life of subjects that speech will divulge not a harmony without fissure between its components but a fissure steeped in matters of sex.

B The sign and sexual difference

In the *Course in General Linguistics*, the oblong encircling and uniting signifier and signified is retained throughout the graphic renderings of the theory, including in the often-cited example in which the upper part of the oblong (in Saussure's terms, the signified) is occupied by a sketch of a tree, and the lower part (in Saussure's terms, the signifier) is occupied by the spelt-out word 'arbour.'[38]

Lacan, when citing this example as a 'classical' form of introducing the relation between signifier and signified, silently omits the unifying oblong while turning the diagram on its head.[39] But even when the dominance of the signifier is asserted and the symmetrical oblong, as compelling (and horrifying) an image of satiating union with a lost complement as Aristophanes's 'primitive double-backed creatures in which two halves are fused together as firmly as those of a Magdeburg sphere,'[40] is dropped from Saussure's graphic rendering of the sign, his illustration remains, for Lacan, 'faulty' and 'erroneous.'[41] This is because Saussure's rendering fails to take into account the 'surprise'[42] that emerges when Lacan replaces Saussure's diagram, in which the image of the tree allegedly exemplifies any signifier, with one in which the example for the signifier is redoubled by

> the image of two twin doors that symbolize, with the private stall offered Western man for the satisfaction of his natural needs when away from home, the imperative he seems to share with the vast majority of primitive communities that subjects his public life to the laws of urinary segregation[43]

That when the signifier at stake involves sexual difference something goes awry in the seemingly neat correspondence between signifier and signified is further affirmed by the following account of a childhood memory that comes to Lacan's attention:

> A train arrives at a station. A little boy and a little girl, brother and sister, are seated across from each other in a compartment next to the outside window that provides a view of the station platform buildings going by as the train comes to a stop. 'Look,' says the brother, 'we're at Ladies!' 'Imbecile!' replies his sister, 'Don't you see we're at Gentlemen?'[44]

The anecdote, like the drawing preceding it, is ocular – which gives one pause. It is perhaps not only because Lacan's polemical allusion is to a graphic illustration that in drawing out the consequences of the diagram of the twin doors symbolizing the imperative for urinary segregation and the ensuing anecdote, his focus should be the visual field. 'One would have to be *half-blind*,' Lacan writes, 'to be confused as to the respective places of the signifier and the signified here,'[45] and shortly before: 'in having to move closer to the little enamel plaques that bear it, the *squinting gaze of a nearsighted person* might be justified in wondering whether it is indeed here that we must *see* the signifier.'[46] For it is indeed the field of the gaze, field of the scopic drive and its object, that is mobilized in the encounter with the signifier, whether manifest as graphic illustration or as a word written or auditivated but attaining the status of a word read (that is to say, first of all seen) by virtue of the analyst's floating attention which is nothing but, Jacques-Alain Miller teaches, a *savoir-lire*.[47] In the drawing of the two doors which Lacan asserts is a 'more correct' rendering of the structure of the signifier-signified relation than the tree from the *Course in General Linguistics*, the signifier at stake is indeed, as Lacan suggests, encountered visually, but, as he also insinuates, not in the plaques attached to the doors and designating the sites of urinary segregation nor in these doors themselves nor in the additional line of doors of the stalls sometimes extending behind it, but in what these doors are designed to hide or veil and which determined urinary segregation in the first place: the corporeal mark of sexual difference – which is not what it may seem.

Freud indeed speaks of an 'accidental sight' of particular genitals, the female genitals,[48] as a pivotal moment of the castration complex, psycho-textual apparatus in which man is seized, but without which 'he could not identify with the ideal type of his sex or even answer the needs of his partner in sexual relations without grave risk.'[49] But this sight is nothing but the visual encounter not with an organ but with an absence, with the missing penis of the mother, the phallus in the imaginary register.

More precisely still, the *Eindrücke* or imprint of this sight leads to the destruction of the primary psychic text of a body without lack, equipped with the penis as a '*Gemeingut*,' a possession or goods common to all things.[50] The castration complex is the psychic mechanism which repeatedly generates attempts on the part of the subject to 'gloss over' [*beschönigen*, colour or whitewash][51] the ensuing damage to this primary text with imaginary productions in the form of narrative patches of which Little Hans's '"When she grows up it'll get bigger all right!"'[52] is perhaps the best known example. In cases which do not turn out to be psychoses, these attempts cease at an unforeseeable moment of subjective consent. The consent at stake is the agreement to underwrite the damage to the archaic *ursprüng* of a maternal body lacking nothing[53] by means of which man 'aim[s] at being whole'[54] and to register the absence of what was never there. What the subject consents to at this moment, so shattering that its aftermath is the dissolution (not without residue) of the entire castration complex as revisionary writing apparatus, simultaneous with the 'smashing'[55] of the psycho-textual mechanism of the Oedipus complex with which the castration complex is interlocked (*Zusammenhänge*, literally 'hangs together with'),[56] is what Freud calls the '*Kastrationsmöglichkeit*,'[57] the possibility of castration. Caught up in possibility, in a calculus of modal logic which includes what might not be and what might not be had, the phallus is displaced from the register of what Lacan calls 'con-sideration,' where its image is glued to other components forming the imaginary constellation of a maternal body lacking nothing to that of the 'designation,' of 'something to be desired' because it is not there, of what Lacan hence denominates 'desideration.'[58]

The consent to register castration is the most momentous of the psychological consequences of the anatomical distinction between the sexes of which Freud writes. It installs sexual difference symbolically: not as image of the penis as the most important component in the constellation of a maternal body but as the possibility of the penis being or not being there as possession of the subject. Henceforth, the '*Kastrationsmöglichkeit*,'[59] the possibility of the absence of the real phallus (the penis), or otherwise put, the possibility of not having it, will forge different destinies for the two sexes. Man, haunted by the possibility of not having, will need to forge, out of the debris of the shattered psycho-textual mechanisms of the Oedipus and castration complexes, the phallus as what Lacan (after Lévi-Strauss) calls a 'logical instrument,'[60] a symbolic apparatus which might allow him to approach the Other sex in the sexual act without fear of 'blowing himself loose.'[61] Woman will need to forge a limit to a ravaging Other jouissance that assails her,[62] relic of that savage archaic dyad Freud calls the pre-Oedipal and locates as the *verso* of the Oedipus complex,[63] and will sometimes retain an 'imaginary nostalgia' for what she does not have.[64] Hence, in the anecdote of the girl and the boy on the train approaching a station a different imaginary scenario with respect to the symbolic phallus will emerge as the signified of the closed door of the site of urinary segregation that appears in one of the station platform buildings. '[F]or these children,' Lacan writes, 'Gentlemen and Ladies will henceforth be two homelands toward which each of their souls will take flight on divergent wings.'[65] Horror of losing what one has, especially if the orifices and body of the partner are not cast in phallic form that might delimit a space posited so that ejaculation would not destroy the subject,[66] possible nostalgia for what one has not—such are the signifieds, imaginary and subjectively particular dimension of the sign, that will be generated for a man or woman respectively at the sight of the closed restroom door. For if it is 'irregardless of … sex'[67] that the subject's destiny is determined, it is clear why in this case the signified would have a constancy durable till death and hence, as Lacan wryly remarks, 'be paid its last respects by the solemn procession in two lines from the upper nave.'[68]

The point is not only, however, that contrary to Saussure's claim, the signified is not soldered to the signifier by universal bonds of social convention but generated by it in subjectively particular ways in which sexual difference plays a decisive role. It is that this difference which makes two and that plays a role in the generation of signification as well as in the beyond of any relation between man and woman is only ever sustained by a reference point which is one and whose essence is absence: the phallus as what is and is not there, that is, as symbolic. In Freud's account this reference point is the missing penis of the mother, whose absence from the archaic ideal ego the castration complex struggles to gloss over and which is always registered last. Lacan, in at least two points of the *Écrits*, chooses to speak of it via mythological allusion as 'the member forever lost of all those—Osiris, Adonis, and Orpheus—whose fragmented body must be reassembled by the ambiguous tenderness of the Mother-Goddess.'[69] What this choice emphasizes is that the passage of the phallus from consideration to desideration, from most cherished item in an ideal image to possible absence such as operative in any generation of signifieds is not only a cataclysmic event in infantile sexuality but an instance of an impossible question to which humanity's response, as Lévi-Strauss teaches, had been myth[70] many centuries before Little Hans forged the little myths of the plumber that finally assuaged his phobia, born of an anxiety of castration.[71] A member forever lost to the subject at the moment of the transformation of consideration to desideration, the symbolic phallus as partaking in the generation of signification is a single reference point for both sexes. This is why, in analysing the anecdote of the two children on a train as a sequel to his corrective replacement of the tree diagram with which Saussure's theory of the sign is usually explicated by the drawing of the two restroom doors, Lacan remarks that although for the two

children in question 'Gentlemen and Ladies will henceforth be two homelands,' the homelands in question are 'in fact the same.'[72]

Unheimlich homeland of the *Kastrationsmöglichkeit* which is always, and
differently, at play for men and for women in the generation of signification; desolate homeland where 'indignation and scorn'[73] cannot but 'hiss' in
the face of the once resolute belief in what was never there – this is the
topography of what Lacan teaches us to read as the mainspring of significations, that are ever 'incomplete'[74] because for all the force of social convention with which Saussure would have them soldered to signifiers, they can
vary with sexual difference and other determinants of subjectivity. 'Radiant
center,' Lacan ironically calls this mainspring from which 'the signifier
reflects its light.' For it can 'radiate' only because it has taken the place
where something else (the mother's penis that never was) was stubbornly
believed to subsist.

C The phallic signifier

What takes the place of what never was is the 'instrument' of the phallus as
stand-in, pieced together or sutured, upon the subjective assumption of castration, from the debris of the psycho-textual apparatuses of the Oedipus
and castration complexes which leave a residue behind. But why is it, other
than the allusion to Lévi-Strauss, that Lacan calls this instrument 'logical'[75]?
What is 'logical' in subjective life, Jacques-Alain Miller suggests in 'Suture,' is
so insofar as it answers to the same structure as what 'sutures logical discourse,' at least as Gottlob Frege articulates it: the operator of the number
zero as stand-in for the absolute zero.[76] The 'zero number,' Miller explains, is
'the suturing stand-in' that displaces absolute nothingness.'[77] This suture
involves a double emptiness. The displacement that makes the standing in
possible leaves an empty place in its wake and the zero number that comes
into this empty place is a numerical emptiness. What this double emptiness
makes possible is movement in the numerical sphere: the zero number is that
element in the series of whole natural numbers, Miller explains, 'to which we
can assign their progression.'[78]

Taking into account 'analytical reasoning,' Miller erotematically asks,
might we not regard the 'relation of the zero to the series of numbers,' that is
at the foundation of the 'logician's logic,' represented here by Frege's
Foundations of Arithmetic, for all of its empiricist exclusion of the subject,
'the most elementary articulation of the subject's relation to the signifying
chain?'[79] If this is so, it is only because this logician's logic unwittingly and
perhaps inevitably repeats the structure of what it excludes, or perhaps better,
as Miller suggests, represses:[80] the displacement, at the moment of the consent to register castration, of what is logically equivalent to the absolute zero,
the mother's penis that never was that makes the archaic *ursprûng* a seamless
ideal ego, by the symbolic phallus, patchwork of remnants of the two

foundational psycho-textual apparatuses operative in the infantile genital organization. Unlike the non-existent penis of the mother it displaces, the imaginary phallus which has the modal status of necessity, of what must be there to sustain a primordial fiction that circumvents narcissistic injury, this patchwork phallus is so crucial for the sexuation of both men and women precisely because it is only ever a possibility (what might or might not be there, depending on subjective choice), that is, because it is taken up in the alternation of presence and absence subtending the symbolic. But unlike the imaginary phallus, the penis of the mother, the symbolic phallus, motley wear, to use the words of Shakespeare's Rosalind, that is the 'only wear'[81] of the neurotic subject, is an emptiness. It 'does not correspond to anything real,[82] just as in the foundations of arithmetic the zero number that replaces and displaces the absolute zero is 'the first non-real thing in thought.'[83] More precisely still, as Lacan indicates in his sixth seminar, the zero number that is the logical equivalent of the phallus is an 'irrational number' that as such, can never be written either as a real or as a natural number. Yet it is on such an irrational number, which Lacan identifies as the square root of minus one, that the calculation of human life subsists.[84]

The symbolic phallus is the 'thing of nothing' such as Lacan does not fail to note in the words of Shakespeare's Hamlet[85] when referring to the king who had usurped the place of his father:[86] 'a king of shreds and patches,'[87] a king made up of debris tacked together, a king, that is, who shares the structure metapsychology has recognized as what displaces the primary text of the castration complex revolving around the imagined penis of the mother with an instrument assembled from its remnants. King of shreds and patches, Claudius in Shakespeare's play is a sham stand-in for an unrepresentable whose other dramatization is the spectre, isomorph of the zero number (or its square root) which displaces the absolute zero. The symbolic phallus whose isomorphs seem to appear at different corners of the manifestations of civilization, from the foundations of logic and arithmetic to a drama which owes its lasting appeal, Freud suggests, to its dramatization of the unconscious conflict of every neurotic,[88] attesting to its pivotal role in civilization itself, thus divulges itself as an emptiness displacing an illusion whose very emptiness, irrational mainspring of subjective calculation, is crucial to this calculation's very possibility. Paradoxical calculation in which, in the cases of neurosis, the quotient of desire is maintained as either impossible or unsatisfied but that at the end of an analysis may emerge as what might make absolute difference emerge as the subject's singular symptom no less than in the remainder of jouissance that operates as mainspring of the analytic act and that Lacan denominates the desire of the analyst.

That to say the symbolic phallus is a thing, even of nothing, does not imply it is graspable in any conceivable way is poetically articulated, Lacan points out, in another of Hamlet's only seemingly cryptic statements about his usurping uncle: 'the body is with the king, but the king is not with the body.'[89]

'I would ask you simply to replace the word "king" with the word "phallus,"' Lacan says,

> to realize that it is the phallus that is involved here. For the body is tightly bound up in this business of the phallus, and how, but on the other hand, the phallus is bound to nothing, and always slips between your fingers.[90]

Unlike the phallus as organ whose unpredictable vicissitudes propel Little Hans into inhibition and phobia, and which for every male, Michèle Montrelay writes, is 'subject to the fluctuations of desire and thought' and hence 'runs the risk of too rapid a fall,'[91] but which is nevertheless, both for a man and for a woman, tangible 'object of little sense ... marked by the sign of death,'[92] unlike the imaginary phallus which, so long as castration is not registered in the unconscious, the subject endeavours to uphold in the face of any encounter with its possible absence, the symbolic phallus, instrument made of shreds and patches whose essence makes it a thing of nothing, is, for the neurotic, never quite in its place. Like the purloined letter of Poe's tale, it is never where one feverishly looks for it, for its very function is to leave that place empty even of its own emptiness. '"'Tis here' ... 'Tis here'... 'Tis gone'" are the exasperated cries of the guards on the walls of Elsinore castle in the opening scene of Shakespeare's play, as it is precisely with the attempts to 'strike at it,' at the phallus precisely dramatized as a ghost, that it disappears.[93]

The result of the disappearance of the phallus as the effect of the very attempt to seize it is of course not its obliteration but its hiding. In Shakespeare's *Hamlet*, after the first act, the ghost of the dead father disappears almost completely from the script, save a fleeting appearance in the third act, at the very moment of Hamlet's reference to the 'king of shreds and patches,' to 'whet [Hamlet's] almost blunted purpose,'[94] to propel him, that is, not to reference the phallus but to put it to use in the act whose deferral constitutes the (non)-action of the play as of every neurotic, especially of the obsessional variety. But this fleeting (re)-appearance of the phallus, emerging, as always, only to 'steal ... away,'[95] is synecdochic of the operation of the spectre throughout the play and indeed of the phallus as impelling cause of 'the dialectic of the subject with the object of his desire.'[96] For it is the ghost who propels the action of the play not only and not so much in the apparitions that 'can only subsist in the flash of an instant,' what Lacan calls 'apparitions of the phallus, phallophanies,'[97] but in his non-appearances, in the beyond of what can be staged, as what Shakespeare's language adequately names 'this fellow in the cellarage.'[98] The spectre of the phallus, the phallus as spectre, operates in the beyond of the Shakespearean stage as mainspring of the drama of Hamlet, less dramatic personage that can be seen as an analogue of a clinical case than 'a hub where a desire is situated.'[99] In this too, the ghost in *Hamlet* is isomorphic with the phallus as what 'can play its role only as veiled,' as evidenced also in the ancient mysteries, because, since it is an emptiness without referent, it is only the concealing veil that gives it substance. What functions in the play as a surface that conceals what can operate only as concealed because, being nothing, it is the concealment that gives it substance, is not the arras that causes the tragicomic death of Polonius in the third act, but the stage itself, propped as it is over the empty space of the trapdoor or 'cellarage' at its centre. In *Hamlet*, that is, the Shakespearean stage as a whole functions as the veil permitting the phallus to play the leading role from a beyond, or more literally, a below.

But it is of course not only with respect to desire that the phallus plays its role as veiled. The 'advent of desire' from beyond demand, not as what in the demand fails to be satisfied but as the quotient of the subtraction from demand of the very possibility of satisfaction, Lacan says, is wedded to 'the mark of Logos.'[100] For it is in speech that desire is articulated. Hence the phallus is not only thing of nothing, motley instrument made of the shreds and patches of a primordial fiction without reference that can hence operate only thanks to a veil that makes its absence present. As an absence made present, the phallus partakes of the structure of signification, is in effect paradigmatic for it, for it is a sign, Lacan writes, 'of the latency with which any signifiable is struck, once it is raised [*aufgehoben*] to the function of signifier.'[101] What this means is that any account of signification that does not exclude the subject of the unconscious must take into account not only the consequences of the different modes of sexuation, but also the phallus as operator that, as Lacan shows in *Encore*, functions differently in each of them. This is precisely what Lacan does, and not only in the essay explicitly concerned with 'The Signification of the Phallus,' but also and more implicitly in 'The Instance of the Letter,' site of his programmatic explication of the structure of language as encountered in psychoanalytic experience. For the phallus is at stake in the drawing of the entrance to the site of urinary segregation and the ensuing anecdote of the two children arriving at a station not only as the 'radiant centre' from which 'the signifier reflects its light'[102] but also as what does so from behind closed doors. Challenging the assumption that the place of the signifier in the production of signification might be illustrated by any nominal type, Lacan replaces the 'faulty'[103] drawing in the *Course in General Linguistics* by one that exemplifies the structure of the signifier itself because it involves not only sexual difference but a surface of interposition: the veil without which, Lacan emphasizes, the phallus cannot play its role, either as object of desire or as mark of Logos and paradigm of the signifier.[104] Like the piece of cloth shrouding the simulacrum of the phallus in the Eleusinian mysteries, like the Shakespearean stage in *Hamlet* which, unlike the arras in Gertrude's bedroom, covers what cannot be killed because it is already an absence, the restroom doors in Lacan's 'Instance of the Letter' manifest what Lacan points out as 'truly one of the most fundamental images of the human relation to the world,' the curtain or veil, what incarnates the 'relation of interposition' which renders 'what is aimed at' ever 'beyond what presents itself.'[105]

What the boy and the girl sitting opposite one another in the train in Lacan's anecdote in 'The Instance of the Letter' 'see' is indeed not the words imprinted on 'the little enamel plaques' of the restroom doors but the veil these doors (and these plaques) constitute: the veil owing to which, Lacan explains in

Seminar 4, 'what is beyond, as masked, tends to realize itself as image.'[106] What is beyond those doors for every speaking being is the phallus not as anatomical marker of sexual difference but as the precipitate of the ceasing of the efforts to replace this difference with narrative patches designed to preserve intact a primary fiction of sexual equality in which the penis is a *Gemeingut*, common property of all things,[107] a precipitate whose nature is absence.

D The phallus in the visual field: Self-portrait of an absence

Lacan implies that the absence of the phallus is an active absence, and that this absence causes a difference in the visual field. For absence, Lacan says, is what 'paints itself' on the veil thus indexed as canvas or other substrate of painting,[108] hence qualifying self-portraiture in visual art as involving something other than the oft-assumed physical presence of the painter. In the history of art, this presence is accentuated, for example, in Bartolomé Esteban Murillo's self-portrait of 1670, in which the painter's hand holds the painted frame of his torso painted on the canvas, seemingly trying to break through the substrate of painting towards his palette and paintbrushes with which it was painted, to be in the portrait as physical presence beyond appearing in it

Figure 1.1 Bartolomé Esteban Murillo, *Self-Portrait*, c. 1670. Oil on canvas, 122 x 107 cm.
Source: © The National Gallery, London.

as representation. In a book on painting at the threshold of modernity, Victor Stoichita uses this painting as an example of a self-portrait that aspires to push the boundaries of representation to a point at which the act of self-portraiture would bring about the presentification of the painter himself.[109]

But the history of self-portraiture also includes examples which are perhaps the truth of the insistence on the presence of the painter of the self-portrait on which Murillo's painting protests so much. To Murillo's self-portrait, in which the painter's hand seems to exceed the frame towards a plaque attesting to the painter's act of self-representation, Stoichita opposes Annibale Carracci's self-portrait of 1604, in which the artist's portrait appears on an easel in the studio, colour palette hanging on its right, the easel, palette and painted canvas sole indexes to his presence.

Far from working towards a transformation of painted self-image to the flesh and blood persona who had painted it, staged fantasy of Murillo's self-portrait, self-portraiture, as Stoichita shows by means of Carracci's self-portrait, may operate precisely as what generates the absence of the artist painted in it.[110] Self-portraiture, that is, is the manifestation in the visual field of what Paul de Man called 'Autobiography as Defacement.'[111]

Figure 1.2 Annibale Carracci, *Self-Portrait on an Easel*, Italy, 1603–1604. Oil on panel, 42.5 x 30 cm.
Source: © State Hermitage Museum. Reproduced with the kind permission of the State Hermitage Museum, St. Petersburg.

Even generating an absence by means of self-portraiture as visual autobi-ography, however, is not the same thing as absence painting itself that Lacan talks about in the fourth seminar. Diagonally from the easel bearing Carracci's self-portrait, indicated as situated behind it at some distance, a bright-coloured square emerges from the sombre backdrop, perhaps a canvas. A thin silhouette appears in front of the square, the outlines of its head sug-gesting the propped up hairdo of a woman from which a locket escapes. Behind the woman in the shadows, the canvas is empty. If the absence of the painter is the precipitate of self-portraiture as positive act, as Stoichita sug-gests, the canvas behind the self-portrait on the easel is perhaps an instance of the veil as interposing plane on which absence paints itself.

Another such instance is the Berlin version of Georg Friedrich Kersting's *Caspar David Friedrich in his Studio* of 1819, where the painter, leaning on the back of a chair in an ascetically bare studio and holding a brush and palette, contemplates a canvas on an easel before him.[112]

The canvas on the easel dominates the centre of the painting in a composi-tion resembling Carracci's self-portrait, but unlike in Carracci's self-portrait, in this case what is visible to the viewer is not an image of a painter but a dark plane empty of an image, the obverse side of the canvas contemplated by Friedrich. What image, if any, is painted on the canvas contemplated by Friedrich is hidden from the viewer, yet the painter of the canvas itself is not Friedrich but Kersting, indicated by the painting's perspective as situated diagonally across from Friedrich. The dark blank plane on the easel is thus not only the obverse side of a canvas on which Friedrich may or may not have painted something. It is a plane on which the painting's author, Kersting, paints himself as absence. The visual artworks of both Carracci and Kersting feature a painted plane on which the absence of the painter paints itself, bear-ing out Lacan's statement in the fourth seminar concerning the nature of the interposing plane that in visual art is the canvas as substrate of painting as a site where, prior to any brushstroke, the absence that is the phallus (in the subjective structure of painter and then viewer) paints itself.

The history of portraiture, self-aware as it sometimes is in Stoichita's terms, occasionally exposes the projection of the phallus as absence on an interposing plane as an act preliminary to any self-portrait. But what visual art thus exposes, for instance in the paintings of Carracci and Kersting dis-cussed above, is structurally at stake for the neurotic subject in any ocular encounter with an interposing surface such as a door or plaque. The phallus as painter of a self-portrait hidden by the canvas it paints on, which shows nothing but its image as absence; it is this that the speaking being, affected by the signifier, encounters in every encounter with a door such as that of the site of urinary segregation, a door whose function is an interposition which concerns the body as sexuated. The 'surprise' of unexpected signification which is produced by this door as Lacan speaks of it in 'The Instance of the Letter' is thus not only signification as determined not, as Saussure would

Figure 1.3 Georg Friedrich Kersting, *Caspar David Friedrich in his Studio* (in the Dresden suburb Pirna, An der Elbe 26). Painting, c. 1812. Oil on canvas, 51 × 40 cm. Berlin, SMB, Alte Nationalgalerie.
Source: © akg-image.

have it, by total social fact but by the particular subjective consequences of the registration of sexual difference. The unexpected signification that emerges is of the phallus as active absence which, by means of the veil (in this case manifest by the plaque and the door) and from beyond it, does not cease to register 'the sentiment of nothing' at play in 'all of man's relations with his desire.'[113]

The veil as interposing plane on which the absence that is the phallus 'projects itself,' Lacan adds in the fourth seminar, is in the end a captivating idol. Commonly metaphorized as the illusory veil of Maya,[114] the veil is testament to a pervasive sentiment of a 'fundamental illusion' at play in all relations of desire.[115] For even if the interposing plane does show, does function as a canvas on which absence paints itself as a positive image, it still has an obverse side that is not only not seen but that can prevent one from truly seeing. The 'squinting gaze of a near-sighted person might be justified in wondering whether it is indeed here' – on the two plaques on the twin doors, on the twin doors themselves – 'that we must see the signifier,'[116] because there is more at issue in the generation of the signifier even than the self-portrait of an absence that projects itself on these interposing planes: the real stake of castration.

E The signifier as slash: Lacan with Fontana

In Freudian terms, castration may be said to be the subjective consent to register the possibility of not having, which never comes without discontent. Remnants of the castration complex as mechanism of writing and revision designed to keep intact a primary text of an ideal body without fissure remain operative in the form of an 'essential disturbance in human sexuality that is the "irreducibility—in any finite [*endliche*] analysis" of the fear of losing the penis in a man's unconscious and of *Penisneid* in woman's unconscious.'[117] Fear and envy, irreducible affects, are, as affects, nothing but the precipitates of the dismantling of a mechanism of representation. What they ultimately index, however, is not simply the shattering of the primary text of a maternal body without lack but what generated the shattering in the first place: the puncturing of the primary text subsequent to the subject's 'acceptance' of the '*Kastrationsmöglichkeit*,'[118] a moment of holing. Other than the possibility of absence, then, castration in its Freudian declension is a hole in an illusory archaic ideal that once was.

To underscore the mainspring of the signifier as a hole is more than to mark its topology, instituted by an operation not of gluing or soldering implicit in Saussure's theorization of the signifier and signified as two sides of a sheet of paper, but of a puncturing that changes topological structure. Any signifying production, Lacan writes, rests on a 'moment of cutting'[119] that is nothing but the moment of the institution of castration. This cutting slashes through the primary text of a body without lack, leaving open the hole that had been repeatedly glossed over by revisionary narrative patches generated in an attempt to preserve it. As topological operation, this puncturing alters the structure of the subject, precipitating the smashing of the textual apparatus of the castration complex and the construction from its debris of the phallus as logical instrument, condition at once of signification and of the limitation of excess jouissance. And yet the puncturing involved in the generation of signification pertains not only to the textual, or, more precisely, pertains to the textual only insofar as textuality itself is a product of an operation performed on of zooic matter that palpitates and moves, that enjoys and acts.

The conditions for the production of the phallus, Lacan explains in the fifth seminar, is the sacrifice of a 'vital surge,' which is 'more male than female and nevertheless of which the female herself may become the symbol.'[120] Whether it takes the imaginary form of an erect penis or of a seductive goddess, what is sacrificed to produce he phallus is a 'privileged object ... of the world of life, which moreover in its Greek appellation is linked to everything which is of the order of "flux and sap."'[121] By 'virtue of its turgidity, the piece of flesh sacrificed in the production of the phallus as signifier is the image of the vital flow as it is transmitted in generation.'[122] And yet, Lacan stresses, taking his cue from the mysteries of antiquity, 'this extreme point of the manifestation of desire in its vital appearances,'[123] that is to say, the penis in turgid form of vital tumescence or fertile goddess, 'can play its role only when veiled'[124] – and for reasons which are not of the order of prudery.

The point is not that in the Eleusinian mysteries, the veiling of the simulacrum of the penis in its tumescent form obstructs obscenity from view, but that this veiling makes possible the operation of unveiling that changes the semiotic status of what is veiled. As veiled, the penis signifies, that is to say, reveals itself in its nature as signifier. This is because, as Lacan explains in the fifth seminar, a signifier is nothing but what emerges from the operation of cancellation, which far from obliterating what is hidden, sublates and raises it to a second power.[125] The veiled and then unveiled penis of the ancient mysteries thus becomes, for Lacan, paradigmatic of the procedure of the production of a signifier as such,[126] visually indexed by a drawing of what in the modern world displaced the veil of the Eleusinian mysteries: the twin doors of sites of urinary segregation.

To posit the 'the organism of life,' the penis as 'sprouting' or 'vital surge' as semiotically operative only on condition of its veiling or cancellation, its extraction from the realm of palpitating zooic matter, is to isolate it as precisely what finds itself able 'to enter into the field of signifiers only by unleashing the bar in it.'[127] The phallus, Lacan goes on to say, 'finds itself covered by a bar placed over its accession to the domain of signifiers.'[128] These two statements in effect seemingly synonymize veil and bar, collapsing the doors and plaque in Lacan's diagram with the line above them. But the synonymy ultimately discloses a significant difference in the categories it seemingly synthesizes. The bar in Lacan's account is not only what cancels or veils signifiable organicity to recreate it as the presence made of absence that is the signifier. As component of the mechanism of the signifier's generation, the bar not only conceals organicity but cuts into it.

The bar which in Saussure's diagrams of the sign remains unnamed, Lacan initially states in 'The Instance of the Letter,' is a 'barrier resisting signification' which separates signifier and signified not as symmetrical complements but as components of two 'distinct orders' of semiosis.[129] The resistance to signification, however, does not render the bar completely identical with another category defined by its inability to enter the arena of the signifier: the real phallus (the penis) in its vital flow, for the bar is identified precisely with what can be 'unleashed' to make the entry of the phallus into this arena possible after all.[130] It is the ancient mysteries, more specifically, the frescoes of the Villa of Mysteries at Pompei to which Lacan turns as source of knowledge concerning the genealogy of the signifier, that clarify the relation of bar to phallus as neither synonymous nor synecdochic. If the phallus in the mysteries can play its role only as veiled, the dropping of the veil at the moment of initiation is simultaneous with its replacement. In the 'famous painting in the Villa of the Mysteries in Pompeii,' Lacan writes in 'The Signification of the Phallus,' the 'demon of Aιδoς (Scham) springs forth at the very moment the phallus is unveiled,' a peculiar demon, Lacan points out in the fifth seminar, 'winged, booted, not helmeted, but almost, and in any case armed with a *flagellum*,' with which it is 'beginning to administer the ritual punishment to one of the applicants or initiates who are in the image.'[131] The *flagellum*, then, is what replaces the veil in the genealogy of the signifier as extractable from the murals of the mysteries. In the reference to the Pompei frescoes in 'The Signification of the Phallus,' the instrument with which 'the demon's hand strikes' is identified as the bar.[132] Veil and the *flagellum* displacing it both affect the phallus, but differently. Where one hides, making possible a continued operation *sous rature* of a palpitating piece of flesh, the other gives rise to 'a fantasy of flagellation … in the most direct of forms,'[133] in which flesh is wounded and torn, as it is, Lacan points out, in other attestations from the ancient cults in which the approach to the phallus as 'fruitful potency' involves 'amputations' and 'marks of castration,' of which the 'eunuch character of the priests of the great goddess' is a case in point.[134] In the genealogy of the generation of signification for which visual depictions of the ancient mysteries give Lacan imaginary signposts, the bar is not what hides but what hurts, consequence of an act of amputation in which a piece of flesh is detached from the body. If, in the anecdote of the boy and the girl on the train in 'The Instance of the Letter,' 'the rails … materialize the bar in the Saussurean algorithm in a form designed to suggest that its resistance may be other than dialectical,'[135]

Figure 1.4 Pompei, Villa of Mysteries, detail of salon decoration.
Source: Reproduced with the kind permission of the Ministero per i Beni e le Attività Culturali e per il Turismo – Parco Archeologico di Pompei.

it is also because their crossing might entail irretrievable corporeal loss that is not signifiable but that makes signification possible.

Nor is this corporeal loss, except phantasmatically, inflicted by the Other. What the bar cuts off, Lacan says, is something that 'the Other does not have at its disposition,'[136] and that hence cannot be 'given back ... by the Other.'[137] What the bar cuts off belongs to the subject's very life.[138] It is a pound of flesh which is 'sacrificed,'[139] not to the obscure gods of a sombre jouissance Lacan evokes at the end of the eleventh seminar[140] but so that the signifier might be born at the moment this pound of flesh 'takes on a signifying function.'[141] It is this pound of flesh, cut off not from any place but from a 'privileged place' that Shakespeare's Shylock locates as 'nearest to [the] heart'[142] because it pertains to the very fact of biological subsistence that in the life of the neurotic appears wherever the bar on the Other is found.[143]

The bar, then, is the name of what is operative at the moment of rupture in which a surge of life palpitating in the flesh is lost to the benefit of the signifier. Trou-matic moment which, as such, effects a topological change in which what was zooic matter alone is made symbolic, occulted cause of a chain whose concatenation proceeds according to the logic of ancestral lineage. But if the bar is operative at the inaugural point where the organism gets caught up in ancestry, in inherited lines of fate mercilessly repeating the phantomatic, it also makes a second(ary) appearance as inaugurator not of ancestry but of bastardy. Operating, like the pleasure principle, at the boundary between this chain and the piece of flesh excised so as to make this chain possible, the bar also shows up between signifier and signified, effectuating what seems to be another *Aufhebung* but isn't. Instead of propelling the emergence of a symbolic lineage (the unconscious chain of signifiers), the bar in this secondary appearance is capable of 'demot[ing]' a signifier from its 'function in the line or in a lineage.'[144] In addition to the signified, the bar can generate 'bastard offspring'[145] that have nothing to do with the transmission of the ancestral in which the unconscious is bound up.

The bar, then, is not what solders and separates signifier and signified, as the Saussurean algorithm silently suggests, but what generates them[146] as orders that are both distinct and discordant[147] and between which 'any possibility of establishing a term-by-term equivalence is aprioristically obviated,'[148] at two different moments of transformation. The second (the passage of the signifier into the signified),[149] jettisons the illusion that the signifier serves [*répond à*] the function of representing the signified, or better, that the signifier has to justify [*répondre de*] its existence in terms of any signification whatsoever,'[150] and involves the bar's crossing.[151] This crossing is not a shattering productive of jouissance. Nor is it the exchange of the connection of a signifier to other signifiers constituting the unconscious for the socially conventional 'mediation of the relationship of the signifier to the referent.'[152] The crossing of the bar productive of the signified is nothing but the isolation and extraction of an unconscious signifier from the signifying battery of its subjectively particular connections with other unconscious signifiers whose corollary is its substitution for another signifier which remains unconscious, an effect of this substitution being the emergence of signification.[153] As Lacan's anecdote of the boy and girl on the train indicates, however, this emergence depends on more than substitution alone: the subjection of the signifier extracted from the unconscious chain whose links follow laws that are particular to the no less subjectively particular mechanism of sense-making Lacan would come to call the phantasm. Narrative ensemble of unconscious signifiers, the phantasm, unless traversed in an analysis, generates signification with a univocal insistence, usually painful to the subject. The univocity of the phantasm as generator of signification is the reason that in the order of the signified, what 'dominates ... is the unity of signification,' whereas in the order of the signifier, each unit of unconscious representation 'takes on its precise usage ... by being different from the others.'[154] Determinant of subjective reality which is nothing but a defence against an even more unbearable real, the phantasm that goes into operation when the bar is crossed and a signifier extracted from the unconscious generates significations that always refer to other significations[155] whose subjective mainspring is the same. Hence both the unity that characterizes the domain of the signified and its constitutive inability to ever 'come down to a pure indication of the real.'[156]

The real, doubly covered over by the phantasm put into play by the bar's second operation is, however, precisely what is effected by the first, which is not the crossing of the signifier but its production by a cut. For if the subject incurs what Lacan calls 'symbolic debt',[157] it is insofar as, as Freud puts it in the essay on narcissism, he is 'an inheritor of an entailed property, who is only the temporary holder of an estate that survives him.'[158] He not only, unless analysis intervenes, always settles this debt with his flesh,[159] but also comes into his inheritance in the first place by paying a price that is not symbolic. For ancestral property to be entailed, a piece of enjoyment in the flesh must be left on the threshold, 'reject[ed]' by the subject with all his being.' This rejection of 'something of himself' so that it might '[take] on the value of signifier'[160] is but another name for the first operation of the bar, not a crossing but a slashing.

Zooic matter slashed by the bar fails to disappear behind it once the bar's operation effects its accession to the value of signifier. Involved in more than a logic of sublation in which what is cancelled out continues to operate under erasure, it haunts what displaces it. The 'moment of cutting' in which the bar produces the 'signifier of signifiers,' the symbolic phallus, the phallus as signifying and typifying the structure of any signifier, Lacan writes in 'The Signification of the Phallus,' 'is haunted by the form of a bloody scrap ... impossible to restore, as such, to the imaginary body; ... the lost phallus of embalmed Osiris.'[161] If the veil involved in the generation of the signifier determines the symbolic phallus as an absence, the bar in its inaugural function of slashing is a reminder that this absence is not pure abstract sterility, but trails an image indexing a real loss in flesh and bone. This is the image of the penis cut off and made 'bloody scrap,' for which the genitals of the mother Freud speaks of in 'Medusa's Head' from which it is imagined to have been cut off[162] are an apotropaic displacement, the image of a hole or wound torn open on the body's surface at the site of sex which is not the feminine orifice, protective limit, for the man, in the sexual act.

What this means is that if, as Lacan puts it in the fourth seminar, the phallus that operates as condition for any signifying production 'depicts itself,' operates as an agent of self-portraiture, its resultant self-portrait would be, perhaps even more than the blank side of the canvas such as that of Friedrich in his studio, an instance of absence painting itself on an interposing surface, an isomorph of one of the slash works of Lucio Fontana, traces of moments of an act of cutting in which rather than a paintbrush covering the canvas, a blade scores it at multiple points. Fontana, Lacan says in ...*or Worse*, 'was surely not one of those who completely misrecognize structure,' which is the structure of the subject not as split but as 'gash,' not, as Lacan maintained in his early teaching, represented by one unconscious signifier to another, but 'gaping' between signifiers as a result of the operation of 'the little a-object,'[163] opening up onto a real that is impossible to bear. Both cut object and what effects the cut, the object a in Lacan's reference to Fontana's work in his later teaching condenses what in the earlier teaching had been divided between the bar in its inaugural function of cutting and the 'bloody scrap' it slashes off so that it might accede to the function of a signifier. Nevertheless, Lacan's commentary on Fontana in ... *Ou pire* retroactively clarifies an aspect of the generation of the signifier in its relation to the flesh as it appears in accounts of the bar in the early teaching: the bar's extracting a pound of flesh as price for the emergence of the word, the deal effecting a topological change in the organism now marked by the signifier, whose speaking body will henceforth be a slashed surface made of flesh whose structure, Lacan implies, Fontana's works captured so well.

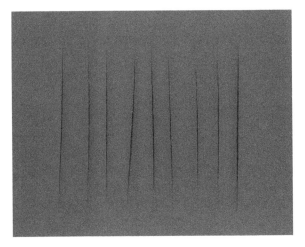

Figure 1.5 Lucio Fontana, *Concetto Spaziale, Attese*, 1964. Water-based paint on canvas, 73 x 92 cm, catalogue no. 64 T 10.
Source: © Fondazione Lucio Fontana.

Figure 1.6 Lucio Fontana, *Taglio*, Milan, 1964. 567 x 787 cm.
Source: Photo Ugo Mulas © Ugo Mulas Heirs. All rights reserved.

What at a first moment cuts off a piece of flesh at a privileged point of the organism which manifests life in its most vital flow so that it might turn signifier and at a second extracts a signifier it had produced so that, in becoming input of the phantasm, it participates in the generation of signification univocal in a subjectively particular way – such is the bar in its double operation. What conceals what had been cut off, enabling it to appear only as an absence – such is the veil in Lacan's account, in his early teaching, of the generation of the signifier. Both bar and veil leave something behind, a piece of life at its most vital, most satisfying, that can never be retrieved because its loss is precisely the condition of the birth of the symbolic. Where this lost piece of life lives on is as cause, cause of what Lacan calls the 'endless perpetuation of the subject's desire.'[164] It is this perpetuation that is the ultimate effect of the joint work of bar and veil. Excluding, extracting and occulting a portion of life in its most vital surge that hence becomes precisely what is wanting, together they perform the 'banishing summons' which constantly brings the subject back to his desire.[165]

Neither bar nor veil feature in Saussure's account of the structure of the sign, the first present as an unnamed line in the illustrative diagrams, which give Lacan his cue. But what unfolds from this cue – the cutting, crossing, occluding operations of bar and veil on living flesh that haunts the signifier and the signified that is its bastard offspring in the form of a bloody scrap – is thus Saussurean linguistics' scandal, what dis-concerts it, literally disturbs the concert of intimate union, of a harmonic and symmetrical relation, that is the fantasy animating it as modern linguistics' version of the fable of the 'all round' primeval man-woman attributed to Aristophanes in Plato's *Symposium*, ancient articulation of the perennial mirage of a sexual ratio between man and woman. But if the *Course in General Linguistics* tries to preclude the dis-concert of a 'sound-image' (Saussure's phenomenological description of the signifier) standing alone by summoning the signified as its partner in a fantasy of intimate and harmonic union, in Freud's *Project for a Scientific Psychology*, which lays the foundations for metapsychology as theory of language, such dis-concert is a principle of structure.

Notes

1   Lacan, J. (1957). 'Psychoanalysis and its Teaching,' *Écrits: The First Complete Edition in English*, trans. B. Fink et al., New York, Norton, 2002, p. 372.
2   Lacan, J. (1957). 'The Instance of the Letter in the Unconscious or Reason Since Freud,' *Écrits*, Op. cit., p. 426.
3   Lacan, J. (1958). 'The Signification of the Phallus,' *Écrits*, Op. cit., p. 578.
4   Lacan, J. (1955). 'The Freudian Thing, or the Meaning of the Return to Freud in Psychoanalysis.' *Écrits*, Op. cit., p. 345.
5   Lacan, J. (1955–1956). *The Seminar of Jacques Lacan Book 3: The Psychoses*, trans. R. Grigg, New York, Norton, 1993, p. 203.
6   Ibid, p. 204.
7   Ibid.
8   Lacan, J. (1972–1973). *The Seminar of Jacques Lacan Book 20: Encore*, trans. B. Fink, New York, Norton, 1998, p. 21.
9   Lacan, J. (1956). 'Seminar on "The Purloined Letter,"' *Écrits*, Op. cit., p. 21.
10 Lacan, J. (1957) 'The Instance of the Letter in the Unconscious or Reason Since Freud,' *Écrits*, Op. cit., pp. 372, 598.
11 Lacan, J. (1956). 'The Situation of Psychoanalysis and the Training of Analysts in 1956,' *Écrits*, Op. cit., p. 391.
12 Lacan, J. (1960). 'The Subversion of the Subject and the Dialectic of Desire in the Freudian Unconscious,' *Écrits*, Op. cit., p. 676.
13 Lacan, J. (1956). 'The Situation of Psychoanalysis and the Training of Psychoanalysts in 1956,' *Écrits*, Op. cit., p. 391.
14 Lacan, J. (1957). 'Psychoanalysis and its Teaching,' *Écrits*, Op. cit., p. 373.
15 Lacan, J. (1957). 'The Instance of the Letter in the Unconscious,' *Écrits*, Op. cit., p. 419; see also *Seminar 3: The Psychoses*, Op. cit., pp. 238–239.
16 Lacan, J. (1955–1956). *Seminar 3: The Psychoses*, Op. cit., p. 239.
17 de Saussure, F. (1916). *Course in General Linguistics*, trans. W. Baskin, New York, Columbia University Press, 2001, p. 13.
18 Lacan, J. (1957). 'The Instance of the Letter in the Unconscious,' *Écrits*, Op. cit., p. 419.
19 Lacan, J. (1955–1956). *Seminar 3: The Psychoses*, Op. cit., p. 244.
20 Ibid.
21 Lacan, J. (1958). 'On a Question Preliminary to Any Possible Treatment of Psychosis,' *Écrits*, Op. cit., p. 481.
22 Lacan, J. (1959–1960). *The Seminar of Jacques Lacan Book 7: The Ethics of Psychoanalysis*, trans. D. Porter. New York, Norton, 1992, p. 67.

23   Lacan, J. (1955–1956). *Seminar 3: The Psychoses*, Op. cit., p. 244.
24   Jakobson, R. (1935). 'The Dominant,' *Language in Literature*, ed. K. Pomorska and S. Rudy, Cambridge, Mass., Harvard University Press, 1987, p. 41.
25   de Saussure, F. (1916) *Course in General Linguistics*, Op. cit., p. 114.
26   Lacan, J. 'The Freudian Thing, or the Meaning of the Return to Freud in Psychoanalysis,' *Écrits*, Op. cit., p. 345; see also Lacan, J. (1955). 'Variations on the Standard Treatment,' *Écrits*, Op. cit., 299.
27   Lacan, J. (1958). 'The Signification of the Phallus,' *Écrits*, Op. cit., p. 578.
28   Lacan, J. (1958). 'The Direction of the Treatment and the Principles of its Power,' *Écrits*, Op. cit., p. 519.
29   de Saussure, F. (1916). *Course in General Linguistics*, Op. cit., p. 66.
30   Lacan, J. (1957). 'Psychoanalysis and its Teaching,' *Écrits*, Op. cit., p. 365.
31   Lacan, J. (1939). 'The Mirror Stage as Formative of the *I* Function as Revealed in Psychoanalytic Experience,' *Écrits*, Op. cit., p. 78.
32   Lacan, J. (1969–1970). *The Seminar of Jacques Lacan Book 17: The Other Side of Psychoanalysis*, trans. R. Grigg, New York, Norton, 2007.
33   Montrelay, M. (1977). *L'ombre et le nom: sur la féminité*, Paris, Minuit, p. 34, my translation.
34   Ibid.
35   Lacan, J. (1958) 'The Direction of the Treatment and the Principles of its Power,' *Écrits*, Op. cit. p. 366.
36   Lacan, J. (1972–1973). *Seminar 20: Encore*, Op. cit., pp. 78–89.
37   See Freud, S. (1923). 'The Infantile Genital Organization (An Interpolation into the Theory of Sexuality),' *The Standard Edition of the Complete Psychological Works of Sigmund Freud*, trans. J. Strachey et al., London, Vintage, 2001, 24 Vols., Vol.19, pp. 139-146, henceforth SE; references in German are in the German edition of Freud's complete works, *Gesammelte Werke*, ed. A. Freud, Frankfurt, Fischer Verlag, 1999, henceforth GW; Freud, S. (1924). 'The Dissolution of the Oedipus Complex,' SE 19, pp. 171–180; Freud. S. (1925). 'Some Psychical Consequences of the Anatomical Distinction between the Sexes.' SE 19, pp. 241–258; Freud (1931). 'Female Sexuality,' SE 21, 221–244; Freud, S. (1933). 'Femininity,' *New Introductory Lectures in Psychoanalysis*, Lecture 33, SE 22, pp. 112–135.
38   de Saussure, F. (1916). *Course in General Linguistics*, Op. cit., p. 67.
39   Lacan, J. (1957). 'The Instance of the Letter in the Unconscious, or Reason Since Freud,' *Écrits*, Op. cit., p. 416.
40   Lacan, J. (1964). 'The Position of the Unconscious,' *Écrits*, Op. cit., pp. 716–717.
41   Lacan, J. (1957). 'The Instance of the Letter in the Unconscious,' *Écrits*, Op. cit., p. 416.
42   Ibid.
43   Ibid., p. 415.
44   Lacan, J. (1957). 'The Instance of the Letter in the Unconscious,' *Écrits*, Op. cit., p. 416.
45   Ibid., p. 417, my emphasis.
46   Ibid., p. 417, my emphases.
47   Miller, J.-A. 'Reading a Symptom.' http://ampblog2006.blogspot.com/2011/06/nls-messager-24-20112012-towards-tel.html
48   Freud, S. (1923). 'The Infantile Genital Organization,' SE 19, pp. 143–144.
49   Lacan, J. (1958). 'The Signification of the Phallus,' *Écrits*, Op. cit., p. 575.
50   Freud, S. (1923). 'The Infantile Genital Organization,' SE 19, pp. 143–144; GW 13, p. 296.
51   Ibid., p.143; GW 13, p. 296.
52   Freud, S. (1909). 'Analysis of a Phobia in a Five-Year-Old Boy,' SE 10, p. 11.

53 Freud, S. (1923). 'The Infantile Genital Organization,' Op. cit., SE 19, p. 141;
    GW 13, p. 293
54 Lacan, J. (1958). 'The Signification of the Phallus,' *Écrits*, Op. cit., p. 580.
55 Freud, S. (1925) 'Some Psychical Consequences of the Anatomical Distinction
    between the Sexes,' SE 19, p. 257.
56 Freud, S. (1924). 'The Dissolution of the Oedipus Complex,' SE 19, p. 175; GW
    13, p. 398.
57 Ibid., p. 176.
58 Lacan, J. (1957–1958). *The Seminar of Jacques Lacan Book 5: The Formations of
    the Unconscious*, trans. R. Grigg, Cambridge, Polity, 2017, p. 324
59 Freud, S. (1924). 'The Dissolution of the Oedipus Complex,' SE 19, p. 176; GW
    13, p. 397.
60 Lacan, J. (1956–1957). *Le séminaire de Jacques Lacan livre 4: la relation d'objet*,
    Paris, Seuil, 1994, p. 266, my translation.
61 Montrelay, M. (1981). '*L'appareillage*,' *Cahiers Confrontation* 6, p. 38, my
    translation.
62 Lacan, J. (1972–1973). *The Seminar of Jacques Lacan Book 20: Encore*, trans. B.
    Fink, New York, Norton, 1998, pp. 74, 87.
63 Freud, S. (1931) 'Female Sexuality,' Op. cit., SE 21, p. 226.
64 Lacan, J. (1956–1957). *Séminaire 4: La relation d'objet*, Op. cit., p. 266, my
    translation.
65 Lacan, J. (1957). 'The Instance of the Letter,' *Écrits*, Op. cit., p. 417.
66 Montrelay, M. (1981). '*L'appareillage*,' Op. cit., p. 38, my translation.
67 Lacan, J. 'Seminar on "The Purloined Letter,"' *Écrits*, Op. cit., p. 21.
68 Lacan, J. (1957). 'The Instance of the Letter,' *Écrits*, Op. cit., p. 417.
69 Lacan, J. (1959). 'In Memory of Ernest Jones: His Theory of Symbolism,' *Écrits*,
    Op. cit., p. 599; 'The Signification of the Phallus,' *Écrits*, Op. cit., p. 526.
70 Lévi-Strauss, C. (1955). 'The Structural Study of Myth,' *The Journal of American
    Folklore*, 68.270, pp. 428–444.
71 Freud, S. (1909). 'Analysis of a Phobia in a Five-Year-Old Boy,' Op. cit., SE 10,
    pp. 65–66, 97–100, 105, 127, 131; Montrelay, M. (1981), '*L'appareillage*,' Op. cit.,
    p. 38, my translation.
72 Lacan, J. 'The Instance of the Letter.' *Écrits*, Op. cit., p. 417.
73 Ibid., p. 418.
74 Ibid., p. 417.
75 Lévi-Strauss, C. speaks of myth as a 'logical tool' or instrument produced at
    moments when civilization faces an impossible question. See Lévi-Strauss, C.
    (1955). 'The Structural Study of Myth,' Op. cit., p. 434.
76 Miller, J.-A. (1966). 'Suture: Elements of the Logic of the Signifier,' trans. J.
    Rose, *Screen* 18, 1978, p. 26.
77 Ibid., p. 25.
78 Ibid., p. 26.
79 Ibid., p. 32.
80 Ibid., p. 25.
81 Shakespeare, W. (1599). *As You Like It*, ed. Juliet Dunsiberre, London, Arden,
    2006, 2.7.35.
82 Lacan, J. (1958–1959). *The Seminar of Jacques Lacan Book 6: Desire and its
    Interpretation*, trans. B. Fink, Cambridge, Polity, 2019, p. 327.
83 Miller, J.-A. (1966). 'Suture,' Op. cit., p. 30.
84 Lacan, J. (1958–1959). *Seminar 6: Desire and its Interpretation, Op cit.*, p. 327.
85 Shakespeare, W. (1601). *Hamlet*, ed. H. Jenkins, London. Arden, 1982, 3.4.103.
86 Lacan, J. (1958–1959). *Seminar 6: Desire and its Interpretation*, Op. cit., p. 354.
87 Shakespeare, W. (1599). *Hamlet*, Op. cit. 3.4.103.

88   Freud, S. (1906). 'Psychopathic Characters on the Stage,' SE 7, p. 309.
89   Shakespeare, W. *Hamlet*, Op. cit., 4.2.29.
90   Lacan, J. (1958–1959). *Seminar 6: Desire and its Interpretation*, Op. cit., pp. 353–354.
91   Montrelay, M. (1977). *L'ombre et le nom*, Op. cit., p. 151, my translation.
92   Ibid., my translation.
93   Shakespeare, W. (1601). *Hamlet*, Op. cit., p. 1.1.153–157.
94   Ibid., 3.4.127.
95   Ibid., 3.4.154.
96   Lacan, J. (1957–1958). *Seminar 6: Desire and its Interpretation*, Op. cit., p. 354.
97   Ibid.
98   Shakespeare, W. (1601). *Hamlet*, Op. cit., 1.5.171.
99   Lacan, J. (1958–1959) *Seminar 6: Desire and its Interpretation*, Op. cit., p. 290.
100 Lacan, J. (1958). 'The Signification of the Phallus,' *Écrits*, Op. cit., pp. 580–581.
101 Ibid., p. 581.
102 Lacan, J. (1957). 'The Instance of the Letter,' *Écrits*, Op. cit., p. 417.
103 Ibid., p. 416.
104 Lacan, J. (1958). 'The Signification of the Phallus,' *Écrits*, Op. cit., p. 581.
105 Lacan, J. (1956–1957). *Séminaire 4: La relation d'objet*, Op. cit., p. 155, my translation,
106 Ibid., my translation.
107 Freud, S. (1923). 'The Infantile Genital Organization,' SE 19, pp. 143-144.
108 Lacan, J. (1956–1957). *Séminaire 4: La relation d'objet*, Op. cit., p. 155, my translation.
109 Stoichita, V. (1997). *The Self-Aware Image: An Insight into Early Modern Painting*, Cambridge, Cambridge University Press, p. 215. See also Biberman E. and Zisser, S. (2018), *Art, Death, and Lacanian Psychoanalysis*, London, Routledge, pp. 65–67.
110 Ibid.
111 de Man, P. (1984). 'Autobiography as De-Facement.' *The Rhetoric of Romanticism*. New York, Columbia University Press, pp. 67–81. See also Biberman, E. and Zisser, S. *Art, Death, and Lacanian Psychoanalysis*, Op. cit., pp. 67–69.
112 I wish to thank Efrat Biberman for this reference.
113 Lacan, J. (1956–1957). *Séminaire 4: La relation d'objet*, Op. cit., p. 155, my translation.
114 Ibid., my translation.
115 Ibid., my translation.
116 Lacan, J. (1957). 'The Instance of the Letter,' *Écrits*, Op. cit., p. 417.
117 Lacan, J. (1958). 'The Signification of the Phallus,' *Écrits*, Op. cit., p. 575.
118 Freud, S. (1924). 'The Dissolution of the Oedipus Complex,' SE 19, p.176.
119 Lacan, J. (1958). 'The Signification of the Phallus,' *Écrits*, Op. cit., p. 526.
120 Lacan, J. (1958–1959). *Seminar 6: Desire and its Interpretation*, Op. cit., p. 300; see also Lacan, J. (1957–1958). *Seminar 5: The Formations of the Unconscious*, Op. cit., p. 363; Lacan, J. (1958). 'Signification of the Phallus,' *Écrits*, Op. cit., p. 581.
121 Lacan, J. (1957–1958). *Seminar 5: The Formations of the Unconscious*, Op. cit., p. 327.
122 Lacan, J. (1958). 'The Signification of the Phallus,' *Écrits*, Op. cit., p. 581.
123 Lacan, J. (1957–1958). *Seminar 5: The Formations of the Unconscious*, Op. cit., p. 327.
124 Lacan, J. (1958). 'The Signification of the Phallus,' *Écrits*, Op. cit., p. 581.
125 Lacan, J. (1957–1958). *Seminar 5: The Formations of the Unconscious*, Op. cit., p. 324.
126 Lacan, J. (1958). 'The Signification of the Phallus,' *Écrits*, Op. cit., p. 581.
127 Lacan, J. (1957–1958). *Seminar 5: The Formations of the Unconscious*, Op. cit., p. 327.

128 Ibid.
129 Lacan, J. (1957). 'The Instance of the Letter in the Unconscious,' *Écrits*, Op. cit., p. 415.
130 Lacan, J. (1957–1958). *Seminar 5: The Formations of the Unconscious*, Op. cit., p. 327.
131 Ibid.
132 Lacan, J. (1958). 'The Signification of the Phallus,' *Écrits*, Op. cit. p. 581.
133 Lacan, J. (1957–1958). *Seminar 5: The Formation of the Unconscious*, Op. cit., p. 327.
134 Lacanm J. (1957–1958). *Seminar 5: The Formations of the Unconscious*, Op. cit., p. 327.
135 Lacan, J. (1957). 'The Instance of the Letter,' *Écrits*, Op. cit., p. 417.
136 Lacan, J. (1958–1959). *Seminar 6: Desire and its Interpretation*, Op. cit., p. 299.
137 Lacan, J. (1958–1959). *Seminar 6: Desire and its Interpretation*, Op. cit., p. 300.
138 Ibid.
139 Ibid.
140 Lacan, J. (1964). *The Seminar of Jacques Lacan Book 11: The Four Fundamental Concepts of Psychoanalysis*, trans A. Sheridan, New York, Norton, 1999, p. 275.
141 Lacan, J. (1958). 'The Signification of the Phallus,' *Écrits*, Op. cit., p. 581.
142 Shakespeare, W. (1600). *The Merchant of Venice*, ed. J. Drakakis, London, Arden, 2001, 4.1.265.
143 Lacan, J. (1958–1959). *Seminar 6: Desire and its Interpretation*, Op. cit., p. 299. Ibid.
144 Lacan, J. (1957–1958). *Seminar 5: Formations of the Unconscious*, Op. cit., p. 323.
145 Ibid.
146 Lacan, J. (1958). 'The Signification of the Phallus,' *Écrits*, Op. cit., pp. 578–579.
147 Lacan, J. (1954). 'Introduction to Jean Hyppolite's Commentary on Freud's "*Verneinung*,"' *Écrits*, Op. cit., p. 310.
148 Lacan, J. (1957). 'Psychoanalysis and its Teaching,' *Écrits*, Op. cit., p. 371.
149 Lacan, J. (1957). 'The Instance of the Letter in the Unconscious,' *Écrits*, Op. cit., p. 429.
150 Ibid., p. 416.
151 Ibid., p. 429.
152 Lacan, J. (1964–1965). *The Seminar of Jacques Lacan Book 12: Crucial Problems for Psychoanalysis*, trans. C. Gallagher from unedited typescripts, lesson of 2.12.64, www.lacaninireland.com
153 Lacan, J. (1957). 'The Instance of the Letter in the Unconscious,' *Écrits*, Op. cit., p. 429.
154 Lacan, J. (1957). 'Psychoanalysis and its Teaching,' *Écrits*, Op. cit., p. 371.
155 Lacan, J. (1955). 'The Freudian Thing,' *Écrits*, Op. cit., p. 345.
156 Ibid.
157 Ibid., p. 360.
158 Freud, S. (1914). 'On Narcissism: An Introduction,' SE 14, p. 78.
159 Lacan, J. (1962–1963). *The Seminar of Jacques Lacan Book 10: Anxiety*, trans. A.R. Price, Cambridge, Polity, 2014, p. 220.
160 Lacan, J. (1958–1959). *Seminar 6: Desire and its Interpretation*, Op. cit., p. 321.
161 Lacan, J. (1958). 'Signification of the Phallus,' *Écrits*, Op. cit., p. 526.
162 Freud, S. (1922). 'Medusa's Head,' SE 18, pp. 273–274.
163 Lacan, J. (1971–1972). *The Seminar of Jacques Lacan Book 19:....Or Worse*, trans. A. R. Price, Cambridge, Polity, 2018, p. 206.
164 Lacan, J. (1953). 'The Function and Field of Speech and Language in Psychoanalysis,' *Écrits*, Op. cit., p. 262.
165 Ibid., p. 206.

Chapter 2

'Written in the sand of the flesh'

On modes of writing in the psychic apparatus

A Introduction: Two primal scenes of psychic writing

> How is it that orthography exists? It is the most stupefying thing in the
> world
>
> – Jacques Lacan,
> 'Geneva Lecture on the Symptom'[1]

If, as Lacan emphasizes, 'Freud's opus ... is absolutely unthinkable unless we
place the signifier's dominance in analytic phenomena at centre stage,'[2] this
stage, at once that of Freud's opus and of the Other scene this opus supposes
and makes emerge, is not empty of other protagonists. If 'everything pertaining to the psychological pregiven follows willy-nilly the signifier's train, like
weapons and baggage,' as Lacan writes in the 'Seminar on "The Purloined
Letter,"'[3] what this means is that the unconscious signifier trails along a
momentous entourage whose nature is semiotic. This entourage of the unconscious signifier as it emerges from the work of Freud is even more divorced
from signification than the unconscious signifier as Lacan reconceptualizes it
via his critique of Saussure. Nor is this entourage of the unconscious signifier
less embroiled than the signifier with the 'bloody scrap' caught up in semiosis
at the moment of the signifier's emergence, analysed in this book's previous
chapter. As theorized by Freud, both the unconscious signifier (in Freud's
terms, *Vorstellung*) and its entourage, whose semiotic nature is not separable
from the flesh and blood of which they are formed, are instances of a carnal
writing that does not mean but that determines a destiny.

In Letter 52 to Wilhelm Fliess, which slightly postdates the *Project for a
Scientific Psychology*, Freud proclaims the operation of semiosis and inscription in the psychic apparatus to be his most radical innovation to date. 'What
is essentially new in my theory,' he writes, 'is the thesis that memory is present
not once but several times over, that it is registered in various species of
'signs,' [*Zeichen*], elements of semiosis.[4] The most primal form of semiosis
Freud postulates, the '*Wahrnehmungszeichen*'[5] (what Strachey translates as
the 'signs of perception' and Lacan, more precisely, as an 'initial putting into

DOI: 10.4324/9781003037958-3

signs'[6]) has an affinity with the pictural: the German *zeichnen* means drawing or sketching. That Freud should shortly after rename this drawing '*Niederschrift*'[7] (literally 'underwriting') grants it calligraphic inflection. In Letter 52, Lacan notes in his examination of Freud's early metapsychology in the seventh seminar,

> the impression of the external world as raw, original, primitive … is effectively inscribed in something that, it is quite striking to note, Freud expresses right at the beginning of his thought as a *Niederschrift* … of something which makes a sign and which is of the order of writing. And I wasn't the one who made him choose that term.[8]

Nor is the reference to components of the psychic apparatus as instances of a writing peculiar to this early Freudian text. Almost every time Freud speaks about the processes of the psychic apparatus, Lacan says in the sixth seminar, he uses terms such as *niederschreiben*, has recourse to the language of what is inscribed and imprinted.[9] That in Letter 52 the most fundamental form of semiosis in the psychic apparatus is described as pictorial as well as inscriptorial, however, is not without relation to the postulation of fundamental modes of psychic inscription as scenes, metapsychological processes that can be imagined as seen. 'It is always with the help of words that man thinks,' Lacan says in the 'Geneva Lecture on the Symptom,' 'and it is in the encounter between these words and his body that something takes shape' ['*se dessine*,' literally 'draws itself'].[10] Seizing the body's organicity in its movement, writing as it first appears in psychoanalytic theory is inseparable from a drawing or sketch. Psychic writing, that is, is carnal and corporeal, and it appears in the flesh as a drawn scene, in effect – as two scenes.

These scenes, detailed in the *Project for a Scientific Psychology* (1895), are constitutive occurrences of whose derivatives the entire chain of unconscious signifiers is 'inhibit[ory].'[11] Freud names these scenes the experience of satisfaction [*Befriedigungerlebnis*], and the experience of pain [*Schmerzterlebnis*].[12] The first involves an 'endogenous stimulus' originating in a '*Not das Lebens*' [need of life] which the subject is initially 'helpless' to satisfy himself and which requires a 'specific action' to be carried out in the external world by means of a 'helpful person,' a primordial Other.[13] The second is conceptualized only as the failure of 'contrivances of a biological nature.'[14] Pain for Freud, that is, is a constitutive subjective experience which involves the shattering of biological limits that might have provided protection. Satisfaction, on the other hand, is an experience which has no less 'radical results on the development of the individual's functions,' but that is predicated on the succouring presence of the Other.

Both these primal scenes of psychic life have a psychological 'residue' and a metapsychological correlate. The residual yield of the experience of satisfaction is a 'wishful state' and its metapsychological correlate is a 'positive attraction towards the object wished-for,' towards the Other who had dispensed the experience of satisfaction that had relieved the vital need.[15] The experience of pain leaves behind the residue of an unpleasurable 'affect' which Freud describes as a 'repulsion.'[16] The metapsychological correlate of the experience of pain is the 'irruption' of 'excessively large' quantum into the psychic apparatus and a 'large rise' in the level of excitation in it.[17] It is a breaking in, a shattering which is on the side of a positivity that increases to a surplus. The primal experience of satisfaction, for its part, results in the negativity of a 'state of desire' [*Begierdezustand*].[18]

One of the foundational scenes of the unconscious, then, is metapsychologically underlain by an axiomatics of negativity, of a minus; the other – by an axiomatics of excess presence Lacan would later call a *plus de jouir*.[19] One has to do with the work of subtraction, the other – with the work of addition.

Addition and subtraction are also fundamental to the operation of giving form to matter as a distinctly human activity, the activity of art. In the Italian Renaissance, addition and subtraction were explicitly conceptualized as techniques of the visual art of sculpting by major theorists of art such as Leon Battista Alberti and Leonardo da Vinci. In *Della Statua* [Of Sculpting] of 1443, Alberti theorizes two ways of giving form: the *via di levare* (way of subtraction) and the *via di porre* (way of addition). Sculpting or the way of giving material a form that 'remain[s] continuously stable and firm,' Alberti says, proceeds 'through two paths.'[20] Some proceed *per via di levare*, by 'removing that material which is deemed superfluous.' These, he goes on, 'we call Sculptors, brothers perhaps of those who carve into seals the features of faces once buried.' Others 'work by adding, like silversmiths, beating silver with hammers, stretching or extending it to the form they desire.'[21] If, as Freud puts it in the *Project*, components of the psychic apparatus both find their paradigm in a pictorial scene of either addition or subtraction and, as he puts it in Letter 52, are forms of transcription and retranscription, *Niederschrift* and *Wiederschrift*, one may describe these components in Albertian terms as ways of writing and/as drawing that proceed by *via di porre* and *via di levare*.

Nor did the relevance to psychoanalysis of the distinction, formulated by Renaissance theorists of art, escape Freud. In his 1904 essay 'On Psychotherapy,' Freud has recourse to the distinction between *via di porre* (or *pone*) and *via di levare* as formulated by Leonardo in his 'The Practice of Painting' (c. 1540) to clarify the schism between suggestion and psychoanalytic treatment. 'The sculptor,' Leonardo writes, 'produces the light and shade from taking off from the block in carving [*levare*]' so that the shadows are produced not by him but by 'nature itself,' while in painting shading is the result of the imposition of layers of paint, by *via di porre*.[22] Sculpting that proceeds by way of subtraction, Leonardo implies, manages to implicate nature itself in the production of an aesthetic effect.

Freud finds in Leonardo's distinction between art formed by addition and art relying on subtraction a conceptual grid for formulating the crucial difference between the therapeutic technique of suggestion, which proceeds by 'superimposing' ['*legt*', also emphasizing] a suggestion 'in the expectation that it will be strong enough to restrain the pathogenic idea from coming to expression.'[23] Suggestion, in other words, works by adding signifiers to those articulated by the subject, preventing the surfacing of a 'pathogenic idea' which might be painful for the subject at the price of clogging up his unconscious. Analytic treatment, on the other hand, Freud writes, 'does not seek to add or to introduce anything … but to take away something.'[24] The jouissance that plagues the subject in his symptomatology appears as a surplus, a surge of too much life. Analytic treatment seeks to subtract from this jouissance. That is why its voiding is an operation not only of subtraction but also of mortification. Hence Lacan's assertion that the 'symbol first manifests itself as the killing of the thing, and this death results in the endless perpetuation of the subject's desire.'[25]

Both in sculpting as Leonardo speaks of it and in analytic work as Freud speaks of it in 'On Psychotherapy' and elsewhere, subtraction is a technique economically preferable to addition because it effects a new element (shadowing in the case of sculpture, a hitherto unknown unconscious signifier in the case of analytic treatment). But in analysis subtraction is not only economically prudent. It has an ethical slant, for the experience of analysis is nothing if not an experience of loss, subtraction, castration, in which, in traversing his phantasm, the subject progressively cedes the menacing jouissance that had saturated it, thereby gaining more access to the desire that inhabits him.

There are, of course, significant differences between the theory and experience of a psychoanalysis and the techniques of sculpting, painting, and empirical writing to which Freud has recourse in his theorizations of the structure of the psyche and analytic technique. Most obviously, the material involved in the transcriptions and retranscriptions whereof Freud speaks and which proceed by either addition or subtraction is not the marble, silver, clay, or wax Alberti and Leonardo mention. The psychic apparatus, Freud writes in the *Project*, is 'taught *biologically*,'[26] emphasizing that it is within the *bios* that the *logos* metapsychologically manifest as writing by way of addition or subtraction emerges. Psychic inscription is a writing that lives, a writ(h)ing that is an index of the Thing beyond representation.

In the 'Geneva Lecture on the Symptom' of 1975, Lacan specifies the emergence of this writ(h)ing as a process of double addition. The fundamental addition, Lacan writes, is the 'debris' or 'detritus' left in the subject by the 'water of language,' which 'he will be forced to cope with.' To this addition, he continues, '*there will be added* … problems that will frighten him because he is premature,' of which Little Hans's precocious involuntary erections are perhaps a signal example.[27] The result of this double addition is what Lacan calls the 'coalesce[nce]' of 'sexual reality and language.'[28]

This coalescence is manifest as the various forms of psychic writ(h)ing enumerated by Freud and Lacan: the character and the unary trait (*einzinger zug*); the memory trace, the unconscious signifier whose Freudian names range from *Darstellung* to *Vorstellung* to *Vorstellungsräpresentanz*, the effect of the 'stereotype plate' Freud finds operative in the transference owing to which, if he so chooses and perseveres, the subject may be set on the path of what is wanting. These forms of psychic writ(h)ing proceed by way of addition to the fundamental double addition of language to flesh, of precocious sexual encounters to flesh traversed by language, or they proceed by subtraction from the flesh. They proceed, that is, by way of jouissance or of desire, and at times by way of both.

The following three sections of this chapter will seek to specify these forms of psychic writ(h)ing, enquiring throughout after the traces of the Thing in psychic orthography. They will also seek to delineate the traces of organicity that remain in the forms of writ(h)ing that mortify it, correlatives in psychic life of the facial features of those buried that are carved into seals that Alberti speaks of in *De Statua*. For in its writ(h)ings, the psyche always already mourns.

B *Per via di porre*: The writ(h)ing of jouissance

a Sculpture and pain

The experience of pain, Freud writes in the *Project*, is the experience of a surplus that irrupts, causing a noticeable increase in quantum experienced as unpleasure.[29] It has to do with an intense presence of what is there in excess, hence its conceptual alignment with modes of psychic insculpture or giving form by way of addition. But in the seminar on the *Ethics of Psychoanalysis*, Lacan precises a different metapsychological aspect of the art of insculpture and the statuesque. In Freud's terms in the *Project*, the psychic apparatus has 'a most decided inclination to a *flight from pain*'[30] by means of the effort to release the excess quantum pain is. This release takes place in part by means of the 'motor neurones which, when they are filled to a certain amount, conduct $Q\dot{\eta}$ into the muscles and accordingly discharge it,' that is to say, via the operation of components of the psychic apparatus that trigger the movement of the limbs.[31]

Yet not all of the excess excitation brought about by pain can be discharged motorically. About a quarter century before *Beyond the Pleasure Principle* and the formulation of the metapsychological findings concerning the apparatus's tendency to retain, not discharge, precisely what is unpleasurable, Freud already finds himself led to postulate the 'puzzling but indispensable hypothesis' that some of the excess excitation generated by the irruption of pain passes not to the motoric neurons that trigger motion in the musculature but to neurons of another type that Freud calls the 'key neurons' [*Schlüssen-Neuronen*] which 'do not discharge $Q\dot{\eta}$ but supply it in roundabout ways,' that is – that retain the excess excitation whose Lacanian name is jouissance.[32]

As in the case of 'sexual release' – the example to which Freud has recourse to confirm his hypothesis concerning the key neurons – in the case of pain as Freud theorizes it in the *Project* not all excess excitation is released motorically. Some of the jouissance involved in pain is retained, cannot be fled from; and while Freud hypothesizes that pain not released by movement is secreted by a gland,[33] Lacan provides an account of the destiny of this pain whose cue is provided not by biochemistry but by the arts. 'We should perhaps,' Lacan says, 'conceive of pain as a field which, 'in the realm of existence, opens precisely onto that limit where a living being has no possibility of escape':

> Isn't something of this suggested to us by the insight of the poets in that myth of Daphne transformed into a tree under the pressure of a pain from which she cannot flee? Isn't it true that the living being who has no possibility of escape suggests in its very form the presence of what one might call petrified pain? Doesn't what we do in the realm of stone suggest this? To the extent that we ... make of it something fixed, isn't there in architecture itself a kind of actualization of pain?[34]

The lesson Lacan draws from the arts is that the pain that cannot be fled from or completely discharged is not secreted but congealed. The cultural correlate of pain as Lacan describes it is what is given form in the realm of stone. This realm teaches Lacan about the experience of pain, however, not in itself but as it is transformed by human activity into an object of art, that is to say as matter made to manifest the distinctly human substance that Hegel, in theorizing art, called the Spirit.[35] Specifically, it is in matter made into thresholds and walls, objects of architectural art, and in sculptures, that Lacan finds his instruction concerning the experience of pain, especially as these appeared in the Baroque. Despite the period's aesthetic goals of providing pleasure, its products in stone are, and not incidentally, Lacan points out, referred to as '"tortured."'[36] For Lacan, this denomination confirms the status of works of architecture and sculpture as actualizations of a metapsychological process wherein an excess jouissance that irrupts through defensive mechanisms and cannot be fled from is cathected and fixed.

In the *Ethics of Psychoanalysis*, it is at Baroque architecture that Lacan wonders as an objective correlative of pain. But perhaps what best exemplifies Baroque stone-work as an artistic manifestation of petrified pain or frozen torture is not the ornate 'masonry and building' Lacan mentions but the creation of a Baroque master sculptor he silently alludes to: Bernini's 'Apollo and Daphne,' stone rendering of the myth of a woman petrified in a moment of torture, her face revealing the same suffering ecstasy, same jouissance experienced but not expressible in words Lacan would years later find in the face of one of Bernini's other great creations, the *Ecstasy of St. Teresa*.[37]

Figure 2.1 Gian-Lorenzo Bernini, Apollo and Daphne, 1622–1625, Rome, Galleria
Borghese, MiBACT – Borghese Gallery/photo: Luciano Romano.
Source: Reproduced courtesy of the Borghese Gallery, Rome.

Figure 2.2 Gian-Lorenzo Bernini, The Ecstasy of St. Teresa, 1647–1652, sculpture
in marble, stucco, and gilt bronze, height 350 cm, Church of Santa
Maria della Vittoria, Rome.
Source: Photo © Bibliotheca Hertziana – Max-Planck-Institut für Kunstgeschichte,
Rome.

Although like all of Bernini's great works, the statue is technically speaking an instance of sculpting *per via di levare*, the subtraction of material from a marble slab whether by drill or scalpel at which Bernini excelled,[38] metapsychologically speaking it is an instance of the emergence in art of the petrification of a *plus de jouir* and hence of the order of excess, of addition, *per via di porre*. Baroque sculpture upon its frozen movement is thus a cultural manifestation of the metapsychological scenario of the destiny of an excess jouissance that irrupts and cannot be fully discharged as Freud speaks of it in the *Project* and as Lacan specifies it in the *Ethics* seminar.

Freud's metapsychological works detail several forms this destiny of the petrification of excess jouissance can take when its matter is not stone but the living organism affected by language, and its scale not the momentous proportions of architecture and Baroque sculpture but the miniature measurements of letters and instruments of embossing. It is to the specification and analysis of these metapsychological insculptures, produced by way of addition, that I now turn.

b The character typed by the drive

What Freud calls 'character' is a category on whose divorce from the signifiable Wilhelm Reich, in proposing a theory and practice of *Character Analysis*,[39] paused hardly enough. Reich's theory of character is predicated on an attempt to seek an 'ineffable organic substance beyond speech,' and beyond what he calls the 'character armour.'[40] Seeking to short-circuit the register of the semblant so as to achieve direct access to the real, Reich pays with a loss of his own hold on the symbolic in the bargain.[41]

Yet it is from the writings of Freud that Reich drew the metapsychological category of character he developed to the point of delirium. In Freud's work, character is an instance of metapsychology where the coalescence of sexual reality and language is theorized as the product of a pulsating *via di porre*. 'What we describe as a person's "character,"' Freud writes towards the end of the *Three Essays on the Theory of Sexuality*, 'is built up [*aufgebaut*] to a considerable extent from the material of sexual excitations and is composed of instincts [*Trieben*] that have been fixed since childhood of constructions achieved by means of sublimation, and of other constructions.'[42] Character as Freud first theorizes it is a building or construction, and its constituents, in themselves constructions, are comprised of blocks that are sexual because their materiality is that of the drives that transform portions of organicity from instruments of survival to sites of peculiar satisfactions, into the erotogenic organs Freud would later theorize as the drive's source [*Quelle*].[43]

Early experiences relating to erotogenic organs and the objects ceded from them – pleasure in retention, pleasure in defecation, pleasure in the products of the excretory process – are at the foundation of characterological tendencies such as procrastination alternating with periods of feverish activity, or the habit of collecting. Such is the contention of Freud's early disciples – Ernest

Jones, Karl Abraham, Sandor Ferenczi and Isidor Sadger – who, following Freud's cue in the article of 1908, produced detailed and laborious accounts of the correspondences and interrelations between particular configurations of the anal zone and modes of conduct.[44] The axiomatics of the metapsychology assumed by these psychoanalysts seem to be, as Jacques-Alain Miller puts it, 'give me an organ and I will deduce you the world.'[45] In these articles as in Freud's study of character and anal erotism, the erotogenic organ seems to assemble into itself 'all the most elevated properties of a personality.'[46]

Far from only establishing 'an immense anal coding of all existence,' however, these articles by the early Freudians, Miller suggests, are the unarticulated backdrop of Lacan's characterological portraits of the obsessional and the hysteric in the last chapters of his seminar on *The Formations of the Unconscious*.[47] Against this backdrop, the findings of the early Freudians concerning the basis of tendencies of conduct in precocious peculiarities of the pleasure of an organ are silently utilized but also displaced. For if in the investigations of Abraham and Jones, as in Freud's article on character and anal erotism which is their theoretical foundation, character appears as the direct derivative of the libidinal permutations of an organ, as if by a short-circuit, Jacques-Alain Miller says, of the labyrinths of the symbolic,[48] Lacan insinuates that the symbolic is always already operative in the formation of character in its incidence as the demand of the Other – that the breast be taken, excrement given, gaze averted. 'The case of the obsessional,' Lacan says in the last lesson of *The Formations of the Unconscious*, 'hangs precisely on the precocious formation at th[e] horizon of the relationship to demand.'[49] For instance, while

> a suckling does not begin to be an obsessional from the moment that he is first suckled ... from the time he is first suckled he can already very well begin to create this gap which will bring it about that it will be precisely in the refusal to feed himself that he will find the evidence he requires of the love of his maternal partner.[50]

What this means is that the relation to an erotogenic organ which is at the foundation of character only ostensibly escapes the axis of psychic life extended between subject and Other. For it is in relation to an Other who demands that the mouth refusing to suckle just as the anus joying in retention is erogenized in the first place, its erogenization nothing but a defamiliarization with respect to algorithms of anatomical and physiological function. The erotogenic organ is a portion of organicity made strange to anatomy and physiology, caught up in the Other. It is as such that it operates at the roots of character.

The erotogenic organ, however, only ever operates as part of the drive as, in Lacan's terms, a montage,[51] a combinatory of four constituents (pressure, source, aim and object)[52] into which instinct is splintered when impacted by the signifier. Hence while foregrounding what he would come to call the source of the drive in the formation of character, Freud also speaks of this formation as derivative of the operation of the drive in its entirety. What appear as 'permanent' qualities of a subject, Freud writes, are nothing but 'either unchanged prolongations [*Fortsnetzungen*] of the original [drives], or sublimations of those [drives], or reaction-formations against them.'[53] These permanent qualities of behaviour are 'formed out,' [*Formel angeben*, literally 'given form'] Freud writes,[54] of constituent drives, subjected to an operation of a forming, which in the case of prolongation is precisely the stretching or extending Alberti uses to exemplify the technique of sculpting by addition, *per via di porre*.[55] In 'Transformations of Instinct,' Freud speaks of the outcome of this forming as a '*Gepräge aufdrückte*,'[56] the imprint of an imprint, an imprint in the second power, for its addition to the constitutive addition that is the detritus language leaves in the spoken subject is the stamp of a character grounded in a particular erotogenic organ. This pattern is at once the instrument onto which a pattern is moulded (by a subjectively particular modulation of an erotogenic organ affecting the vicissitudes of the drive of which it is a part) and the result of the operation of this instrument on the subject's flesh. A peculiar comportment, or on occasion, as Karl Abraham suggests in the conclusion of his article on the anal character, a morose expression, the appearance of sniffing at something traceable to a coprophilic pleasure in smell – the anal character, Abraham writes, sometimes 'seems to *stamp itself* on … physiognomy,'[57] that is to say, operates as a relief moulded by way of addition which imposes its imprint on features of a face, producing a grimace which is nothing but a way in which jouissance announces its hold on a body that speaks.

Character as metapsychological category is a procedure of writ(h)ing involving multiple additions: the moulding of what functions as a relief of a stamp by way of addition out of archaically acquired modes of satisfaction of an erotogenic organ and as addition to the fundamental addition of the detritus of inherited signifiers, and the idiosyncrasies of conduct resulting from putting this relief into operation. That what is at stake in character for Freud is a form of writing by additions is suggested also by his granting its product the double name of an inscription: 'character traits' [*Charakterzügen*] [*Charakter* = also 'letter' + *zügen* = traits or marks].[58] The character trait is the congealing, or in Freudian terms, fixation, of a primal mark that proclaims nothing but the memory of the mode of satisfaction of an organ and seeks to repeat or rewrite it. A writing by way of multiple additions that writ(h)es with an urgency of repeating a primal satisfaction of an erogenous zone while adding not only instances of this behaviour of an organ but forms of its trans-formation: prolongation, sublimation, reaction formation. The Freudian notion of character as rooted in the drive, J.-A. Miller says, is the 'parent' of the Lacanian notion of a *mode de jouir*.[59] It has to do with a mode of satisfaction different from the mode of satisfaction in the symptom *strictu sensu*, a mode of satisfaction 'more archaic than the symptom, anterior to the stage of the formation of symptoms, a stage where the drive is satisfied not in the symptom but in action.'[60]

Almost a decade after 'Character and Anal Erotism,' in 'Some Character Types Met with in Psychoanalytical Work,' Freud would qualify the additions at stake in character temporally as well as mechanically or procedurally. Character traits, Freud writes there, are 'peculiarit[ies]' of conduct whose temporality is double. Traceable to an archaic satisfaction which is not that of an organ but of a highly cathected 'experience of suffering,'[61] such as he would later find at the perverse core of the neurotic's unconscious phantasm, the character type as Freud theorizes it in this article also involves a second time, which is that of a grafting. The examples of this grafting, taken from the literary sphere, include a sense of entitlement supplementing the sense of an early injustice incurred (Shakespeare's Richard III) or the guilt attendant upon primal unconscious phantasies of an interdiction transgressed followed by an inability to tolerate these phantasies' realization (Shakespeare's Lady Macbeth).[62] These two instances of grafting seem antithetical: the first is an unabashed claim of a right to jouissance, the second is jouissance's interdiction. Both, however, are of the order of what appears clinically in the register of the subject's *plus de jouir* and is not amenable to the curative work of the signifier.[63]

Both for Freud in 'Character Types' and for Reich in *Character Analysis*, the structure of character in its metapsychological declension is that of a double addition. It consists of a core of enjoyment inherited and sedimented over time which Lacan qualifies as the arms the subject receives[64] and whose weight the subject retains even after analysis, and the defence against this enjoyment, which analysis can deconstruct.

What distinguishes the character trait metapsychologically is neither the experience of suffering at its core nor what is grafted on to it, but its intractability, its non-dialectic opaqueness to sense. The character trait, Freud writes, proves impervious to an analytic deciphering enquiring after the cause of symptoms, seeking to know 'what instinctual impulses are concealed behind them and are satisfied by them, and what course was followed by the mysterious path that has led from the instinctual wishes to the symptoms.'[65] The character trait as Freud defines it in the article on 'Character Types' is at base an archaic jouissance that receives form in a way that does not involve a subtraction. Like the character trait as Freud theorizes it in 'Character and Anal Erotism,' this form of enjoyment engenders a supplement: an avowed 'right to disregard the scruples by which others let themselves be held back,' a will to a sadistic jouissance which follows a sense of 'congenital and infantile disadvantages'[66]; an ambition that reigns only on condition it is unfulfilled, because its realization would confront the subject with a jouissance of transgression, much more shattering if it takes the form not of a phantasy but of a past event.

It is this supplement to a mode of jouissance acquired early on that years later Wilhelm Reich would qualify as a character 'armour,'[67] a term Lacan, accentuating this supplement's inscriptorial nature, would correct to 'a coat of arms'[68] or an 'armorial.'[69] The economic function of this armour, Reich writes, is to 'gain ... mastery over the libido, which is continuously pushing forward,' that is, to protect the subject from archaic jouissance which constantly seeks to erupt as suffering ecstasy and with which, Reich points out, anxiety is bound.[70] Because of the protective function of the character armorial, coat of arms displaying the blazon of the singularity of a conduct, Reich writes, this armorial is not amenable to the conventional analytic technique of free association under transference in which formations of the unconscious emerge and can be deciphered. Indeed, analysis constitutes a danger to the libidinal 'balance' (with the quantum of archaic jouissance in suffering) the character armorial as second moment in the formation of character achieves.[71] Unlike the symptom whose kernel is similarly made of a jouissance congealed by libidinal investment, but which is experienced as an ego distonic intrusion, an obstacle in life, an 'internal scission in the subject's being,' character in the metapsychological sense is ego syntonic, 'harmonized with the ego' and 'integrative of subjective identity.'[72] Hence the opposition to 'the doctor's efforts' Freud finds posed by character traits.[73] 'In the analysis,' Reich too writes, 'the neurotic character traits as a whole prove to be a compact defence mechanism against our therapeutic efforts.'[74] Character is encountered in psychoanalytic work as an obstacle. It is hence that Jacques-Alain Miller finds the legitimacy of situating it as related to the experience of the real in the analytic cure.[75]

If the second time in the formation of a character trait is that of the constitution of what Lacan precises as an armorial or heraldic sign, is it not the time of an addition to what it conceals as protection? Is it not, that is, an instance of unconscious inscription that proceeds *per via di porre*? No less significantly, what the character armorial protectively conceals, the suffering ecstasy always on the verge of a re-eruption that would shatter it, is itself, Reich specifies, the product of an accumulation. While like the symptom, Reich writes, character can be 'traced back to and understood on the basis of drives and experiences,' the symptom 'corresponds solely to one definite experience' (or rather, one could precise, a chain of several representations of such experiences, whose interconnections can be unravelled in the transference, as Freud showed already with the case of Emma in the *Project*).[76] Character, for its part, is not traceable to a definite sequence of representations tangled around an opaque kernel of enjoyment (in Reich's terms, the symptom's 'basis in the character'), but is 'an expression of the person's entire past.'[77] Character, that is to say, is the cumulative product of a particular mode of drive satisfaction along a temporal continuum. The symptom synchronizes a definite number of unconscious signifiers and a kernel of jouissance in a paradigm whose structure is rhetorical. The jouissante component of character as Freud theorizes it in 'Character Types,' and after him, Reich in *Character Analysis*, is the precipitate of a diachronic process of indefinite duration. It is the product of the sedimentation of a painful pleasure – as is the protection against this painful pleasure that Freud points to and exemplifies by the sense of entitlement of those bearing a primal wound. The protection can also be the will to jouissance of those plagued by the guilt of its achievement whether phantasized, experienced, or inherited as symbolic debt, and that Reich calls 'armour.' Character upon its two constituent parts, both products of a process of accumulation, is thus an inversion extended in time of what Freud in the *Project* theorizes as one of the two foundational *Ur* scenes of the psychic apparatus: the experience of pain [*Schmerzerlebnis*].[78] If pain for Freud in the *Project* is excess quantum (Q), later qualified as *Triebregung* or motion of the drive,[79] irrupting through 'screening contrivances,'[80] character as Freud theorizes it in 'Character Types' and Reich in *Character Analysis* is just those screening contrivances and the excess jouissance ever threatening to irrupt through them *as they sediment over time* to form part of a subject's singular mode of enjoyment: shattering pain plus what protects the subject from it. Freud defines the products of this sedimentation by means of signifiers from the semantic field of writing and imprinting: he calls them character *traits* [*züge*][81] and character *types* [*typen*].[82] Traits and types that are the product not of a subtraction but of an accumulation, devices that are reliefs formed by way of addition out of what is by its very nature a positivity: the subject's jouissance, always a *plus de jouir*. Character as Freud theorizes it, Jacques-Alain Miller says, is 'a subjective position with regard to jouissance.'[83]

The relief as device of inscription cannot but engender repetition. Even if it is, as Freud puts it with respect to the relief he finds operative in an amatory history, 'not entirely insusceptible to change in the face of recent experiences,'[84] the only form of writing it can generate in a given state is its own imprint. Indeed the reference to the imprinting of a relief (a 'stereotype plate') as a method of inscription which strikes the opening note to Freud's essay on the dynamics of transference runs throughout Freud's essay on character types. The first example in the essay that draws its 'types' not from the analytic work referenced in its title but from the canonical dramas of Shakespeare and Ibsen, an extract from Gloucester's soliloquy at the opening of *Richard III*, is shot through with the vocabulary of inscription *per via di porre*:

> But I, that am not *shaped* for sportive tricks,
> Nor *made* to court an amorous looking-glass;
> I that am *rudely stamp'd*, and want love's majesty
> To strut before a wanton ambling nymph;
> I, that am curtail'd of this fair proportion,
> Cheated of feature by dissembling Nature,
> *Deform'd, unfinish'd*, sent before my time
> Into this breathing world, *scarce half made up*,
> And that so lamely and *unfashionable*,
> That dogs bark at me as I halt by them;[85]

What interests Freud in this excerpt – the longest literary excerpt he cites in the 'Character Types' essay – is its profiling of Gloucester's early 'privation' or 'damage in infancy'[86] what Gloucester bitterly refers to as his having been 'curtail'd of … fair proportion' and 'Cheated of feature by dissembling Nature.' In terms of Freud's metapsychological account in the 'Character Types' essay, and Reich's development of the notion of character in *Character Analysis*, what is at stake in Gloucester's speech is the jouissante kernel of character, the sedimentation of bad encounters in the sphere of the drives (the privation of an object of satisfaction Gloucester names being 'curtail'd' or 'cheated') made possible by the more fundamental detritus left by language as it traverses the speaking being, to which the manifest part of character Reich calls the character 'armour' is added as protection.

But Shakespeare's text that Freud chooses to cite, with its references to what is 'made,' 'shaped,' or 'de-formed,' emphasizes that what is at stake for Freud in character in its metapsychological sense of the sedimentation of sexual reality over the detritus left in the body by language is also its operation as character in the orthographic sense of a writing device made by moulding, *per via di porre*, the 'character type' to which he alludes in his title or the 'stamp' of Gloucester's speech. It is this character type as writing device, of course, that constitutes Gloucester as 'character' in the sense of a literary protagonist, a *dramatis persona*, for as such he is made up of nothing but the characters or letters of the English language, as is Hamlet, Freud's key example in another essay on 'character': 'Psychopathic Characters on the Stage.'[87]

The conceptual connection, confirmed by equivoque, between orthographic, literary, and psychological character that speaks through Freud's citation of part of the opening soliloquy of *Richard III* is not by any means an idiosyncrasy of this most tragic of Shakespeare's history plays. *The Taming of the Shrew* is a comedic play that, as the name of one of its characters, Cambio (Italian for 'change') underscores, reflects throughout on the possibility of the change of roles: from drunkard to lord in the frame, 'from a wild Kate to a Kate / Conformable as other household Kates'[88] in the well-known inset play. A conversation among the many suitors of Kate's sister Bianca accentuates the nature of this change as an imprinting. 'Take you assurance of her / *cum privilegio ad imprimendum solum*,'[89] one of the suitors says to his peer while alluding to the age's practices of book licensing, granting resonance to the main plot's Aristotelian insistence on woman as matter to be (dis)figured by the figural pattern of her husband[90] by casting Bianca as a white or b(l)ank page on which her husband has the sole privilege to 'imprint,' as well as the b(i)ank in which he could deposit the coinage of his sperm. Rhetorical treatises of the English Renaissance have recourse to the mode of conduct dramatized by Shakespeare's Bianca to theorize a form of simile qualified as 'shamefest and as it were maidenly, that it may seem to led by the hand to another signification.'[91] Opposite this micro-narrative theorizing of 'shamefest' rhetorical comparison the character of Bianca embodies in Shakespeare's play is a micro-narrative theorizing which receives its full dramatization in the character of Kate – 'Kate the curst,'[92] a qualification that in the play's rhetorically-laden vocabulary resonates with the name of a rhetorical form, catachresis, whose Latin name is, appropriately for this play which stages the vicissitudes of the sadomasochistic drive in rhetorical terms, 'abuse.'[93] The play's final scene, in which the previously catachrestic Kate turns 'maidenly' as her sister had been while Bianca begins to assume the catachrestic qualities of a shrew abusing her husband is thus in effect an exchange of character imprints between two sisters qua *dramatis personae*. A change in the conduct of a *dramatis persona*, that is, is equated with the stamping of a page with a seal, a relief or a stereotype plate, the unspoken signifier 'character' knotting the three.

This signifier knotting conduct, protagonist and letter in a polyvalent equivoque becomes manifest in one of Shakespeare's later, and less canonical tragedies, *Timon of Athens*, which ends with a scene in which Alcibiades, the new ruler of Athens, reads an epitaph which the play's protagonist, now dead, had inscribed on his grave as synopsizing what he had been: 'Here lie I, Timon; who, alive, all living men did hate.' What Alcibiades reads from is not the tombstone itself but an 'impression' that is taken 'with wax' and 'brought away' by a soldier who discovers the grave. Though he 'cannot read,' the soldier identifies what he encounters on the grave as 'insculpture': what is sculpted in stone and can be impressed on pliable material as a text to be 'interpret[ed].' What the illiterate soldier brings away as *tessera* identifying him to the city's next ruler is at once a relief of sculpted letters and an apophtegmatic statement of the mode of existence of the play's major *dramatis persona*; it is triply, as the soldier puts it, a 'character.'[94]

The Shakespearean notion of character as repeatable imprint was not limited to the unveiling of dramatic personages as constructed out of letters, characters made of characters. As the Prologue to Shakespeare's *Henry V* suggests, Shakespeare conceived of the theatrical stage ('this wooden O,' 'this unworthy scaffold') itself as a blank page on which the texts spoken by the actors is 'printed,'[95] on which the character as mode of conduct of a *dramatis persona* as character appears as the result of the articulation of a text made up of alphabetical characters which the spectator introjects and projects.

Nor was the triple equivoque of character as letter, personage and mode of conduct foreign to Shakespeare and his contemporaries, emphasized as it was in the Theophrastan genre of character sketches which enjoyed renewed popularity in Elizabethan and Jacobean England. Character, Thomas Overbury writes at the opening of what was one of period's most popular books of sketches of the conduct of personages such as an actor, a moralist, or a rogue – typologies antecedent to Freud's 'Character Types' – 'signifieth to ingrave, or make a deep Impression. And for that reason a letter (as A, B) is called a Character.' Character, Overbury adds, 'is also taken for an Egiptian Hierogliphicke, for an impresse, or a short Embleme.'[96] Character, Shakespeare and other Elizabethan men of letters were well aware, is of the order of a mode of conduct that is ultimately an impress made of characters qua letters. What they could not have articulated is the localization of the inscribed characters at the foundation of peculiarities of conduct in the materiality not of books but of bodies that speak. It was not till four centuries later that Freud would articulate this localization. Appropriately, Freud would do so via a reading of Shakespearean texts.

What this means is that Freud's choice to exemplify 'Character Types Met with in Psychoanalytic Work' by means of Shakespearean texts has to do with more than the clinical discretion he suggests.[97] If Freud takes 'the opportunity of pointing to a figure created by the greatest of poets' to exemplify one of the peculiarities of human character, it is also because for this greatest of poets 'character' is the name at once of a personage, a mode of conduct, and a letter. So it is for Freud, who in citing, borrows the Shakespearean language synchronizing the formation of dramatic and psychological character with an inscription of character by 'stamp[ing]' to exemplify the first of his 'Character Types,' and who in exemplifying the second, not only alludes to another Shakespearean personage, Lady Macbeth, but takes on this language, describing her as a 'character which had seemed *forged* [*geschmiedet*] *from the toughest metal*' that then 'broke.'[98] Adopting as well as relying on the Shakespearean conception of the nature of a dramatic protagonist which has a ramified legacy in English Renaissance culture, Freud theorizes 'Character Types' as types also in the typographical sense, stamps forged from metal *per via di porre* and imprinted to make letters emerge on a surface.

But Freud's essay is not, of course, an essay in *belles lettres*, nor even a psychoanalytical inquiry into the legacy of a literary work such as his 'Psychopathic Characters on the Stage,' but a metapsychological work whose source and horizon is the clinic. What is psychoanalytically significant about Freud's recourse to and adoption of the Shakespearean language of character as device of inscription is not the unveiling of the *dramatis personae* who were to be canonized as some of the greatest sources of 'knowledge of the mind'[99] as made not of the flesh and blood where the mind manifests itself but of printed letters constitutive of Shakespearean drama.

The psychoanalytic significance of Freud's essay on character types is the displacement of this numismatic meta-theatrical language to the register of metapsychology, where what it helps reveal is the imprinting of character as precipitate of the drive in the organism itself. For Freud, Lacan says in the second seminar, 'the organism is essentially impressionable; the impression is elementary, and it is by virtue of that that it comes into play in what takes place at the level of symptoms.'[100] The Shakespearean character is the idea of the protagonist – what Freud in 'Psychopathic Characters on the Stage' describes as 'the hero in his struggles ... or defeat'[101] that emerges for the spectator as a result of the imprinting of the Shakespearean text, made of characters qua letters and spoken by an actor, on the blank apron stage. The Freudian character is the peculiarity of conduct that emerges in the life of the subject as a result of the imprinting of a type made of the sedimenta-tion, over time that may be the time of many generations, of residues of the drive in the subject's very flesh. Both are cases of an imprinting that involves the body, but in the first the body (of the actor) is the vehicle of an imprint-ing that takes place elsewhere; in the second, Freudian case, the subject's body is both the source of the imprinting stamp and the surface for its imprinting, the very stage for onto which the psychopathic character liter-ally mounts.

c The erotics of the stereo-type

Character as theorized by Freud, character in the metapsyhcological sense, Jacques-Alain Miller says in the course on *The Experience of the Real in the Analytic Cure*, which includes an extensive analysis of the category of char-acter in the work of Freud and his early followers, is 'ultimately the closest way in which analysts attempted to conceptualize, to respond by means of a concept, to what they encountered as the incidence of the body on the uncon-scious.'[102] The incidence of the body in what becomes part of the psychic apparatus, of the *bios* on (and in) the *logos*, is the case also in Freud's theori-zation, in 'The Dynamics of Transference,' of another form of psychic inscription: the 'stereotype plate [*Klichee*] (or several such)' that is 'constantly reprinted afresh—in the course of [the subject's] life.' This stereotype plate is none other than the subject's 'method for falling in love' – effectively the sub-ject's erotic 'preconditions' and the drives implicated in his amatory scenar-ios.[103] These constitute, Freud says, a device enabling a writ(h)ing to appear.

Since transference is a form of love, since the analyst is nothing if not a member in the 'psychical "series"' of the analysand's love objects,[104] it is in relation to the analyst that this writ(h)ing, the imprint of the stereotype plate of the analysand's erotic conditions, will emerge. The dynamics of transfer-ence whereof Freud speaks are thus but the clinical chronicle of the residues left behind by the subject's erotic conditions in which the analyst is caught up as dynamic, movable and moving object.

What causes erotic conditions of which the subject knows nothing to appear on the scene of the transference as pulsating hieroglyphic, moreover, is not only an instrument for but also the effect of a writ(h)ing by addition. For what is a 'stereotype plate' such as Freud refers to when conceptualizing the subject's mode of erotic conduct that appears on the scene of the transfer-ence but a matrix of letters cast in solid form? In the case of the stereotype plate that is the subject's erotic style, the source of the material accumulated in this matrix is initially said to be double: the influences brought to bear on the subject during his early years, and the subject's innate disposition. This disposition itself, however, Freud says, is 'a precipitate from the accidental effects produced on the endlessly long chain of our ancestors,'[105] part of what, in the essay on narcissism, he calls the 'entailed property,' the estate of which the individual subject is 'only the temporary holder.'[106] What this means is that if 'Δαίμων καὶ Τύχη [daimon kai tyché, Endowment and Chance] determine a man's fate,'[107] as Freud puts it when speaking of the stereotype plate operative in love life, it is only insofar as the daemonic power of inherited disposition is ultimately itself the product of contingencies long since forgotten.

In *The Ego and the Id*, Freud would specify the initially contingent psychic property that is inherited, that constitutes part, that is, of what in 'The Dynamics of Transference' he describes as the stereotype plate operative in amatory life, as the 'impressions' [*Eindrücke*, literally 'imprints'] made of the 'residues' [*Reste*] of 'the existences of countless egos' harboured in the id. These residues themselves, Freud later precises, are of the order of the '*Triebregungen*' (motions of the drive), and are subject to 'resurrect[ion]' [*Auferstehung*] as the superego[108], thus revealed to be yet another product of psychic writing by way of addition, an accretion of stamps made of ancestral remainders that remain concealed from consciousness but that return as imperatives to enjoy in the field of love, as long as this field remains clad in the thick fog of the phantasm. The stereotype plate of amatory life is what, as long as the phantasm has not been traversed, never ceases to seize objects of love (and hate) from which it manufactures the series of prints that are a subject's erotic history. In a subject's psychic life, such objects are the bearers of the imprint left by the plate that is made by the accretion of residues of the drive, encountered early on or inherited, and that in the phantasm, answers to the command 'thus shall you love.' The dissipation of this command in an analysis – never without residue – is the possible point of emergence of a new love, a new relation to the partner whose source of satisfaction is not phantasmatic but symptomatic, or better, sinthomatic.

d Copying jouissance: The unary trait

Neither character nor stereotype plate, however, are for Lacan the most crucial Freudian terms for precising the function of inscription in psychic life and in civilization more generally. It is the unary trait, Lacan's translation of the *Einziger zug* Freud theorized in the chapter on identification in 'Group Psychology and the Analysis of the Ego,' that Lacan singles out as the form of inscription that the whole question of the written revolves around.[109] Identification, Freud explains, 'behaves like a derivative [*Abkömmling*, also child] of the first *oral* phase of the organisation of the libido, in which the object that we long for and prize' – the love object constitutively surrounded by ambivalence – is assimilated by eating and is in that way annihilated as such.'[110] The consequences of such orally accented identification, Freud concludes later, in *The Ego and the Id*, appear as a form of psychic writing he had first theorized as a construction whose material is the drive and more specifically the erotogenic organ that is the drive's source. 'An interesting parallel to the replacement of object choice by identification,' Freud writes in a footnote to the third chapter,

> [i]s to be found in the belief of primitive peoples ... that the attributes of animals which are incorporated as nourishment persist as part of the character of those who eat them.[111]

What is incorporated [*einverleibten*] remains [*verbleiben*]. It is part of the *leib* resonating in Freud's qualification of identification, the body of the being affected by the verb (verb-*leiben*). Initially indistinguishable from object cathexis, Freud writes, identification becomes for the subject the sole condition under which wrenched objects can be given up. Set up within the ego as retheorized in Freud's second topography – the beyond of the symptom as disturbance which had been Freud's focus in the first – the object whose cathexis had to have been abandoned becomes what the ego absorbs. It is as such that it plays a role, Freud writes, in the 'building up' [*herzustellen*] of character.[112] Identification with wrenched objects is addition by absorption, the incorporation of living remains. Character traits that are vestiges of cathexes of objects given up are identification's precipitate: what remains of these remains as what is permanently written as what lives on as peculiarities of conduct.

Throughout Freud's work, character remains for him what is 'built' [*aufgebaut, herzustellt*], written by way of addition from material originating in the domain of the drive. But where the early work inflected this material as the forms of satisfaction of an organ, the drive's source, in Freud's later theorization of character it is the object (more precisely the cathexis of an object) by means of which the drive achieves its aim of satisfaction that is specified as the material from which character is constructed. The building blocks of character become for Freud less the erotogenic organ and more the cathexis of the object, cast as love object and conjugated as oral. Comportment becomes a matter less of the organ through which a subject prefers to enjoy, more of libidinally invested objects of love the subject inevitably incorporates, that is to say enjoys orally. If Freud's early work on character, though taking anal erotism as its model, implies that conduct may be the issue of various erotogenicities conjugated through the drive's source, his late work restricts conduct's constituent material to oral erotogenicity as it operates in the field of object cathexes. The subject's permanent and intransigent idiosyncrasies of behaviour, that is, are written by way of addition from how he psychically eats, destroys so as to preserve, portions of his libidinal investments in objects.

Freud teaches, however, that at times it is not the object of hate and love in itself that is incorporated and hence annihilated so as to persist but only an 'extremely limited' [*höchst beschränkte*] part of that object.[113] What Freud calls the *Einziger zug* is the product of precisely such a synecdochic incorporation. In its Freudian declension, the *Einziger zug* is an inscription of a select portion of the object in the subject's own body by way of an incorporation or swallowing. Its paradigmatic example, for Freud, is Dora's assumption of her father's cough. Freud describes this synecdochic inscription as what the subject has 'copied' [*kopiert*][114] from a libidinally invested object.

In Lacan's treatment of the *Einziger zug* in the seminar on transference, however, the synecdochic inscription that is the unary trait is delimited and specified in a way that aligns it with the primordial experiences Freud posited at the foundation of the psychic apparatus in the *Project for a Scientific Psychology*. It is a particular portion of the libidinally invested object that becomes ingested as a unary trait for the subject – that portion in which the subject seeks the most preliminary response to his distress, the Other's gaze. The Other's response in the scopic field to a signal of *Hilflosigkeit* can be the 'sign of the Other's assent,'[115] a foundation of an experience of satisfaction that breeds the wishful state of encountering its copy in the gaze of those who in seeing us, make us at once seen and deserving of love.[116] Obviously, this 'little sign' of being deserving as seen is not always at the subject's disposal, as the primordial Other from which it is sought may 'at any moment change its preference.'[117] When the subject emits signs of distress, there is no guarantee of these signs' encountering, in the gaze of an Other, the sign of assent that can become the foundation of a sense of being loved. The portion of a libidinally cathected Other that is then introjected is a gaze that does not see, prone to be repeated in ravaging encounters in the love life of the subject who, for all that, does not cease to seek, and on occasion miraculously finds, a gaze of another order that can supplant or at least veil the ravaging unary trait. This is the miracle of love Lacan speaks of in the seminar on *Transference*, and it may emerge at any point in the subject's life. In its wake, the chain of unconscious signifiers to which the *Einziger zug*, albeit not a signifier, bears the relation of a determining initiator,[118] may come to organize itself differently.

What this treatment of the *Einziger zug* in Lacan's eighth seminar indicates is that for Lacan, the unary trait as a mode of psychic writing that is a 'primordial symbolic term' that, for all that, is not a signifier but a sign, is not synecdochic but iterative. For Lacan, that is, the copying at stake in the *Einziger zug* seeks not to indexically preserve an entity (the Other who responds to the signal of distress) through the gaze as object of the drive by means of which this Other responds, but to multiply the registration of this part. Its logic, that is, is the logic of repetition, that is to say, in analytical terms, of jouissance beyond the pleasure principle. The unary trait, Lacan says in *From the Other to the other*, is 'the essential of the effect of what for us analysts … is called repetition.'[119] It is repetition's origin and end – both what is sought for in repetition and the reason repetition takes place.[120]

But the synecdochic declension of the *Einziger zug* in Freud's text is only seemingly discrepant with the iterative accent of the category's Lacanian formulation. In terms of elocutionary structure and theory, both synecdoche and repetition are forms hinging on unicity or sameness. For instance, in

Richard Sherry's *Treatise of Schemes and Tropes* (1550), the first rhetorical treatise to be published in the English vernacular, *intellectio* (Latinate synonym for synecdoche) is defined 'when *one* thyng is vnderstand by another y^t is of the *same* maner and kind,' and repetition [*Repeticio*] is said to occur 'when in lyke and diuerse thynges, we take our begynnyng continually at *one* & the *selfe same* word.'[121] In another influential rhetorical treatise of the English Renaissance, Abraham Fraunce's *Arcadian Rhetorike,* one of the forms of synecdoche is said to occur when 'by *one* integrall member the whole is signified.' Forms of repetition, for their part, occur in different levels of the microstructure of the signifier. They can be 'the continued repetition of the *same* word in one or diuers sentences,' or 'the seuered repetition of the *same* sound.' Examples for this return of the same include '*Anaphora* ... a bringing back of the same sound, when the *same* sound is iterated in the beginning of the sentence,' or '*Epistrophe* ... turning to the *same* sound in the ende,' or '*Symploce* ... when the *same* sound is repeated both in beginnings and endings,' or '*Epanados,* ... turning to the *same* sound, when *one* and the *same* sound is repeated in the beginning and middle, or middle and end.'[122] What the theorizations of the rhetoricians from the time of rhetoric's apex in civilization make clear is that synecdoche and repetition, the seemingly different elocutionary forms by means of which Freud and Lacan theorize the unary trait as a form of psychic inscription, in effect constitute different modes of the linguistic use of the One. The *Einziger zug*, Lacan says, is '*mono*-formal or *mono*-semantic.'[123]

   Each of these linguistic forms of unicity, however, is situated differently in the taxonomy of elocution prevalent in theory of language in the West since Quintilian's *Institutio oratoria*. Both Sherry and Fraunce, who utilize this taxonomy, note that synecdoche is a trope, while the various forms of repetition are figures or schemes. What this means is that synecdoche is recognized as a linguistic form which involves the 'turning' of a word 'from his naturall signification ... to some other'[124] or as Henry Peacham puts it, 'an artificall alteration of a word, or a sentence, from the proper and natural signification to another not proper,'[125] while repetition is situated as a use of language that has to do not with signification but with the '*forme* of words, oration, or sentence,'[126] what Sherry and Fraunce call their 'fashion'[127] – their use as material for an aesthetically pleasing act of *poesis*.[128]

   Synecdoche, that is, is a linguistic form situated on the axis of the signified which Fraunce names as such long before Saussure was to theorize it for modern linguistics and psychoanalysis. It is an elocutionary form that as trope, involves an operation on semanticity. The various forms of repetition, on the other hand, are classified as pertaining to the figural axis of language that is apportionable into units of different size – an entire oration, sentences, words or the sounds comprising words – but that does not involve semantic transformation.

This is not to say that rhetorical theory does not recognize distinctions among forms of repetition. For instance, polyptoton, a repetition of 'the selfe same words and sence' in units that vary syntactically is considered a virtue of language because its constituting words 'haue diuers fallings or terminations.'[129] On the other hand, repetition without variation, the 'repeting agayn of one word or more in all one sentence,' is described as *Inutilis repeticio* and listed as linguistic fault.[130] Theorists of rhetoric, that is, distinguish between forms of repetition involving some measure of diversity, variation, alterity, and those that do not, or in psychoanalytical terms, between forms of repetition implicating something of the Other and those which are purely of the One. What this means is that while synecdoche is unequivocally an instance of the linguistic use of the One, in the case of repetition it is only those forms whose only utility is the iteration of the same without variation that are purely of the One. They are the rhetorical manifestation of what Lacan calls the return of the same, of a jouissance serving nothing beyond itself, a Macbethian jouissance signifying nothing.

These forms of repetition are the ultimate consequence of the logic of the One as it manifests itself in elocutionary theory. It is to this manifestation of the One beyond the veils of sense that Lacan is led when he extracts the category of the *Einziger zug* from Freud's 'Group Psychology and the Analysis of the Ego' and follows its structure to its logical conclusion. This operation of extraction and exhaustion leads Lacan to displace the category of the *Einziger zug* from a rhetoric of synecdoche which assumes a concealment to a rhetoric of inutile repetition, that is to say, from the domain of sense to what is beyond sense, and in psychoanalytical terms, from incorporatory identification to the insistence and iteration of a jouissance. The *Einziger zug* in its Lacanian declension becomes a 'trait that is a One,'[131] a unity that recurs as always identical to itself, even when it has a 'relationship to the signifying battery' that it sets in motion.[132]

Nevertheless, the *Einziger zug* as Lacan theorizes it retains the synecdochic genealogy of its first, Freudian formulation. For if the *Einziger zug* can be said to be 'the *son* of enjoyment [jouissance] that's found in psychosomatics,'[133] it is only insofar as it is the memory trace of a body event of intense satisfaction that the subject isolates from others in what amounts to a synecdochic operation. This isolation, however, is followed by a hypercathexis in which the synecdochized trace of a body event such as the encounter with a loving gaze or its absence is assumed as site of a '*Fixierung*' [fixation]. In this hypercathexis, the memory trace at stake is 'frozen'[134]: in effect extracted and cut off from other memory traces at the same time that it becomes charged with excess libido, turns into a site of *plus de jouir*. It is as so subjectively fixed that the memory trace of a body event becomes a trait susceptible of producing what Freud calls copies, and these are not only identificatory but iterative. Fixation of libido in the isolated memory trace is hence in effect the metapsychological point of the *Einziger zug*'s transformation from a synecdochic operation to the site of a repetitive copying of a *plus de jouir*, from the isolation of a One to the reproduction of a profusion of Ones, each charged with jouissance in abundance. The repeated copying of what is already copious (with enjoyment) makes the *Einziger zug* as Lacan specifies it after Freud a metapsychological correlate of what Renaissance theorists of rhetoric termed '*copia*': a profuse use of language, to which Erasmus devoted a treatise,[135] and whose discursive resonances involve both the bounty of the cornucopia and the chthonic deity Ops, goddess of abundance.[136]

Manifest physiologically at the same time that it is the product of a rhetorical mechanism involving the transformation of a synecdoche into a *repetitio inutilis*, the *Einziger zug* as subjective *copia* is indeed, as Lacan puts it, a manifestation of 'the body in the signifier'[137] – or perhaps even more precisely, of the body in what is of the order of semiosis, of inscription. This inscription, Lacan writes in 'The Youth of Gide' is of a particular kind: it registers instances in the subject's life where 'the fire of an encounter has etched his coat of arms'[138] – the same inscriptorial term Lacan uses to precise the characterological defence Reich imaginarily termed 'character armour' (see above). That this should be so serves to accentuate not only the heraldic functioning of character type and unary trait as forms of psychic inscription that can recur in families (see below), but also the common metapsychological derivation of both these forms of psychic inscription in a moment of jouissance. Both are instances of psychic inscription that proceeds through accretion – whether of satisfaction or of pain – rather than loss, *per via di porre* and not *per via di levare*.

The inscriptorial specifications of the *Einziger zug* as Lacan theorizes it after Freud, however, extend beyond the copy, etching, and coat of arms. The unary trait, Lacan writes in 'The Youth of Gide,' may be thought of in terms of a hieroglyph, which as such 'may be transferred from one text to others.'[139] The unary trait, that is to say, is an inscription that is not only opaque to sense but that can be transferred, in its opacity, across subjects (as in the case of Dora's assumption of her father's cough),[140] and also across generations, as in the instances of traits repeated in the histories of families or nations of which the salvation from destruction marked in most Jewish holidays may be a signal example. The differences between unary traits, to a significant extent accounting for the clinical differences between one analysis and another, are incidental, Lacan implies, to their structural functioning as transmissible opacities of enjoyment. 'Whether the hieroglyph is Egyptian or Chinese is in this respect the same,' he says, 'it's always a question of a configuration of the trait.'[141]

The transmissibility of the unary trait qua hieroglyphic which Lacan accentuates in its retheorization is more precisely thought of, he implies, in terms of a form of inscription differing from the one to which Freud had recourse when first conceptualizing it, in terms of the forming not of a copy but of a 'print.'[142] For if the notion of copying implies the duplication of the same, that of printing specifies a duplication that involves the pressing of a plate to a surface. The functioning of the unary trait, Lacan says, 'ought to be recalled' in terms of the pivotal moment in the history of writing that is the invention of Gutenberg's printing press in 1436, for it is this invention which made it possible to think in cultural terms of what metapsychology always reveals: the recurrent 'imprinting of surface schemas' which have proven to yield a satisfaction.[143] Originating in the body's surface, these schemas also take this surface, which in the being traversed by language is distinct in its being 'impressionable,'[144] as the site on which they imprint themselves.

The unary trait as Lacan precises it is thus a psychic instance where 'the body lets itself go,' abandons the algorithms of biological subsistence, 'to write something of the order of the number,' to congeal in itself a semiotic element that does not mean but whose recurrences can be counted.[145] It is precisely as countable element that is not of the predictable order of biological schemas of stimulus and response that the unary trait is repeated in a subject's life, its instances constituting a series of marks branded in the flesh whose isomorph Lacan finds in the archaeological discovery of the 'little row' of marks 'on what seemed to be the rib of an antelope.'[146] But in the life of the subject, the row is not of grooves in bone but of signs of miraculous instances of a loving gaze, and all too often, of paroxysms of pain made to congeal by the quantum of libido invested in them, Baroque insculptures of the history of the subject's painful jouissance.

These insculptures, Lacan teaches, 'enslave the subject'[147] both to the petrified pain they repeat or to the loss of the satisfaction they register and to the anticipation of its repetition or reinscription, for which they 'are content to make us wait.'[148] Yet the anticipation they generate also has another function in psychic life, to do with the destiny of the signifier in neurosis. For the neurotic subject, Lacan teaches, the structure of the unconscious signifier is anticipatory, its equivalent in conscious speech the sentence 'interrupted before the significant term: "I'll never...," "The fact remains...," "Still perhaps..."'[149] This is because, as Jacques-Alain Miller points out in 'Interpretation in Reverse,' the unconscious interprets, and it wants to be interpreted, each of the signifiers constituting it seeking the sense another signifier would confer upon it.[150] The anticipatory structure of the unconscious signifier is not a *différance* as Derrida speaks of it, that elusive motion between the differential components of writing and speech that never halts at a point of 'presence-being.'[151] For the postponement unconscious anticipation involves is not endless, just as interpretation, as Lacan points out in the eleventh seminar, is not 'open to all meanings.'[152] Sentences such as those by means of which Lacan exemplifies the unconscious signifier's anticipatory structure 'nevertheless make sense,' he writes.[153] But this is a peculiar sense, which 'all the metaphors in the world cannot exhaust,' because it does not have any, 'since it is the mark of the iron with which death brands the flesh when the Word has disentangled flesh from love.'[154] What Lacan thus intriguingly describes in inscriptorial terms is the archaic moment of the emergence of a unary trait of the kind that does not register a satisfaction. This is, rather, an archaic moment when the scenario of satisfaction is undone, becomes unmaintainable even as hallucination, and turns experience of pain. At such a moment, the fulfilment of the *Not das Lebens* by a helpful Other, registered as the Other's gaze that loves in its seeing, is suddenly disentangled from this love because the Other fails to respond to the cry or motion of distress. All that remains at such moments is flesh writhing, caught in the paroxysms of what in psycho-grammatological terms is the death inscribed in it by way of addition, of an excess suffering that is congealed. Writhing flesh, a portion of organicity seized in unpleasure is mounted onto the scene of an Other who does not love – who disrespects, judges, abandons, violates, abuses. Libidinal investment in the product of this mounting causes it to congeal, precipitating the insculpture that is the unary trait, petrified pain, susceptible of iteration – but not of sense-making interpretation. In effect, the sense-making interpretation sustaining long years of analytic deciphering is nothing but a delirium whose function is to cover this insculpture of the first pains just as painting, Lacan teaches in the eleventh seminar, covers the gaze.

This is why in the analytic cure, the isolation of the insculpture that is the unary trait in its declension as libidinally invested scene of pain which the subject intakes as a most loved unloved object brings the delirium of deciphering that had covered it to a halt. The non-susceptibility to further deciphering of the insculpture written in the sand of the flesh that is the unary trait, the unary trait's non-sense, then, is precisely the anticipated sense structuring the unconscious signifier: what is beyond the sense oppressive for a neurotic subject as long as he is caught in his phantasm or its traversal. If 'the mental is discourse,' as Lacan puts in *L'insu*, that is to say, the enchainment of memory traces into the phantasm or mechanisms of producing unconscious formations such as dreams or symptoms, there is also the experience of 'lesions of the body ... which suspend' this discourse. The metapsychological name of these lesions is the unary trait.[155]

At the end of neurotic sense-making upon its often ravaging, usually masochistic scenarios of which 'a child is being beaten' is the Freudian paradigm, is the metapsychological isomorph of Bernini's ravaged Daphne, frozen in a scene of pain she cannot escape, always already turning into leaves that can carry the imprint of her torture. An actualization of the *Ur*-scene of pain copied by incorporation, the unary trait isolated at the end of analysis in the field of the neuroses is an 'elementary phenomenon of the subject,' as it was, Miller says, 'before it was articulated in the formation of the unconscious which gives it a sense of delusion.'[156] It is as so isolated that a painfully repeated unary trait can serve as premise of a renewed relation to the world. This can be a relation to the painful unary trait that is no longer the insistence on its repetition. It can also be the substitution of this wounding unary trait by the subject's assent to encounter and register the sign of what was sorely absent in the beginning: a gaze that suddenly emerges in response to a signal of *Hilflosigkeit*; a gaze that sees, and in so seeing, beckons the subject to assume the dignity of being worthy of being loved.

C *Per via di levare*: On the hysterical inscription of the unconscious symbol

a Myths of the origin of mnemonic writing: Phaedrus and Simonides

What is writing? The question of the written that to Derrida bespeaks a history of debasement with respect to speech which he dubs a 'logocentrism,'[157] repeatedly leads Lacan to superlatives indexing a proximity to the impossible, in particular where its origin is concerned. That orthography exists at all, Lacan says in the 'Geneva Lecture on the Symptom,' is the 'most stupefying thing in the world.'[158] To think of its primordial emergence, he says in *From the Other to the other*, 'is the most difficult thing.'[159] Two years later, however, Lacan would offer what is his most sustained meditation on writing, '*Lituraterre*,' in which he makes explicit what writing is for him at that relatively late period of his teaching, where the focus shifts from the symbolic to the real, from the signifier to jouissance, from the order of representation to what can never be represented even as unconscious. Most notably, Lacan in '*Lituraterre*' rejects the collocation of writing and the signifier that is a cornerstone of Freudian metapsychology. 'Writing is not impression,' he says emphatically, invoking Freud's *Project for a Scientific Psychology* and Letter 52 to Fliess, texts which suggest as much.[160] In stating so, Lacan contravenes, as he often does, the position he had taken in his earlier teaching, notably in such texts as 'The Instance of the Letter in the Unconscious,' where the unconscious is specified as the realm of writing,[161] to the benefit of foregrounding the jouissance at stake in what is written or ceases to be – to which I shall return.

This shift in Lacan's treatment of the question of writing from the written letter as component of the unconscious signifier to the letter as real inscription of jouissance in the flesh also constitutes a movement away from an ancient tradition of the thinking of writing which is an unspoken genealogy of Lacan's early treatments of writing. A major textual site where this geneaology unfolds is those old manuals of rhetoric which Lacan in his early teaching points out as part of the lineage and legacy of psychoanalysis because of their similar preoccupation with the relation of the subject to the signifier.[162]

It is the written letter not as a remainder of jouissance but as what Miller calls a 'presentification of the symbolic,'[163] register of the signifier, such as would appear in Lacan's early teaching, that receives pride of place in some of the ancient answers proposed to the vexed question of writing's origin. Some of these answers take the form of those narratives that appear in human history, Lacan teaches in *The Relation to the Object*, to explicate 'the invention of the great human resources,' in particular those connected to 'the power of signification,' that is to say, of myths.[164] Ancient myths of the invention of writing, attempted answers to the impossible question of its origin, relate it to a category that would become central in Freudian psychoanalysis, that of memory.

In what is perhaps the best known of these myths of origin of writing, Socrates tells Phaedrus the following story:

> I heard, then, that at Naucratis, in Egypt, was one of the ancient gods of that country, the one whose sacred bird is called the ibis, and the name of the god himself was Theuth. He it was who invented numbers and arithmetic and geometry and astronomy, also draughts and dice, and, most important of all, letters [γράμματα, *grammata*] Now the king of all Egypt at that time was the god Thamus, who lived in the great city of the upper region, which the Greeks call the Egyptian Thebes, and they call the god himself Ammon. To him came Theuth to show his inventions, saying that they ought to be imparted to the other Egyptians. But Thamus asked what use there was in each, and as Theuth enumerated their uses, expressed praise or blame, according as he approved or disapproved. The story goes that Thamus said many things to Theuth in praise or blame of the various arts, which it would take too long to repeat; but when they came to the letters, 'This invention, O king,' said Theuth, 'will make the Egyptians wiser and will improve their memories [μνημονικωτέρους, *mnēmonikōterous*]; for it is an elixir [φάρμακον, *pharmakon*] of memory and wisdom that I have discovered.'[165]

In his magisterial reading of the *Phaedrus*, Jacques Derrida points out that in Socrates's account, 'writing is proposed, presented, and asserted as a *pharmakon*,' that is to say, as at once a remedy and a poison.[166] Derrida destabilizes conventional readings of the dialogue as 'simply condemning the writer's activity'[167] because in his response to Theuth in the myth, Thamus ostensibly chastises Theuth for offering his pupils not memory but *hypomnēsis* [*hupomnēseōs*, ὑπομνήσεως],[168] what Derrida glosses as 're-memoration, recollection, consignation,'[169] a monument to what was once a living memory and not the living memory itself.[170] What Plato dreams of, Derrida affirms, 'is a memory with no sign, that is, with no supplement. A *mnēme* with no *hypomnēsis*, no *pharmakon*.'[171] Nevertheless, Derrida writes, between *mnēme* and *hypomnēsis*, between memory and its supplement, the line is more than subtle; it is 'hardly perceptible.' It is precisely this more than subtle line that opens onto 'the space of writing, space as writing.'[172] It follows that the grapheme or written letter that comes to inhabit the space within this line may come perilously close to the consignatory substitute of *hypomnēsis*, the less than living trace that Plato longs to excise from the realm of memory as its *pharmakos* or scapegoat. What the *gramma* can never do, however, is elide the relation to mnemonics. In Derrida's reading of the *Phaedrus*, it seems, writing is bound up with the possibility of a living memory it does not cease to betray; *gramma* always carries the dream of pure *mnēme*, the slice of life it can never be.

But it is precisely as hypomnestic and less than living that the grapheme receives pride of place in another narrative attempting to respond to what Lacan calls the stupefying question of the emergence of the orthographic: the myth of the invention of memory as the fifth canon of rhetoric that circulates in the rhetorical tradition from Cicero's *De Oratore* onwards. Invention in this case is credited not to a god but to a poet, mortal maker with what is the most distinctly human matter of words: 'I am grateful to the famous Simonides of Ceos,' Antonius says in Cicero's text, 'who is said to have first invented the art of mnemonics.'[173] The maker of memory is the maker with words, a pre-Socratic poet whose poem on becoming is a topic of conversation in the *Protagoras*.[174] The occasion for this invention, however, is not the authoring of a poem but precisely a momentous disturbance to *poesis*, a catastrophe in the literal sense of a cut in the strophe and antistrophe of verse:

> There is a story that Simonides was dining at the house of a wealthy noble-man named Scopas at Crannon in Thessaly, and chanted a lyric poem which he had composed in honour of his host, in which he followed the custom of the poets by including for decorative purposes a long passage referring to Castor and Pollux ... the story runs that a little later a message was brought to Simonides to go outside, as two young men were standing at the door who earnestly requested him to come out; so he rose from his seat and went out, and could not see anybody; but in the interval of his absence [*hoc interim spatio*] the roof of the hall where Scopas was giving the banquet fell in, crushing Scopas himself and his relations underneath the ruins and killing them.[175]

The catastrophe at the root of memory, however, is in this myth a real *caesura* not in *poesis* but in what seems to be an action of a different order: the burial of the dead. Cicero writes: 'when their friends wanted to bury [*humar*] them ... [they] were altogether unable to know them apart [*internoscere ullo modo*] as they had been completely crushed.'[176] In the myth as retold at the apex of the English rhetorical tradition, in Thomas Wilson's *Arte of Rhetorique* of 1560, the impossibility of knowing apart which is a knowing between, an inter-knowing [*internoscere*] is cast as the absence of a mark. The collapse of Scopas' hall, Wilson writes

> so crushed their bodies together, and in such sort, that the kinsfolk of those who were dead, coming in, and desirous to bury them every one according to their calling, not only could they not perceive them by their faces, but also they could not discern them by any mark of any part in all their bodies.[177]

In the myth of the invention of memory resonating in the rhetorical tradition, catastrophe takes the form of a contingency leaving in its wake pure unicity, a pure continuity of the real, flesh of no face, anatomy effaced to the point it cannot be made a discrete object for the rites of burial which are nothing but the refusal to forget, Lacan intimates whilst alluding to Sophocles's Antigone, the logical consequences of a living being's having been identified by a name,[178] that is to say, having been seized by language and hence by a particular ancestry. The catastrophe at stake in the myth of the invention of memory is the brutal cessation of the funerary as, in Lacan's terms, 'the total, massive intervention from hell to heaven of the whole symbolic system,'[179] the embodiment, that is to say, of the symbolic, register of language and of difference, as fundamentally sepulchral. No less than Antigone's insistence to bury her dead brother, Simonides's making burial possible thanks to the memory of places underscores the inherent link between the sepulchral and the symbolic, between the practice of burying the dead and 'the break that the very presence of language inaugurates in the life of man' that Lacan identifies as the central problematic of Sophocles's play.[180] Inversely, the impossibility of interment is an instance where the word does not kill the Thing, that hence emerges as pure horror. It is the impossibility not only of poetics but of rhetoric, art of obituaries and funerary orations that veils the Thing and in so doing creates a rim of turns of phrase that turn around the void [Hebrew ריק /rik/] the Thing is, rendering it liveable. The story of Simonides is the story of rhetoric as what broaches upon the void of the Thing so as to circumscribe and emborder it, of the contingent emergence of what ceases not to be written as constructed edge of what would otherwise be the brutally gaping hole of bottomless anxiety. Which is also the story of separation. Cicero writes:

> [T]he story goes that Simonides was enabled by his recollection of the place in which each of them [uniuscuiusque] had been reclining at table to identify them for separate interment.[181]

In the face of the horror of a mangled mass of dead flesh, Simonides resorts to an action that is not martyrological. Unlike the artworks on the walls of churches Lacan evokes in Encore, 'witnesses … of a more or less pure suffering,'[182] this action is not of the order of the testimonial of a disaster. Nor is it of the order of the registering and transmission of a disaster such as Shakespeare invokes through Horatio's vow at the end of Hamlet:

> give order that those bodies
> High on stage be plac'd to the view,
> And let me speak to th'yet unknowing world
> How these things came about. So shall you hear
> Of carnal, bloody, and unnatural acts,

Of accidental judgments, casual slaughters,
Of deaths put on by cunning and by forc'd cause,
... All this can I
Truly deliver.[183]

Neither account nor transmission of a catastrophe, Simonides' action in the wake of the crashing of the roof amounts to the introduction of a separating cut whose structure inaugurates the symbolic as a system of different nominations and whose mythic name is memory. In Thomas Wilson's account, Simonides, 'well remembering in what place every one of them [the guests] did sit, told them [their relatives] what everyone was, and gave them their kinsfolk's carcasses, so many as there were.'[184] Introducing the discontinuities constitutive of the symbolic to what in this case is the literal continuity of the real,[185] Simonides' action is an act – an instance of a *praxis* insofar as it treats the real by means of the symbolic[186] – and it does so not by veiling the real but by operating upon it. It is an act of a rhetor not insofar as he rectifies a subject with a real, as Lacan says of the psychoanalyst as a rhetor of our times,[187] but insofar as he enables a catastrophic real to be encrusted with a symbolic lining, whose name is memory and whose essence is burial.

Simonides' constitutively symbolic act, however, is neither memorization nor burial but what is revealed as foundational to both: writing. What Simonides inferred from the 'circumstance' of his having been able to identify the dead for internment according to his conscious memory of the seating of guests at the table is that

> persons desiring to train this faculty must select localities [*locos*] and form mental images [*effigies*] of the facts they wish to remember and store those images in the localities, with the result that the arrangement of the localities will preserve the order of the facts, and the images of the facts will designate the facts themselves, and we shall employ the localities and images [*simulacra*] respectively as a wax writing tablet [*cera*] and the letters written on it [*litteris*].[188]

What specifies the Simonides myth that would reverberate in the rhetorical tradition, then, is not only the collocation of mnemonics with the possibility of burial as marking the symbolic's intervention in Being. It is also the sublation of this collocation of the mnemic and the sepulchral to the level of writing – specifically, of writing of the kind that involves the creation of crevices and ravines in a pliable substrate – as *hypomnēsis*, of the order of effigies and simulacra as instances of the written *in its symbolic dimension*.

The collocation of memory and writing as a *ravinement* subtending Cicero's sublation of undifferentiated dead flesh to differential marks making the foundational symbolic operation of internment and mourning possible emerges even earlier in the history of grammatology, occurring, for instance, in Plato's *Theaetetus*. Let us suppose, Socrates says in this dialogue,

> there is in our souls [*psukhais*] a block of wax [*kērinon ekmageion*] ... that this is the gift of Memory, the mother of the Muses, and that whenever we wish to remember anything we see or hear or think of in our own minds, we hold this wax under the perceptions and thoughts and imprint [*apotupousthai*] them upon it, just as we make impressions [*sēmeia ensēmainomenous*] from seal rings [*daktuliōn*]; and whatever is imprinted we remember and know as long as its image lasts.[189]

Aristotle's *De memoria et reminiscentia* repeats the theorization of memory as ravining inscription in a pliable surface. The emergence of a memory, for Aristotle, is the effect of an 'imprinting' of a 'stimulus' [*aesthomatos*] in the psyche, operating in a way that is close to a 'seal-ring' [*daktulius*] in 'stamping' [*tupon*].[190] Aristotle's position differs substantially from Plato's with regard to the nature of what is remembered. Where Plato assumes that what is recalled are originary ideas, Aristotle posits only sensory stimuli. Both philosophers, however, speak of the formation of memory as the product of the operation of a *tupon* or *daktulion*, an instrument that creates crevices in pliable material.[191] The theorization of memory as the making of impressions recurs in the *Institutio Oratoria*, where Quintilian speaks of 'the images made on the mind' in terms of an impression of a signet ring in wax.[192] This theorization then resonates in the rhetorical and mnemonic tradition till its apex in the European Renaissance. After his own retelling of the Simonides myth, English Renaissance rhetorician Thomas Wilson writes that the 'places of memory are resembled into wax and paper,' substrates of writing; what is deposited in these places is 'compted like unto letters or a seal,' and the act of depositing or placing itself is 'like unto words written.'[193] Martianus Capella, a medieval humanist involved in the invention of the liberal arts that were to become the foundation of education for many centuries, asserts that 'as what is written is fixed by the letters on the wax, so what is consigned to memory is impressed on the places.'[194] Giordano Bruno's complex and voluminous work on mnemonics is divided into sections he denominates 'seals,'[195] resonating the originally Platonic theorization of memory as the imprinting of a *daktulion* in a pliable substrate, that is to say, as writing, and its reverberations in the rhetorical tradition as of Cicero's *De Oratore* which it supersedes and preserves.

Ancient treatises of mnemonics and rhetoric, then, echo the notion of memory as a writing in pliable material that involves the removal or subtraction of some of this material by the seal that frays it, hollowing out its own shape. What remains is not the living memory Plato dreams of in the *Phaedrus*, in Derrida's reading, but what Cicero explicitly calls effigies and simulacra, hypomnēstic copies of a lost origin which themselves are nothing more than hollows in the material that surrounds them. Hypomnēstic writing produced *per via di levare* – this is how ancient thinkers and rhetoricians theorize memory from the *Theaetetus* through the Renaissance. The myth of the origin of memory retold in the rhetorical tradition since *De Oratore* inflects the hollowing out structuring burial as essential to the social bond. What is bequeathed by early theories of memory and the myth of its origin, then, is the idea of a subtractive writing whose hollowed-out, hypomnēstic, simulacral components are fundamentally sepulchral, acts of grace *in effigie* granting dignity to what would otherwise be pure catastrophe whose sight would be intolerable to the subject.

It is psychoanalysis, however, that would sublate these, and other, early collocations of memory and a sepulchral writing that proceeds *per via di levare*, furrowing out engravings whose prototype is the grave as inaugural symbolic form. Centuries after *De Oratore* and the *Institutio Oratoria*, Freud in 'Note Upon the Mystic Writing Pad' mentions 'the ancient method of writing on tablets of clay or wax' such as invoked also in these rhetorical treatises.[196] He does so in the context of his theorization of the mental apparatus, of which the crucial component is the unconscious, as an apparatus of rememoration. Freud terms the components of this apparatus 'memory traces' or 'representations.' Lacan, after Saussure, renames them 'signifiers.' Their emergence, Freud specifies in 'Negation,' is bound up with the loss of 'things that once brought real satisfaction.'[197]

After Freud, Lacan in the earlier phase of his teaching gives this Freudian specification a thanathic inflection when he accentuates that the loss at stake in Freud's text is the loss of a Thing. This loss 'materializes the instance of death.'[198] A share of jouissance is given up so the signifier might come to be, but this share returns as a cognizance of finitude. The 'coming into play of the signifier in the life of man,' Lacan says in *The Four Fundamental Concepts of Psychoanalysis*, is capable 'of making present the presence of death,'[199] from which the signifier provides a measure of distance. The cultural manifestation of this measure is burial such as the one on which Antigone insists, such as the one which Simonides makes possible. What this means is that in Lacanian psychoanalysis, at whose foundation is Lacan's return to Freud, the relation of the symbolic, register of the signifier Freud had named the memory trace, and the sepulchral, that in the Simonides myth appears as narrative collocation, assumes the form Lacan describes as a 'problem of the second degree.' A problem in the second degree involves reflexivity. In it, 'the subject questions himself about himself.' Such reflexivity, Lacan says, is none other than the subject's 'symbolic assumption of his destiny.'[200] In Freud's theorization of unconscious memory traces in 'A Note Upon the Mystic Writing Pad,' the ancient theorization of memory as a writing *per via di levare* which is a form of burial becomes part of what is no longer a heuristic metaphor but part of a meditation on man's relation to language that departs from and informs the clinical practice that subtends psychoanalysis.

While Freud twice refers to his mode of argumentation in 'A Note Upon the Mystic Writing Pad' as an 'analogy' or 'comparison,'[201] he makes it quite clear that it is not of the order of an illustration. 'All the forms of auxiliary apparatus [*Hilfsapparate*] which we have invented for the improvement or intensification of our sensory functions,' Freud writes, are '*so gebaut*' [so built] as 'the sense organs themselves or portions of them: for instance, spectacles, photographic cameras, ear-trumpets.'[202] What this means, for Freud, is not that better scientific investigation of the sense organs would lead to more advanced instruments for enhancing sensory functions but that the inventions designed to help or intensify such functions work only if they are 'built as' these functions themselves and hence may yield knowledge concerning them. It is thus that Freud's essay on the mystic writing pad opens with the assertion that 'a note made in writing' is a 'materialized portion [*Stück*] of [the] mnemic apparatus.'[203] In other words, the note in question is a fragment of the mnemic apparatus that appears in the outside world. Freud's rhetorical form of its argumentation in 'A Note on the Mystic Writing Pad,' that is, is not analogical but synecdochic. In Peircean terms, it is indexical.

The *Stück* whose structure Freud pursues is what was then the novel contrivance made of a resin slab and layers of celluloid coupled with a sharp stylus which enabled inscriptions to be simultaneously erased and retained. This mystic writing pad, Freud maintains, is a 'concrete representation,' in other words, a synecdoche and index, of the 'functioning of the perceptual apparatus of our mind' where inscriptions repressed from consciousness persist on an Other scene, provided 'we imagine one hand writing upon the surface of the Mystic Writing Pad while another periodically raises its covering sheet from the wax slab.'[204] It is Freud's comments on the operation not only of the covering sheet but also of the surface of inscription, however, that are instructive as to what is at stake, for the psychoanalyst, in the conceptualization of unconscious memory as a form of writing.

Unconscious writing, the writing of 'mnemic traces' that persist beyond perception and consciousness, Freud says in 'A Note Upon the Mystic Writing Pad,' is the production of a 'permanent trace' on a 'receptive surface' by what operates as does a 'pointed stylus.'[205] But it is of course from much earlier in Freud's *oeuvre* that psychic rememoration is conceptualized as a writing. 'What is essentially new about my theory,' Freud writes to Wilhelm Fliess in what has become known as Letter 52, 'is the thesis that memory is present not once but several times over,' that it undergoes a 'retranscription' [*Umschrift*] from one register of the psychic apparatus to another, most importantly, from the unconscious to the conscious.[206] For Freud in Letter 52 to Fliess, that is, the constituents of the psychic apparatus are units of memory that are written, memory traces [*Errinerungspurren*] of subjectively perceived scenes.[207] They are what he would later call mnemic re-presentations [*Vorstellungen*] whose form of presentation is a writing and that can be subject to a rewriting.

It is not in Letter 52 but in the slightly earlier *Project for a Scientific Psychology*, however, that Freud precises the structure of the representations constituting memory traces of which he would find written notes, mystical or otherwise, to be synecdochic. Although as Derrida points out in his analysis of Freud and the scene of writing, the 'system of traces' Freud lays out in the *Project* is not explicitly inscriptorial but 'mechanical,'[208] as Derrida's own analysis makes clear, this system is indispensable for the apprehension of what it evolves to with increasing refinement in Freud's work: 'a configuration of traces which can no longer be represented except by the structure and functioning of writing.'[209] This, it seems, is writing in its Freudian declension: a furrowing in psychic material whose precipitate is the memory trace. This psychical writing is for Freud 'so originary a production,' Derrida says, 'that the writing we believe to be designated by the proper sense of the word—a script which is coded and visible "in the world"' would only be its metaphor,' that is to say, an effigy of the fundamental structure it evinces.[210]

For Derrida, Freud's thinking of the components of the unconscious in terms of a fraying constitutive of written traces is fruitful for the 'deconstruction of logocentrism' in which Freud's thinking, he says, nevertheless remains caught up, especially in its insistence on the category of the subject which, he says, 'necessarily refers to the concept of substance—and thus of presence—out of which it is born.' Derrida thus calls for a 'radicaliz[ation]' of the Freudian concept of trace which would move, beyond effraction and breaching, to the possibility of 'the threat or anguish of [the trace's] irremediable disappearance, of the disappearance of its disappearance,' the total erasure, Derrida says, 'of selfhood, of one's own presence,' which is none other than 'death itself.'[211]

For Derrida, the disappointing limitation in Freud's theorization of writing, what makes it not radical enough, is its insisting that what is erased from the register of perception and consciousness is nevertheless retained as unconscious inscription, and will reappear once it is rubbed over – reappear in dreams, parapraxes, witticisms, and especially in symptoms. 'An unerasable trace is not a trace,' Derrida laments, 'it is a full presence, an immobile and uncorruptible substance, a son of God, a sign of *parousia* and not a seed, that is, a mortal germ.'[212] For Derrida, Freud's theorizing the unconscious memory trace as retained despite its occultation from consciousness as a fraying of a substrate that never reaches the point of that substrate's complete annihilation means his stopping short of embracing the absolute erasure that, in Derrida's terms, is the instance of one's death.

The geneaology of the Freudian thinking of writing as breaching or effraction in the history of mnemonics to which Freud himself gestures in 'Note Upon the Mystic Writing Pad' when invoking 'the ancient method of writing on tablets of clay or wax'[213] however, is in effect inextricably bound up with the thinking of death. As presented by Cicero, writing as fraying in wax is nothing but the raising to the level of a *techné* of the Simonidean operation of the differentiation between mangled corpses that makes their identification possible and thus allows for their subjection to rites of burial. The fundamental structure of the unconscious signifier as written, as paradigmatic of any empirical writing (and not, as is commonly assumed, the other way around), emerging from the legacy of the ancient art of memory of which Freud's argument in 'Note Upon the Mystic Writing Pad' is screen memory, at once cover and index, is that of an (en)graving whose Simonidean prototype is the grave as symbolic shield against an inevitable real of corpses mangled and decomposing. Read with its geneaology in the philosophical and rhetorical tradition to which Freud explicitly alludes, the unconscious signifier as written, far from circumventing death as absolute erasure as Derrida argues it does because it is predicated on a trace that persists beyond the erasure of repression, is precisely, as Lacan says of the signifier in *The Four Fundamental Concepts of Psychoanalysis*, that component of semiosis capable 'of making present the presence of death.'[214] The signifier makes death present – not as real, but as en-graved.

It is not only in prototypifying the grave as culmination of funerary rites as a massive intervention of the whole symbolic operation, however, that the unconscious signifier as written is quintessentially symbolic. Its structure as it emerges from Freud's *Project* and from Lacan's return to Freud at least until the mid-point of Lacan's teaching, and which I will delineate in what follows, pertains to additional manifestations of the humanization of the real and the regulation and limitation of jouissance: the institution of civilization as pact, one of whose conditions is forms of erasure that are of the order not of the fraying Derrida admires in Freud's account but of cessation, limitation, disappearance.

b Sum-ballein: The symbol as a throwing together

The 'constitutive mark of any sign in general and of any linguistic sign in particular,' Roman Jakobson writes in 'The Phonemic and Grammatical Aspects of Language,' 'is its twofold character: every linguistic unit is bipartite.'[215] Freud's theorization of the mnemic trace in the *Project* bears out Jakobson's observation concerning linguistic theory since antiquity. The operation of the conjoining of two parts is indeed fundamental to the system of traces theorized by Freud, as it is, of course, to the Saussurean conceptualization of the sign. Where Saussure postulates the two components as 'signifier' and 'signified,' Freud presents the constituents of the psychical apparatus that he would call '*Darstellungen*' and later '*Vorstellungen*' [representations] and that Lacan, after Saussure, would rename 'signifiers,' as the precipitate of two principal theorems.[216] The theorems in question are the 'particles' Freud calls 'neurons,' of which it is those designated as 'ψ' that are the repositories of memory, and the 'quantity' that passes through and so 'alters' [*verändert*] them.[217] As this already makes evident, Freud locates the split involved in semiosis not between the signifier and another category (the signified) but within the category Lacan would identify with the signifier itself.

What is at stake in the bipartition of the basic unit of semiosis which the Saussurean sign and Freud's unconscious memory trace differently exemplify? Although Saussure uses the term 'symbol' to designate a semiotic element whose relation to the signified is not, like that of the signifier, arbitrary,[218] his theory of semiosis, like Freud's, can be said to be a theory of the symbol not in the Jungian denotation of what 'states or signifies something more and other than itself' which eludes our present knowledge,'[219] but in its archaic derivation of a throwing together [*sum* + *ballein*]. Freud's theorization, however, is at once closer to and more revolutionary than ancient practices of *sumballein* [from '*sum*,' 'with' + '*ballein*,' 'to throw'], where the two components thrown together are not neatly distributed, as Jakobson puts it, between the 'sensible' and the 'intelligible,' between the *signans* (Saussure's 'signifier') and the *signatum* (Saussure's 'signified'),[220] but both grounded in the sensible but senseless, to which signification and intelligibility are supererogatory. In Freud's more radical theory of the symbol, fundamental unit of the register of unconscious representation Lacan would appropriately renominate the 'symbolic,' the signified that makes the Saussurean symbol whole is missing, and the two substances thrown together (resisting and subsequently facilitated neurones and the motion of the quantum that passes through them) engender the conditions for unconscious representation Lacan maps onto the Saussurean signifier.

In using the Saussurean category of the signifier to rename Freud's unconscious memory trace while severing it from the signified which can live a life if its own, in contravention of claims such as Jakobson's that in theories of the sign the sensible and the intelligible 'necessarily suppose and require each other,'[221] Lacan underscores what the fantasy of harmonic union permeating Saussurean linguistics glosses over: the disconcert, in the unconscious, of signifier and signified which renders the signifier not only logically prior to but structurally independent of the signified it might or might not generate, the manifestation in language of what he would years later term the absence of the sexual rapport between man and woman.[222] Speaking of the *Traumdeutung*, Lacan points out that in that book,

> Freud shows us in every possible way that the [dream] image's value as a signifier has nothing to do with its signification, giving as an example Egyptian hieroglyphics in which it would be ridiculous to deduce from the frequency in a text of a vulture (which is an aleph) or a chick (which is a vau) ... that the text has anything whatsoever to do with these ornithological specimens.[223]

Freud's divorcing the unconscious memory trace from sense sets his theorization apart from other theories of semiosis based on bi-partition. But as Lacan shows, it also accentuates its genealogy in yet another ancient practice whose function is not significative but operative: the gift-giving that Lacan locates at the foundation of language.[224] It is anthropology that gives Lacan his cue, specifically Maurice Leenhardt's *Do Kamo: Person and Myth in the Melanesian World*. For the Canaque people of the Pacific, Leenhardt writes, gifts given at the limit points of a life, for instance pieces of bark 'offered on occasion of birth or mourning,' are 'the body of the message [which is] none other than the bark cloth itself.'[225] The giving of these gifts institutes 'exchange' and 'commerce' among human beings and has no declarable sense or function beyond this institution.[226] Like the bark cloths in Leerhardt's account, the objects of gift giving Lacan enumerates – 'vases made to remain empty, shields too heavy to be carried, sheaves that will dry out, lances that are thrust into the ground' — serve no purpose in terms of the propagation of life, are 'all destined to be useless, if not superfluous by their very abundance.'[227] Voiding material objects of use value so as to sublate them to the function of pure exchange value, the action of gift-giving is a throwing together whose precipitate is a new entity in the world: the symbol which in itself means nothing but whose circulation may institute social bonds.

The unconscious representation to which Lacan would give the Saussurean name 'signifier,' however, differs from the Saussurean signifier with which it is isomorphic in its bipartition not only because of its dysfunctionality, as isolated unit, with respect to sense but in particular in its hypothesized materiality – and the procedure to which this materiality is subjected. For Saussure, the two substances thrown together to form the sign are the 'shapeless and indistinct mass' of thought, a 'vague, uncharted nebula' of what is not yet ideas, and the phonic substance which, while 'plastic,' 'is neither more fixed nor more rigid than thought,' is, in fact, 'especially vague.'[228] For Saussure, what slices the two nebulous substances into distinct units and throws together units from each to form what for Saussure is the basic unit of language – what performs the operation of the dotted lines in Saussure's well-known diagram – is 'social fact alone,' the 'usage and general acceptance' of which a single individual is not capable.[229]

For Freud, on the other hand, the two substances coalescing to form the basic unit of semiosis are locatable in a single organism of a being who speaks. These are the neuronic matter he dubs ψ and the quantum in a 'state of flow' [*fließender*] qualified as being subject to 'the laws of motion' [*Bewegungsgeset*].[230] The unconscious signifier, Freud writes in the *Project*, is a product 'of all the influences which ψ has experienced from the external world,' that is to say, the effect of the alteration of ψ by the quantum that moves through and flows in it.

Both Saussure and Freud, then, postulate a basic unit of semiosis that is symbolic in the sense of its being a product of a throwing together of two heterogeneous substances. Both attribute to at least one of these substances a materiality that is ultimately organic. In Freud's *Project*, both components of the substrate for the unconscious memory trace as fundamental unit of semiosis – the ψ neurons and the quantum in motion that frays them – are, to use Jakobson's term, 'sensible.'[231] Even more precisely, they are both physio-logical, made of elements constituting the living flesh (protoplasm, quantum), even if they can never be anatomically locatable. In Saussure's *Course*, only one of the sources of the two components of the sign as fundamental unit of semiosis is clearly sensible. What in Jakobson's terms is the intelligible component of the Saussurean sign, thought, is denominated a 'shapeless *mass*,'[232] but its materiality, if any, is not specified. The materiality of the second component, on the other hand, is clear. It is specified as language's phonic mass.[233] Throughout the *Course*, Saussure insists that 'the spoken form alone constitutes the [linguistic] object.'[234] In other words, throughout the *Course*, as is well-evident to Derrida in his critique, Saussure gestures at speech as the privileged modality in which language manifests itself.[235] Though Saussure does not emphasize this, the phonic mass that he posits as the privileged component of the sign is not only material. It is often grounded in the flesh as the product of the vocal cords and buccal orifice.

The linguistic sign as Saussure's version of the symbol qua throwing together, then, displays a fundamental phonism whose field is that of oral delivery, arena of the ancient orator but also of the much more solitary orator that is the subject invited to speak in an analysis. 'There are no linguistic facts,' Saussure says, 'apart from the phonic substance cut into significant elements,'[236] which are manifest in speech. Writing, for its part, appears to be a phenomenon 'that has to do with speech,'[237] that is to say, is its derivative. In Freud's delineation of the psychic apparatus, on the other hand, the fundamental unit of semiosis, the symbol both of whose components involve organic phenomenality, is quintessentially inscriptorial. Speech is a quality that appears in the psychic apparatus described by Freud only secondarily and subsequently, at the terminal point of the unconscious' folding inside out that Lacan would denominate its syncopating pulsation.[238] It is at the end of the percolation of inscribed memory traces from unconscious to preconscious and conscious strata, Freud explains, that unconscious signifiers (rooted in facilitated ψ neurones) become linked with sound presentations [*Klangvorstellungen*]. This is the process Freud calls 'speech association' [*Sprachbildern*].[239] It is what lends these unconscious signifiers which might have otherwise remained obscure 'presence [and] structure,' even if this presence is prototypically that of a scream.[240]

Both Saussure and Freud theorize a basic unit of semiosis which is a symbol as throwing together in which the materiality of the flesh is involved. However, they differ fundamentally in the ways in which they map writing and speech onto the structure of this symbol. For Saussure, the arbitrary throwing together of sound-image and thought, signifier and signified, manifests itself first and foremost at the joint of speech. 'In the lives of individuals and societies,' Saussure says in the second chapter of his *Course*, 'speech is more important than anything else.'[241] For Freud the mnemic trace that in the *Project for a Scientific Psychology* is theorized as predicated on the product of the coalescence of ψ neurons and quantum is what in Letter 52 or 'Note

Upon the Mystic Writing Pad' is explicitly specified as an inscription, whose mutation into speech involves both the intervention of an additional semiotic component (the sound presentation) and the procedure of the unconscious folding inside out to emit the audible fragment thus produced.

In Derrida's grand project of deconstructing what he calls 'the heritage of that logocentrism which is also a phonocentrism,'[242] Saussure's and Freud's theorizations of the basic unit of semiosis fall on two sides of a conceptual divide. Saussurean linguistics in its insistence on the primacy of speech over writing is taken to task as the epitome of 'the historico-metaphysical reduction of writing to the rank of an instrument enslaved to a full and originarily spoken language'[243] which involves 'the subordination of the trace to the full presence summed up in the *logos*, the humbling of writing beneath a speech dreaming its plenitude.'[244] Freud's theorization of the psychic apparatus in terms of inscription, what Derrida terms his 'psychographic[s],'[245] for its part, while criticized as 'still retain[ed]' in a 'metaphysics of presence ... (particularly in the concepts of consciousness, the unconscious, perception, memory, reality, and several others),'[246] is praised for the 'admirable scope and continuity' with which it 'performs' the scene of writing. Derrida nevertheless insists that writing should be thought of 'in other terms than those of individual or collective psychology.'[247] For Derrida, Freudian psychographics 'fecundates' a thinking of writing whose 'radicalization,' specified as the introduction of the possibility of the total erasure of what is written, none other than one's death, is nevertheless called for.[248]

In terms of Lacanian psychoanalysis, however, there is no such neat divide between the Saussurean and the Freudian theorizations of the fundamental unit of semiosis as a throwing together. In fact, the mapping of Saussure's theorization onto Freud's is the hallmark of Lacan's return to Freud in his early teaching. 'How could Freud have become aware of that structure [of the signifier],' Lacan asks in 'The Instance of the Letter,' 'when it was only later articulated by Ferdinand de Saussure?'

> It is all the more striking that Freud anticipated it as that structure overlaps Freud's own terms. But where did he discover it? In a signifying flow whose mystery lies in the fact that the subject doesn't even know where to pretend to be its organizer.[249]

What Freud anticipated, of course, was not the phonematic accent of Saussure's theorization of the signifier famously critiqued by Derrida but its differential structure which Derrida celebrates. The portion of flesh which involves the 'possibility of representing memory,' Freud writes in the *Project*, is at once 'differentiated protoplasm' and susceptible of further differentiation: 'after each excitation,' Freud writes, 'they may ... be in a different state from before.'[250] Unconscious representation as theorized in Freudian metapsychology, however, differs fundamentally from the Saussurean signifier because unlike the Saussurean signifier onto which Lacan maps it, it is not spoken but inscribed. It is at once differential and written. An inscription that in itself does not mean, the unconscious signifier is the fundamental unit of the psychic register Lacan aptly terms symbolic because it is a throwing together of two units, monument in the unconscious of each subject to the social bond or in Lacan's terms, discourse, whose permutations, always involving something of the order of the semblant but also of the real of surplus enjoyment, Lacan details in *The Other Side of Psychoanalysis*.

c Writing the symbol

How does the throwing together of the two units constituting the unconscious signifier become a writing in which the body is implicated in its enjoyment? Freud's hypothesis in the *Project* rests on a physics of conductivity facilitating an operation of imprinting such as the one described in Plato's *Thaetetus* and Aristotle's *De memoria*. If the production of memory is a procedure best indexed by the operation of a seal or *daktulion*, Aristotle writes, the 'receptive structure' on which it is 'stamped' cannot be too hard, nor can it be 'like running water' on which a seal would leave no trace.'[251] Aristotle, that is, theorizes the inscription of memory by distinguishing between a pliable receptive substrate in which memories are imprinted and preserved and a substrate permeable to the imprinting device to such a degree the collision of the two is never registered.

Freud's hypothesis concerning the psychic apparatus as an apparatus of memory is similar in the physics it assumes. It involves a distinction between two types of components of the psychic apparatus, the ψ and ϕ neurons, distinguished by the degree of their intrinsic permeability (also spoken of as 'faciltation') to a quantity that moves through them. While ϕ neurons are permeable, ψ neurons are initially impermeable and characterized by resistance. The resistance [*Widerstand*] of the ψ neurons, Freud states, is what makes possible their alteration by the quantum passing through them; and it is this alteration, in the course of which the ψ neurons acquire greater facilitation, that is, become more permeable, that grants them 'the possibility of representing memory.'[252]

The precipitate of this process is the memory trace or unconscious representation. The flow of quantum through the 'permeable' ϕ neurons, on the other hand, like the meeting of the *daktulion* with running water described by Aristotle, leaves no trace behind. The effect of its passage, Freud says, 'does not persist for long and disappears towards the motor side,'[253] fading into the muscular action Freud diagnoses as always lesser in intensity than occurrences in the psychic apparatus,[254] in which it leaves no mark.

For Freud, then, the emergence of the basic unit of semiosis as an effect of the throwing together of two substances, that is, as quintessentially symbolic, is dependent upon resistance as a feature of one of those substances. Resistance, as Derrida points out, is for Freud 'an opening to the effraction of the trace.'[255] As Freud's 'Note Upon the Mystic Writing Pad' makes retroactively clear, this effraction as theorized in Freud's metapsychology from the *Project* and Letter 52 onwards is a writing of the kind synecdochized by mystic writing pads as by ancient tablets of clay or wax, substrates that resist but not too much, not as much as the hardened wall which is Aristotle's example of a substrate that will not yield to a *daktulion*'s effraction. Unconscious representation as Freud theorizes it in the *Project*, as Derrida puts it, is the 'violent inscription of a form … in a nature or a matter which are conceivable as such only in their opposition to writing.'[256]

What is the agency that throws resistant neuronic matter and quantum together to form the effraction that is the foundation for unconscious representation as written? Freud writes of a 'choice,' [*Auswahl*], 'preference' [*Bevorzugung*], and 'motive.'[257] Such are the qualities first predicated of the agency operative in the psychic apparatus whose contours Freud inaugurally sketches in the *Project*. They will come to characterize the irreducibly particular subject of the unconscious, never equivalent to an individual but not, as Saussure argues, communal. What this means is that in terms of the *Project* and indeed of Freud's thinking of the unconscious memory trace as writing throughout his work, the subject is not only, as Lacan's well-known definition would have it, what is represented by one unconscious memory trace to another, but even more what emerges in the throwing together of resistant neuronic matter and the quantum that passes through it, increasing the neuron's facilitation or fraying and so transforming it to the substrate of the memory trace itself.

If the passage of quantum through resistant neuronic material, logical *ante* of the conjoining of signifiers, has the subject as its effect, what it has as its precipitate is the unconscious signifier as a fraying or furrowing, that is to say, as written. In 'A Note Upon the Mystic Writing Pad,' Freud specifies this fraying or furrowing as a subtraction. The result of the 'scratching' of the receptive surface of the wax tablet by a pointed stylus in the contrivance that he presents as synecdochic of the mental apparatus is, he says, '*Fruchten*' [grooves] or '*Vertiefungen*' [hollows], that is to say, empty places produced by a removal of material.[258] The unconscious representations as written that Freud theorizes most explicitly in 'The Mystic Writing Pad' and that Lacan would rename signifiers, then, are of the same order of such forms of writing *per via di levare* as a groove in stone, a depression in a slate of wax, a fold of fabric or a curvature of a limb in a statue produced by carving or chiselling such as Alberti theorizes in *De statua*.

What this means metapsychologically speaking is that unlike the modes of psychic inscription proceeding *per via di porre* – the character trait, the unary trait, the stereotype plate operative in the transference – accretions and petrifications of excess jouissance, the inscription of the unconscious memory trace as the furrowing and facilitation of resistant neuronal material by the quantum that passes through it Freud describes in the *Project* is an instance of a voiding of jouissance. What Freud's account of psychic writing in the

Project and its cognates in Letter 52 and 'Note Upon the Mystic Writing Pad' suggests is that the loss of real satisfaction that Freud in 'Negation' would posit as the *sine qua non* of the constitution of psychic reality as an aggregate of unconscious signifiers is already constitutive of each of these signifiers: that every instance of a written signifier in the unconscious is an effect of a subtraction of jouissance, an inscription of what is wanting.

But in the *Project*, which sets out the contours of the Freudian metapsychology of writing, these representations or memory traces are at the same time characterized by an additionality. This is in part because in the *Project* Freud theorizes psychic writing in terms of biology as well as of physics. The substrate of psychic writing, he teaches, not only resists and is then facilitated but is characterized by the 'irritability [*Reizbarkeit*] of protoplasm' of which it is the inheritor.[259] It is, in other words, susceptible of passing from a state of calm to a state of agitated excitation, of being altered by what passes through it. What is removed or subtracted from this substrate as Freud thinks of it in the *Project*, then, is not, as Freud's allusion to grooves and hollows in wax in 'A Note Upon the Mystic Writing Pad' suggests, protoplasm itself. It is the protoplasm's homeostatic quality. What emerges from the encounter of this resisting protoplasm with what passes through it, the quantity in a state of motion that in the 1915 essay on 'The Unconscious' Freud would precise as the '*Triebregung*' or motion of the drive[260] is thus, in terms of the *Project's* biological hypothesis, not only a groove or hollow but an irritation, a writ(h)ing whose field is that of the drive or in Lacanian terms, of jouissance.

The unconscious signifier or memory trace as Freud theorizes it in the *Project*, then, is not entirely the conceptual descendant of the ancient theorizations of memory in terms of a writing in wax that proceeds by way of subtraction he was to invoke in 'Note Upon the Mystic Writing Pad.' Perhaps closest to it of the theorizations of the early writers on the art of memory is that of Giordano Bruno, for whom the author of all mnemonic inscriptions, whose persona comprises, for Bruno, those of the Poet, the Painter, and the Philosopher as creators of memory is 'Phidias the statuary,' described as 'moulding in wax, or constructing by addition of a number of small stones,' proceeding *per via di porre*, but also 'sculpturing the rough and formless stone as though by subtraction.'[261]

The unconscious signifier as written memory trace as Freud theorizes it in the *Project* is at once a hollowing out and an addition, a voiding and an accretion of jouissant material. It involves the coinciding of what in Lacan's teaching would be two distinct and in effect contradictory paradigms of jouissance in its relation to the signifier – the paradigm of jouissance as impossible, absolutely beyond the signifier, the logical conclusion of the 'signifiantization of jouissance' Jacques-Alain Miller identifies in Lacan's early work, and the theorization of the signifier as cause and carrier of jouissance which finds its great moment in *Encore*.[262] Two contradictory articulations of the relation of the signifier to jouissance that in Lacan's teaching would be distributed diachronically find themselves intertwined in what is Freud's inaugural articulation of the unconscious memory trace as written symbol, the fraying of neuronal material by quantum in motion.

The contradiction inherent in this intertwining might seem to be the logical consequence of the operation of two sets of scientific terms, biological and physical, in Freud's articulation of the unconscious memory trace as written symbol. Where the biological account indicates that this writing is of the order of irritation, that is, metapsychologically speaking of the order of addition, of a *plus de jouir*, the physical account explicitized in 'Note Upon the Mystic Writing Pad' suggests an operation of removal of jouissance.

Yet this contradiction – between addition and subtraction, between biology and physics – is neither a shortcoming in Freud's account of the unconscious signifier as written, in the *Project* and beyond, nor a limitation that can be accounted for by discursive tensions between the scientific vocabularies to which he has recourse, nor a condensation of incompatible theorizations of the relations of jouissance and the signifier calling for a clarifying unfolding Lacan's teaching would provide. In the unconscious signifier as written symbol as Freud theorizes it in the *Project* and later formulations of the unconscious scene of writing, jouissant irritation and the effect of the subtraction or voiding of jouissance coexist as incompatible. Indeed, it is their very incompatibility that is constitutive of the unconscious signifier.

Predicated on a heightened quantum or irritation that registers as unpleasure, perennial index of the traumatism with which language strikes the organism and that unless an analysis intervenes, can frequent the speaking being as the monotony of a tormenting jouissance, the unconscious signifier also involves an operation of subtraction of jouissance – but one that is not reducible to a voiding. This operation of subtraction cannot be accounted for in terms of the laws of material physics towards which Freud sometimes gestures in the *Project*. The subtraction which enables Freud, in 'The Mystic Writing Pad,' to speak of unconscious memory traces which in the *Project* he had defined as 'irritations,' as 'depressions,' 'hollows,' or 'grooves' is of the order neither of physics or of biology, not of inert masses in motion nor of such masses when they become palpitating masses, zooic matter. It is of the order precisely of what interferes in the algorithms of biology, produces phenomena which baffle these algorithms: the order of subjectivity which neither biology nor physics nor any other empirical science can account for but that responds to treatment by way of language.

d Scouring and disappearing: The hysterical symptom and the unconscious signifier

It is Freud's first patients, the hysterics he invited to speak rather than to partake of treatments targeting the biological, whose symptoms taught psychoanalysis about the structure and function of that paradoxical entity of a jouissant irritation involving a subtraction of jouissance that is the unconscious signifier. The hysterical symptom as Freud discovered it is the paradigm of the effects of language on what lives. It is, Lacan says in the seminar on the *Logic of the Phantasm*, the 'very principle of any signifying possibility,'[263] that is to say, is instructive concerning the very structure of the unconscious signifier. This is first and foremost because in its simplest form, Lacan says, the hysterical symptom appears to be a *'ragade,'* a fissure in the organism, or more specifically in its natural algorithms: recurrent and specifically localized pain, infection, spasm, convulsion, tic. As organic fissure, Lacan emphasizes, the hysterical symptom is of the same order of any mark on an 'animal body.'[264] For the animal body, Lacan says, 'the first locus in which to put inscriptions,' is in effect 'made to be marked.'[265] But in the case of the organism that is also one that speaks, what marks the body – presides over its 'cutting up' or fragmentation – Lacan says, is not any tool of branding but an instrument 'radical' because it synecdochizes the extreme alterity of sexuality to anatomy: the 'sharp edge' of the signifier saturated in sexuation, always already carrying a morsel of the bloody scrap that enabled it to emerge.[266] It is the inscriptions written in the sand of the flesh that undermine any phantasy of somatic peace, of the blissful silence of organs. In cases of hysteria especially, what is inscribed by the sharp edge of the signifier as sexuated, the irritations produced *per via di levare*, are not contained within the apparatus but are pushed out to its surface. They 'irrupt,' Lacan says, 'on the level of the body.' Subsequently, 'the body breaks into fragments,'[267] its specular unicity destabilized.[268] The result is the curious hybridity of hysteria, wherein the very staging of phallic form in its unicity involves the display of portions of the body as not only erotogenic but hysterogenic, wrenched from their anatomical function, enjoyed precisely in their woundedness, and dramatically displayed as such to an Other who might read.

The hysterical body is a body sliced by language as the subject had experienced it, as incarnated for the subject by the words which had been said around him – or not said but transmitted ancestrally – and that henceforth did not cease resonating in his flesh, were in effect written as irritations in his flesh. As psychoanalyst Jean-Louis Gault puts it, the symptoms into which language carves up the hysteric's body are testaments to the 'traumatism of language that the subject has lived through in his being of flesh.'[269] And it is with his flesh, with the jouissant substance of his body, that the subject is obliged to write them.[270] The subject, Lacan writes in 'The Youth of Gide,' 'pay[s] the price of the signifying operation with the elements of his person.'[271] These elements of the flesh that lives lend material support to the suffering of which the subject complains, Jean-Louis Gault says, just as the putting of pen to paper grants such support to speech.[272]

But the hysterical symptom as paradigmatic is a writing in a way that is more than analogical. Lacan's theorization of the *ragade* typifying the hysterical symptom as part of a structure paradigmatic of the very possibility of the signifier as inscription is in effect a macrostructural version of Freud's theorization of the structure of the memory trace in the *Project for a Scientific*

Psychology. The hysteric's body as body made to be marked, sliced up, by a peculiar relation to sexuation is a macrostructural term for what in terms of psycho-grammatology is the irritable and resistant protoplasm of which Freud speaks in the *Project.* What presides over its cutting up into fissures unknown to anatomy and untreatable by medical methods grounded in it is sexuality as aberration, the peculiarity of the enjoyment of the being who speaks. The sexuality that carves up the hysterical body is a macrostructural manifestation of the quantum in a state of motion, eventually qualified as the motion of the drive Freud postulates as what leaves its mark in the resistant protoplasm he calls the ψ neurons. In both cases, the yield of the irruption of what marks into what is made to be marked is of the order of jouissance: the neuron irritated and made permeable by the motion of the drive, whose large-scale phenomenalization is the recurrently chaffed, inflamed, irritated portion of flesh of which the hysteric complains to the analyst, who knows it to be her secret satisfaction – but that is not only what it seems.

Symptoms, Lacan writes in 'The Direction of the Treatment,' are what 'is written' of the 'censored chapter' of the subject's history that is the unconscious 'elsewhere' rather than in the realm of conscious speech where censorship prevails: in the 'monuments' the hysteric especially erects in her body.[273] The hysteric's symptom, then, is a writing, but one that like the other formations of the unconscious, involves censorship. Parts of this writing, that is, have been removed. Their removal, however, is a form of subtraction that is not effraction but transposition to another scene that remains veiled. Freud's first description of Mrs. Emmy von N. in *Studies on Hysteria*, for instance, is nothing short of a catalogue of *ragades* presented to the analyst:

> This lady, when I first saw her, was lying on a sofa with her head resting on a leather cushion. She still looked young and had finely-cut features… Her face bore a strained and painful expression, her eyelids were drawn together and her eyes cast down; there was a heavy frown on her forehead and the naso-labial folds were deep. She spoke in a low voice as though with difficulty and her speech was from time to time subject to spastic interruptions amounting to a stammer. She kept her fingers, which exhibited a ceaseless agitation resembling athetosis, tightly clasped together. There were frequent convulsive *tic*-like movements of her face and the muscles of her neck, during which some of them, especially the right sterno-cleido-mastoid, stood out prominently. Furthermore she frequently interrupted her remarks by producing a curious 'clacking' sound from her mouth which defies imitation.[274]

At first, Freud describes Emmy as a 'still look[ing] young,' woman with 'finely-cut [*geschnittenen*] facial features [*Gesichtszügen*] that is, one whose appearance is cut out in conformity with the arrangements of physiognomical signs [*zügen*)] conventionally designating a phallic form. But the fineness of features of the initial description is almost immediately breached or frayed by the description of multiple somatic phenomena, some of which are part of her litany of complaints. The mention of the cuts sculpting her features into the finesse of phallic form Freud admires are quickly displaced by description of a panoply of medically denominated cuts that leave phallic form in ruins.

Though the young Freud still treats Emmy with hypnosis and massages, what is significant to what will become psychoanalysis is the clinical knowledge he gleans regarding the connections between the array of somatic paroxysms, the analexias or 'gaps in memory' she explicitly speaks of later in the treatment, and the traumas unravelled in its course (among them a dying brother's repeatedly seizing her when she was a young girl, forced meals, and the sudden death of her husband) – reminiscences which, Freud suggests, contain more than a fragment of the erotic.[275] It is these reminiscences, Freud suggests in his discussion of the case, that are the subject's 'traumas' [literally, wounds]. It is this stock of 'pathogenic reminiscences'[276] that he treats by exhausting them – that is to say, by allowing them to appear, in their strangeness, in speech. The insignia of jouissance in Emmy's body – the spastic speech impediment, the quasi arthetoid fidgetiness of the fingers, the tic-like twitches in Emmy's face and in the muscles of her neck, then, are, to Freud, in effect not the wound but a scar of a wound which subsists in another scene, as the 'sum of excitation[s] impinging on the nervous system.'[277] These excitations, in turn, are what has been subtracted from what is phenomenalized as the monumental and jouissant writing of her panoply of symptoms to be preserved elsewhere, although it is not among them but in the conscious memory about which she testifies to Freud that the gaps indicating them appear. Memory upon its conscious and unconscious strata and somatic symptom thus appear in Freud's writing as phenomena of the same organic substance, segments of the same text that have been torn apart.

The analytic operation of reading the symptom involves first reattaching the gap-ridden conscious memory and the panoply of *ragades* as parts of the same text, then allowing the unconscious 'excitements' of the nervous system to appear as speech under transference. What this also means, however, is that the writing Freud reads on the manifest level of the case of Emmy von N. – the flesh in spasms and tics that interrupts the *finesse* of what is looked at and the gaps and interruptions in memory – emerges only thanks to what it masks, deletes, subtracts so as to preserve in another scene, that is to say, represses. Writing – at least writing in its manifestation as the hysterical structure (well delineated phallic body ravaged by spasms, tics, other displays of enjoyed dis-ease conjoined with a conscious memory riddled with gaps) – is, as Derrida puts it in 'Freud and the Scene of Writing,' 'unthinkable without repression.'[278] But the precise form this repression takes is a form of subtraction peculiar to writing: not the effraction that in the *Project* turns out to be an accretion of quantum, but the *litura* Lacan invokes in '*Lituraterre*,' whose etymology in the dictionary to which Lacan points his audience is not only the waste or 'litter' Lacan accentuates but also 'covering' or 'erasure.'[279]

The written letter as component of the hysterical symptom is litter insofar as like waste in human civilization, it is evicted by being displaced as ob-scene to another scene. But its production, Lacan suggests in '*Lituraterre*,' also involves a subtraction that is other than eviction: the cessation or suspension of writing Lacan marvels at when considering Japanese calligraphy. 'To produce the only, definitive erasure, this is the exploit of calligraphy,' Lacan says in '*Lituraterre*.'[280] This is not because calligraphy is a writing that cancels itself out, leads to an absolute breaching which would leave no trace in another scene such as Derrida gestures towards in 'Freud and the Scene of Writing,' but because mastery of calligraphy is the knowledge not only of how to effect a brush stroke but even more so of when to suspend it.[281] The hysterical symptom as synecdochic of the unconscious signifier that structures it is a calligraphy of unconscious excitations allowed a retracing on the surface of an organism otherwise cut to the design of phallic *haute couture*, which precisely as calligraphy involves suspension as its defining moment. As an accretion of somatically inscribed excitations subjected to suspending *lituras*, hysterical symptoms are indeed, as Lacan puts it in *The Logic of the Phantasm*, the 'very principle of any signifying possibility.'[282] They are the blueprint, daily encountered in the clinic, of the very structure of the unconscious signifier as written. The unconscious signifier as protoplasmic irritation that is nevertheless a writing of a symbol is the synecdoche of the symptom to which analytic interpretation reduces it. This is why analytic interpretation as what Miller calls 'reading the symptom' is effective in curing symptoms. 'Analytic interpretation as reading,' Jean-Louis Gault says, 'is an operation of voiding sense that aims to isolate the signifying matrix, reduced to its literal materiality, which is at work in the symptom.'[283]

In other words, the unconscious signifier as what Freud in *Studies on Hysteria* calls the excitement that affects the nervous system, and in the *Project* – the irritation of the ψ neurons that Freud's developments in Letter 52 and subsequently in 'The Mystic Writing Pad' clarify as a form of writing in the flesh – is a *mise en abŷme* of the hysterical structure as first discovered by Freud. If the surface structure of the hysterical structure as text involves the coalescence of gap and *ragade*, empty points in conscious memory and seizures or lesions in the flesh as equally organic, the unconscious signifier too involves a coalescence: that of the resisting neurons and of the movement of the drive that frays them. Both in the hysterical symptom and in the unconscious signifier, however, the seemingly constitutive coalescence works only on condition of an operation of a subtraction that is not a fraying. For in the unconscious signifier as Freud first theorizes it in the *Project* the fraying or furrowing is precisely what produces not a subtraction but an irritation that is an instance of *plus de jouir*.

What produces the manifest level of the hysterical structure, revealed in the coalescence of gaps in memory and of speech concerning eroticized lesions ravaging the body in its real and imaginary dimensions, as organism and as phallic construct, is a subtraction from this non-subtractive irritation. This subtraction takes the form of the censoring or masking of the irritated portion of flesh that is the unconscious memory precipitating the symptom. This irritation itself, the product of the passage of the motion of the drive in a substrate that resists it depends on what makes the drive emerge in the first place: the splintering of instinct that is the product of language – which involves another operation of subtraction.

In this splintering, something of instinct is lost, henceforth subsisting as a void Lacan would denominate the object a, the object eternally lacking. Other splinters encircle this void in what amounts, Lacan says, to a montage.[284] The result is an irritation, '*Reiz*' in Freud's terms, that is 'different from any stimulation coming from the outside world,'[285] an internal *Reiz* that seeks nothing but the circumvention of this void.[286] It is as an irritation internal insofar as it evinces not a specific action in the world but a topology of circumventing a void whose organic correlates are the apertures in the body insofar as they are erogenized that the drive, Lacan says, 'assumes its role in the functioning of the unconscious.'[287]

The unconscious signifier in its Freudian theorization, then, the unconscious signifier as written, is not divorced from the drive. Indeed, the drive participates in its constitution. If this is so, then the void of the object a around which the drive makes its circuit is part of the unconscious signifier as written. In other words, that the signifier is 'a presence made of absence,'[288] as Lacan puts it in 'The Function and Field of Speech and Language in Psychoanalysis,' means not only that its constitution depends on the loss of a real satisfaction but that this loss remains operative in it, functions as its sustaining cause. The experience of satisfaction [*Befriedigungerlebnis*] Freud specifies in the *Project* as one of the two primal scenes of psychic life and later specifies as what must be ceded for the unconscious representations constitutive of psychic reality to emerge, gives rise, Freud writes in the *Project*, to a *Wunschanziehung* [wishful attraction].[289] The wishful attraction as '*Reste*' or residue of a real satisfaction that can be summoned only as hallucination is the void of the loss of this real satisfaction made operative as mainspring of the act and cause of desire. Not a motivation that can be consciously named, the *Wunschzuständ* [wishful state] is first and foremost the subject's position toward a primordial hole, the consent to allow it to grow scar tissue and become a void, a ריק [*rik*] into which the subject might consent to fall in the operation of the unconscious as a *retour-rik*, rhetorical tour around the void. It is in this void, which the analyst does not seek but into which he falls only to find that something within him has awakened, that the analyst may lodge the jouissance isolated in his cure. It is from that hole and only from that hole that the analyst may act.

In Lacan's terms, what Freud calls the wishful state is nothing short of the position of the subject with respect to the void of the lost object of satisfaction that constitutes him, the consent to make this object operative as cause that propels libido rather than incorporating it into the ego in the melancholic process that tears open a wound from which libido drains out. Not incidentally, Freud calls this state '*Wunschzustände*,'[290] state of wish or desire whose cause Lacan would locate in the void of the object of primordial satisfaction. This void is what sets in motion the quantum Freud in the *Project* theorizes as one of the two components coalescing to generate the unconscious signifier as a fraying and later (in the essay on 'Drives and their Vicissitudes') is specified as one of the four components of the drive as *montage*: its *Drang* or pressure.[291] This *Drang*, however, is only thinkable, Lacan says, in relation to another component of the *montage*, which is localized organically: the drive's *Quelle* or source, the portion of flesh made rim.[292] The rim is what emborders what would otherwise be only tear or wound from which a portion of organicity had been torn, what transmutes it from a hole to the void of the object a as erogenized, that is to say, in Freud's terms in the *Three Essays on the Theory of Sexuality*, as annexed from its anatomical function and used to the end of satisfaction alone. The phenomenal index of this erogenization is the excitation or stimulation of the erogenous zone, the *Reiz* that Freud in the *Project* identifies as a possible state of the ψ neurons. If the drive participates in the structuring of the unconscious signifier as written as the fraying of the ψ neurons that is also their stimulation, then this fraying is not simply the creation of a hollow. It is a scouring that creates this hollow's contours at the same time as it leaves them in a state of irritation.

The circuiting of thrown together segments of a more or less irritated protoplasm around a hole that is no longer a gaping wound but a void, a circomlocution that is constantly aroused – such is the structure of the unconscious signifier as written. Occulted by the conjunction of *ragades* typifying the phenomenology of hysteria, the unconscious signifier itself involves a conjunction (of segments of irritated protoplasm) and a subtraction (that appears as the void of the object at the signifier's center). The unconscious signifier is, as Michèle Montrelay puts it, 'a fragment of jouissance,'[293] but only insofar as this jouissance is subjected to a limiting that takes the form of a cessation or veiling whose prototype in civilization is the cenotaph or grave. If the hysterical symptom, as Lacan puts it in 'The Function and Field of Speech and Language in Psychoanalysis,' 'is a symbol written in the sand of the flesh and on the veil of Maia,'[294] involves a scouring of organic matter and a forgetting that is not a furrowing, so does the unconscious signifier. As Freud had already put it in the concluding sentence in the chapter on Elizabeth von R. in *Studies on Hysteria*, 'it may be that [hysteria] does not take linguistic usage as its model at all, but that both hysteria and linguistic usage alike draw their material from a common source.'[295]

If the hysterical symptom in which portions of the subject's body function as the price of the symbolic operation emerges as an occulting substitute, written in the flesh, for a memory trace too unpleasurable to be translated into conscious thought, this memory trace itself emerges symptomatically, as occulting substitute written in the flesh, for what does not pass the judgment of the pleasure principle and hence ceases to be written at a different limit of the psychic apparatus: not between conscious and unconscious, but between unconscious and a real that cannot be known even in the form of repression. Hysteria attests to writing as the effect of the double operation of a stimulating throwing together and a defensive throwing out (out of conscious thought, out of the unconscious itself). The hysterical symptom – irritated flesh substituting for a signifier whose translation qua retranscription into conscious representation would be too unpleasurable – is indexical of the structure of the unconscious signifier as protoplasm unpleasurably irritated that is at the same time much less unpleasurable than the real, the ultimate horror of a subjective life for which it substitutes, making the real bearable by burying it, occulting it from sight. The combination of irritation with occultation and suspension, excess of life at the hylozooic level of biological matter's indestructibility and partial veiling and the cessation of rewriting are what makes the hysteric's symptomatology, as Lacan puts it, the model of any signifying possibility, and conversely – makes the unconscious signifier indexical of the structure of hysteria, an instance of hysteria *in minima*, a hypomnestic effigy of flesh in suffering ecstasy that also knows very well how to disappear.

D Epilogue: On the unconscious inscription of inherited debt

As deducible from Freud's *Project for a Scientific Psychology* and subsequent developments of the psychic scene of writing in the works of Freud and Lacan, the foundation for the unconscious signifier is organic substrate furrowed by a quantum that irritates as it hollows it. A quantum of the energy Freud would call libido engraves the organism, producing a writ(h)ing that is also the site where libido is bound.

In effect, it is the binding of libido that is primordially crucial for the psychic apparatus as Freud begins to unfold it in the *Project*. The human being, shorn at birth of the ability to sustain itself without the succour of an Other, must have at its disposal a quota of energy that would enable it to signal its distress by means of a motion or scream. In the *Project*, Freud calls this quota 'a store [*Vorrat*] of $Q\dot{\eta}$ sufficient to meet the demand for a specific action.'[296] This store is what later in Freud's work would become the 'great reservoir' [*grosse Reservoir*] of libido referred to in *An Outline of Psychoanalysis* and equated with the 'primary narcissism'[297] Freud had theorized in his introduction to the latter concept.[298] What might ensure that this reservoir not exhaust itself despite the primary tendency of the psychic apparatus to iner-tia[299] that Freud first mentions in the *Project* and that he would come to denominate the death drive?[300] What guarantee that not all contents of this precious store be lost either to the discharge subserving the principle of iner-tia or in the motions striving to support survival?[301]

It is in the differentiation that occurs in what must have initially been 'undifferentiated protoplasm' that Freud, in the *Project*, locates the answer to the question of the enabling condition of 'the accumulation of $Q\acute{\eta}$.'[302] Components of the protoplasm, the substance that lives, Freud argues, ini-tially perform all primary functions of living matter, including respiration and digestion, motility and perception. These components must have origi-nally been self-identical, but at some at some point in evolution they under-went differentiation, including, Freud ventures in the *Project*, the differentiation into portions highly susceptible to conduction, facilitation, and discharge (what Freud calls the ϕ neurons) as distinct from portions which resist the passage of excitations through them (the ψ neurones). Impermeable but not completely, the ψ neurones become more permeable (facilitated) upon their contact with excitations that reach them, and at the same time are able to retain some of these excitations, ensuring that the res-ervoir of energy that might be tapped in states of distress never runs dry. Retained within the protoplasm that resists its passage, the quantum of energy also permanently alters it,[303] the result of this alteration being the foundation for the memory trace or unconscious signifier as protoplasmic irritation.[304] The writ(h)ing that is the foundation for unconscious memory is thus a by-product of the emergence, in the course of the differentiation of living tissue, of portions of the organism less prone to allowing libido to pass through them without leaving a trace behind, portions that hence ensure the perennial availability of quantum necessary to turn to the Other in a state of urgency or distress.

Freud favours a non-essentialist explanation of the emergence of these resistant portions of organicity, arguing that susceptibility to impermeability is not any permanent attribute of these portions but dependent on their 'envi-ronment' or anatomical location in 'the interior of the body,' greater interior-ity spelling greater impermeability and resistance which is nothing other than the inclination to being inscribed.[305] But Freud also mentions what he describes as a 'Darwinian' explanation for the existence of ψ neurones: their being 'indispensable' to the psychic apparatus, as another, less 'modest' pos-sibility alongside his anatomical/topographical explanation of the origin of the characteristic of impermeability of some portions of the *bios*.[306] This argument via indispensability confirms by indirection what the logic of Freud's metapsychology indicates, especially in the wake of the development of the second topography whose roots extend to the *Project*: namely that unconscious inscription as predicated on the irritation of living tissue, espe-cially in the organism's interior, is an offshoot of the existential necessity to ensure a store of libido (primary narcissism) sufficient at least to try and summon help. What is indispensable, that is, is not the psychic writing of memory traces itself but the existential function this writing serves. The memory traces that are the components of the Freudian unconscious, those that are at the foundation of the field of speech and language, are not necessary but incidental to the human organism's prematurity of birth, an aberration of nature. It is this initial status of writing in its Freudian derivation as an incidental by-product of the consequences of *Hilflosigkeit* that perhaps partially accounts for the stupefaction Lacan expresses in the 'Geneva Lecture on the Symptom' in the face of writing's very emergence.[307]

Not only does unconscious writ(h)ing have the status of an incidental by-product; it also comes at a paradoxical cost: its function of binding maintains the organism in a state of heightened quantum which spells unpleasure, belying the system's primary function of releasing as much excitation as possible. 'The principle of inertia,' Freud writes, 'is broken through from the start' so that the apparatus would be able to maintain 'a store of $Q\acute{\eta}$ sufficient to meet the demands for specific action.'[308] Unpleasure is thus the price the human being pays for maintaining a libidinal reservoir (primary narcissism) necessary to signal for assistance (specific action) that would relieve existential distress. And this unpleasure is redoubled. The writ(h)ing that ensures the accumulation of energy sufficient to summon an Other who might simply help one stay alive is protoplasmic irritation, itself unpleasurable. Writ(h)ing hurts and is born of the hurt that is the inevitable consequence of primary narcissism.

Secondary narcissism, for its part, is less the libidinal relation to extraneous objects it is often held to be than the co-optation of the painful by-product of primary narcissism to create what Lacan describes as 'constants' in the psychic apparatus: the ideal ego and ego ideal, both sites of libidinal investment. What constitutes both these constants is no longer the libidinal reservoir itself but conglomerations of its products (unconscious representations coupled with identifications), which replace the insufficiency of birth (Lacan's phrasing for the Freudian *Hilflosigkeit* in his seminal article on 'The Mirror Stage')[309] and by so replacing, continue to treat it. [310] The ideal ego, global body image the infant discovers in the mirror, to which he will develop an erotic relation[311] and which is later observable in his identification with an idealized version of himself that he presents to the world, will not emerge if not for the subject's consent to register as unconscious signifier the experience of satisfaction resulting from a primordial Other's assent to metabolize the screaming signal of helplessness he emits. The ego-ideal too involves an identification. Instead of an idealized image, this identification is with signifiers from one's inheritance, employed as directives or as causes of dissent. In the first case (the ideal ego), what functions as the condition for the emergence of the ideal serving as point of identification of the mask-mirage the subject presents to the world, is the unconscious signifier (of the primordial experience of satisfaction). In the second (the ego ideal), an unconscious signifier which is part of the subject's symbolic debt (unpaid dues, aborted desires, hidden crimes, lost loves) functions as a point of an either positive or negative identification unconsciously orienting the subject.[312] Both these forms of secondary narcissism are amalgamations of identifications, descendants of primary narcissism, that is of libidinal investments not in the world but in the psychic apparatus itself, and of unconscious signifiers. They are liminal components of the psychic apparatus where the symbolic is already emergent, but still steeped in the primordial form of enjoyment Freud calls primary narcissism and Lacan in *Seminar 8*, following a Pindaric Ode, conjugates as the shadow.[313]

The forms of secondary narcissism, that is, treat the helplessness at the foundation of human life not by means of a signal to an Other but by means of an identification wedded to a signifier that is a writ(h)ing in the very entrails of the living being. Used to treat, this writ(h)ing paradoxically hurts, all the more so the more it is invested. This is why, in specifying the ideal ego and ego ideal as two forms of secondary narcissism in his eighth seminar, Lacan speaks of these two forms of the ego in which the signifier is involved as 'the first *lesions* on one's [primary] narcissism.'[314] The signifiers involved in the forms of secondary narcissism that help treat the unpleasure involved in primary narcissism, itself entailed by the human's insufficiency at birth, are themselves lesions, sources of pain or discomfort in the flesh.

Unconscious signifiers subsist also outside the structures of secondary narcissism. Beyond these forms at the cusp of the real and the symbolic is the functioning of unconscious signifiers in what Lacan in the concluding lessons of *Seminar 8* describes as the field of the dream, the field where unconscious signifiers no longer amalgamated with manifestations of the shadow subsist in themselves, enabling the gliding of desire.

Nor are unconscious signifiers as predicated on lesions or writ(h)ings in the body's entrails – whether those caught up in the forms of secondary narcissism or those subsisting as components of the unconscious – the result only of the contingencies of the perceptions or experiences of this body as an *individuum*. In various places in his work Freud insists that the representations comprising the unconscious originate not only in the contingencies of experience he calls 'chance' but also in what he calls 'disposition' or 'constitution.' For instance, in a footnote at the beginning of the article on 'The Dynamics of Transference' Freud emphasizes that what sediments to form the subject's erotic conditions are not only the effects of moments of *tyché*, of contingent encounters in an individual's life, but also what he calls '*daimon*': residues of registrations that accumulated 'in the possibly endless chain of our ancestors,' and that were once, long ago, themselves contingent encounters.[315] 'Constitutional dispositions, Freud similarly writes in the lecture on 'Paths to the Formation of Symptoms,' 'are also undoubtedly after-effects of experiences by ancestors in the past; they too were once acquired.'[316] The subject, as Freud writes in *On Narcissism*, is but the 'temporary tenant of an estate that survives him.'[317] This estate, a reservoir of residues of countless once cathected signifiers, is transferred from one generation to the next via an operation of identification whose organic prototype Freud identifies, in chapter 7 of *Group Psychology and the Analysis of the Ego*, in 'devouring affection.'[318] It is in relation to this paragraph in *Group Psychology* that Lacan says, towards the end of the seminar on *Transference*, that even if man had imagined for a while that he had repudiated cannibalism, he has never ceased to eat the dead.[319]

Far from being a fortune to be saved or squandered, or the condition of luxury, however, this estate is what Freud calls a *daimon*, a signifier whose ancient Greek geneaology points to fate[320] more than to fortune. It plays a part in the formation of symptoms which cause the subject unpleasure of a degree that might lead him to analysis, where he sometimes finds that the deciphering of symptoms brings him some relief. What this means is that in the peculiar economics of the subject, as Lacan puts it in the *Transference* seminar, the operation that binds the generations together involves the transmission of an inheritance as a result of which man still owes. What he owes is what returns in painful symptoms to disturb the banquet of his desires: the vain promises, despairs, failures to act or to love, perversions and betrayals registered as unconscious memory traces and passed on, almost always in silence. It is what Lacan in 'The Freudian Thing' calls 'symbolic debt.'[321]

As delineated in Freud's *Project*, then, unconscious signifiers are lesions or wounds in and on the organism, carved by contingent encounter or the swallowing (oral incorporation) of parts of what was once so carved in the subject's ancestry and that he may choose to confront in the course of his analysis. Or not. As Lacan shows in his magisterial reading of Paul Claudel's Coûfontaine trilogy in the seminar on *Transference*, the subject of the ancient world was at one with his destiny, like Antigone who could not but insist on burying her brother in accordance with her familial ethos or *Até*. It was then too that the function regulating the order of generations, guaranteeing the prohibition of incest as the *sine qua non* of speech, the function Lacan denominates the Name of the Father was, if constitutively never certain, much more firmly in place. But such is no longer the case. It is not only recent decades that have witnessed the decline of the paternal function and the concomitant rise of the object a, object of consumption and enjoyment, to the zenith of civilization.[322] Claudel's bleak trilogy takes place in the wake of the French Revolution, and Lacan's reading of its final play, *The Humiliated Father* [*Le père humilié*] indicates that it is at that point in history that has perhaps somewhat ironically come to be called the Enlightenment that he situates the beginning of the progressive decline, observable already in his lifetime, of the toppling of functions such as Crown and God which had served as anchoring points in civilization. It is thus not only the contemporary, postmodern subject but his antecedent, the modern (post-Enlightenment) subject who inhabits a world in which the function of the father has been humiliated, and with it, the operativity of the signifier and of desire. In such a world it becomes possible, more than possible, for the subject not to confront his symbolic debt, to turn his back on the ancestral signifiers determining his destiny as easily as does Claudel's heroine Sygne de Coûfontaine who in an inexplicable instance exchanges her having taken on the role of (literally) piecing together the entailed property of her noble family almost entirely lost to the guillotine for a consent to marry her family's executioner, the consequences being as disastrous as the guillotine's blade.[323] At the end of the trilogy's first play, L'Ôtage [The Hostage], all that is left of desire for the heroine who turns her back on her signifying legacy, her symbolic debt, is her response to the plea of the executioner whom she had agreed to marry that she give as much as a sign that her throwing herself in front of a bullet targeting him was meant to protect him: the nod of her head signalling a 'no.'

This all but imperceptible facial 'no,' Lacan says, is a 'twitching on the part of life,' desire in its dying throes. What then makes it also and at the same time, the 'extreme derision of the signifier itself'"[324]? Sygne's symbolic debt, first inscribed in the flesh, does not return in symptoms to disturb the banquet of her desires because in her case, the desire that at the outset of The Hostage had been literally manifest in her piecing together the remnants of the familial estate was then relinquished. What this means is that in the case of Sygne as she is staged at the end of 'The Hostage,' what is operative in the signifying function of the unconscious is the additionality of the plus de jouir more than the subtraction constitutive of desire. Rendered almost completely defunct by the subject's defection from it, desire as the effect of the hollowing out of the unconscious signifier which structurally differentiates it from the forms of psychic writing proceeding solely by way of addition is manifest in Sygne's case only in a gesture that mimics desire's negativity. When the subject turns his back on symbolic debt and subsequently on desire as radically as Sygne does, the unconscious signifier becomes nothing but living testament to what Lacan in the seminar on Desire and its Interpretation describes as the 'pain of existence,'[325] a mockery of the subtractions that structure it.

If it is not so mocked but preserved under the bar of repression, the unconscious signifier may vehicle desire under the mask of symptoms. Or it may be retranscribed, as Freud puts it in Letter 52 to Fliess, and in this process not only be voided of some of the cathexis that makes it painful,[326] but, as Freud argues in the Project, make its way towards speech.[327] But speech, the very aspect of language that Derrida argues has always enjoyed a privileged status with respect to writing, is in Freudian terms neither primal nor obvious for the human subject. Nor are all of its manifestations, even under transference, cathartic with respect to jouissance, pure instances of what Lacan would denominate 'symbolic.' It is to the analysis of the spoken aspect of psychoanalytic grammatology that I now turn.

Notes

1   Lacan, J. (1975). 'Geneva Lecture on the Symptom.,' trans. R. Grigg, *Analysis* 1, 1989, p. 24.
2   Lacan, J. (1956–1957). *Seminar 3: The Psychoses*, trans. R. Grigg. New York, Norton 1997, p. 155.
3   Lacan, J. (1956). 'Seminar on "The Purloined Letter."' *Écrits: The First Complete Edition in English*, trans. B. Fink, New York, Norton, 2002, p. 21.
4   Freud, S. (1896). Letter 52 to Wilhelm Fliess, *The Standard Edition of the Complete Psychological Works of Sigmund Freud*, trans J. Strachey et al. London, Vintage, 2001, 24 Vols, Vol.1, p. 234, henceforth SE. References in German are to the German edition of Freud's complete works, *Gesammelte Werke*, ed. A. Freud, Frankfurt, Fischer Verlag, 1999, henceforth GW, save for Letter 52, cited in German from Freud (1962). *Briefe an Wilhelm Fliess, 1887–1904*, Frankfurt, Fischer Verlag, pp. 151–153.
5   Ibid.; Ibid.
6   Lacan, J. (1956–1957). *Seminar 3*, Op. cit., p. 148.
7   Freud, S. (1896). Letter 52 to Wilhelm Fliess, Op. cit., p. 234.
8   Lacan, J. (1959–1960). *Seminar 7: The Ethics of Psychoanalysis*, trans. D. Porter, New York, Norton, 1997, p. 50.
9   Lacan, J. (1958–1959). *Seminar 6: Desire and its Interpretation*. trans. B. Fink, Cambridge, Polity, 2019, p. 66–67.
10 Lacan, J. (1975). 'Geneva Lecture on the Symptom,' p. 13; 'Conférence à Genève sur le symptôme.' *La cause du désir* 95, 2007, p. 12.
11 Freud, S. *Project for a Scientific Psychology*, SE 1, p. 323.
12 Ibid., pp. 317–320; GW 18S, pp. 413–414.
13 Ibid., p. 318.
14 Ibid., p. 320, p. 306.
15 Ibid., p. 322.
16 Ibid.
17 Ibid., p. 320, p. 306.
18 Ibid., p. 321; GW 18S, p. 415.
19 Lacan, J. (1969–1970). *The Seminar of Jacques Lacan Book 17: The Other Side of Psychoanalysis*, trans. R. Grigg. New York, Norton, 2007, p. 175.
20 Alberti, L.B. 1443. *On Sculpture*, trans. J. Arkles, Lulu.com, 2003, p.14.
21 Ibid., p, 10.
22 da Vinci, L. (c. 1540). 'The Practice of Painting,' *The Literary Works of Leonardo da Vinci*, trans. J.P. Richter (1883), London, Low, Marston, Searle and Rivington, p. 656.
23 Freud, S. (1904). 'On Psychotherapy,' SE 7, p. 260; GW 5, p, 16.
24 Ibid.
25 Lacan, J. (1954). 'The Function ad Field of Speech and Language in Psychoanalysis,' *Écrits*, Op. cit., p. 262,
26 Freud, S. *Project for a Scientific Psychology*, SE 1, p. 322; emphasis in the original.
27 Lacan, J. (1975). 'Geneva Lecture on the Symptom,' Op. cit., p. 10.
28 Ibid., emphasis mine.
29 Freud, S. (1895). *Project for a Scientific Psychology*, SE 1, pp. 307, 320.
30 Ibid., p. 307.
31 Ibid., p. 324.
32 Ibid., p. 320; GW 18S, p. 413.
33 Ibid., p. 314.

34 Lacan, J. (1959–1960). *The Seminar of Jacques Lacan Book 7: The Ethics of Psychoanalysis*, trans. D. Porter. New York, Norton, 1997, p. 60.

35 Hegel, G.W.F. (1835). *Aesthetics: Lectures on Fine Art*, trans. T. M. Knox, Oxford, Clarendon Press, 1988, pp. 56–61. For a detailed discussion of art as a distinctly human intervention in the world, upon its roots in Kant's discussion of art in *The Critique of Judgment* (1790), see E. Biberman and S. Zisser *Art, Death, and Lacanian Psychoanalysis*, London, Routledge, 2018, pp. 37–48.

36 Lacan, J. (1959–1960). *Seminar 7*, Op. cit., p. 60.

37 Lacan, J. (1972–1973). *The Seminar of Jacques Lacan Book 20: Encore*, trans. B. Fink, New York, Norton, 1998, p. 76.

38 Cole, M. (2007). 'Bernini Struts,' *Projecting Identities: The Power of Material Culture*, ed. J. Sofaer Derevenski, London: Blackwell, pp. 55–66.

39 Reich, W. (1933). *Character Analysis*, trans. V. Carfagno, New York, Farrar, Straus and Giroux, 1980.

40 See also Lacan's critique of Reich in Lacan, J. (1953). 'The Function and Field of Speech and Language in Psychoanalysis,' *Écrits: The First Complete Edition in English*, trans. B. Fink et al., New York, Norton, 2002, p. 260.

41 Miller, J.-A. (1998–1999). *L'experience du reel dans la cure psychanalytique*, Course in the Department of Psychoanalysis, University of Paris 8, lesson of 2.12.1998. http://jonathanleroy.be/wp-content/uploads/2016/02/1998-1999-Le-reel-dans-l-experience-psychanalytique-JA-Miller.pdf. See also Lacan's critique of Reich in 'Function and Field,' *Écrits*, Op. cit., p. 260.

42 Freud, S. (1905). *Three Essays on the Theory of Sexuality*, SE 7, pp. 238–239; GW 5, p. 139.

43 Freud, S. (1915). 'Instincts and their Vicissitudes,' SE 14, p. 123; GW 10, p. 215.

44 See Jones, E. (1918). 'Anal-Erotic Character Traits,' *Journal of Abnormal Psychology* 13, pp. 261–284, and Abraham (1923) 'Contributions to the Theory of the Anal Character,' *International Journal of Psychoanalysis* 4, pp. 400–418.

45 Miller, J.-A. (1998–1999). *L'experience du réel dans la cure analytique*, Op. cit., lesson of 27.1.1999.

46 Ibid., lesson of 3.2.1999.

47 Ibid., lesson of 27.1.1999.

48 Ibid.

49 Lacan, J. (1957–1958). *The Seminar of Jacques Lacan Book 5: Formations of the Unconscious*, trans. R. Grigg, Cambridge, Polity, 2017, p. 229.

50 Ibid.

51 Lacan, J. (1964). *The Seminar of Jacques Lacan Book 11: The Four Fundamental Concepts of Psychoanalysis*, trans. A. Sheridan, New York, Norton, 1981, p. 169.

52 Freud, S. (1915). 'Instincts and their Vicissitudes.' SE 14, pp. 121–122.

53 Freud, S. (1908). 'Character and Anal Erotism,' SE 9, p. 175; GW 7, p. 208.

54 Ibid.

55 Alberti, L.B. (1443). *On Sculpture*. Trans. J. Arkles. Lulu.com, 2003, p.10.

56 Freud, S. (1917). 'Transformations of Instinct,' SE 17, p. 126.

57 Abraham, K. (1923). 'Contributions to the Theory of the Anal Character,' Op. cit., pp. 417–418.

58 Freud, S. (1908) 'Character and Anal Erotism,' SE 9, p.175; GW 7, p. 208.

59 Miller, J.-A. (1998–1999). *L'experience du réel dans la cure analytique*, Op. cit., lesson of 9.12.1998; lesson of 20.1.1999.

60 Ibid., lesson of 27.1.1999.

61 Freud, S. (1916). 'Some Character Types Met with in Psychoanalytic Work,' SE 14, pp. 311, 313.

62 Ibid., pp. 312–333.

63 Miller, J.-A. (1998–1999). *L'experience du réel dans la cure analytique*, Op. cit., lesson of 20.1.1999.
64 Lacan, J. (1953). 'The Function and Field of Speech and Language in Psychoanalysis,' *Écrits*, Op. cit. p. 232.
65 Freud, S. (1916). 'Some Character Types Met with in Psychoanalytic Work,' SE 14. p. 311.
66 Ibid., pp. 314–315.
67 Reich, W. (1933). *Character Analysis*, Op. cit., p. 48
68 Lacan, J. (1953). 'The Function and Field of Speech and Language in Psychoanalysis,' *Écrits*, Op. cit., p. 266.
69 Lacan, J. (1954). 'Variations on the Standard Treatment,' *Écrits*, Op. cit., p. 284
70 Reich, W. (1933). *Character Analysis*, Op. cit., p. 48.
71 Ibid.
72 Miller, J.-A. (1998–1999). *L'experience du réel dans la cure analytique*, Op. cit., lesson of 16.12.1998.
73 Freud, S. (1916). 'Some Character Types Met with in Psychoanalytic Work,' SE 14, p. 311.
74 Reich, W. (1933). *Character Analysis*, Op. cit., p. 48.
75 Miller, J.-A. (1998–1999). *L'experience du réel dans la cure analytique*, Op. cit., lesson of 20.1.1999.
76 Freud, S. (1895). *Project for a Scientific Psychology*, SE 1, p. 354.
77 Reich, W. (1933). *Character Analysis*, Op. cit., p. 48.
78 Freud, S. (1895). *Project for a Scientific Psychology*, SE 1, 320; GW 18S, p. 413. The other fundamental scene of the psychic apparatus is the *Befriedigungserlebnis*, the experience of satisfaction. Freud, S. (1895). *Project for a Scientific Psychology*, SE 1, pp. 317–319; GW 18S, pp. 410-412. See also previous chapter.
79 Freud, S. (1915). '*Das Unbewusste*,' GW 10, p. 276.
80 Freud, S. (1895). *Project for a Scientific Psychology*, SE 1, pp. 306, 320.
81 Freud, S. (1908). 'Character and Anal Erotism,' SE 9, p. 175, emphasis mine; GW 7, p. 209.
82 Freud, S. (1916). 'Some Character Types Met With in Psychoanalytic Work,' SE 14, emphasis mine; 'Einige Charaktertypen Aus Der Psychoanalytischen Arbeit,' GW 10, pp. 364–391.
83 Miller, J.-A. (1998–1999). *L'experience du réel dans la cure analytique*, Op. cit., Lesson of 10.1.1999.
84 Freud, S. (1912). 'The Dynamics of Transference,' SE 12, p. 100.
85 Shakespeare, W. (1593). *Richard III*, ed. J. Semion, London, Arden, 2009, emphases mine. The quote appears in Freud, S. (1916). 'Some Character Types met with in Psychoanalytic Work.' SE 14, p. 314.
86 Ibid., pp. 312, 315.
87 Freud, S. (1908). 'Psychopathic Characters on the Stage,' SE 7, pp. 303–310.
88 Shakespeare, W. (c. 1592). *The Taming of the Shrew*, ed. B. Hodgdon, London, Arden, 2010, 2.1.267–268.
89 Ibid., 4.4.92.
90 See 'an he begin once, he'll rail in his (t)rope tricks. he'll throw a figure in her face and so disfigure her with it that she should have no more eyes to see than a cat,' or, Shakespeare, W. (c.1592). *The Taming of the Shrew*, Op. cit., 1.2.110–114.
91 See, for instance, Fenner, D. (1585). *The Arts of Logike and rhetorique*, Middleburgh (unpaginated); Hobbes, T. (1637). *The Art of Rhetorike, The Collected Works of Thomas Hobbes*, London, Delphi, 2019, 1.1.
92 Shakespeare, W. (c. 1592). *The Taming of the Shrew*, Op. cit., 1.1.1057.
93 Fenner, D. (1585). *The Arts of Logike and rhetorique*, Op. cit.; Hobbes (1637). *The Art of Rhetorike*, Op. cit.

94 Shakespeare, W. (1605). *Timon of Athens*, eds. A.B. Dawson and G.E. Minton, London, Arden, 2008, 5.5.65–70.
95 See, for instance, the Prologue's instructions to the audience: 'Think, when we talk of horses, that you see them / Printing their proud hoofs i' the receiving earth.' Shakespeare, W. (1599), *Henry V*, ed. T.W. Craik, *Prologue* 13–15, London, Arden, 1995, Prologue, 26–28.
96 Overbury, T. (1615). *Overburian Characters*, ed. J. Hall, London: Routledge, 1924, p. 3.
97 Freud, S. (1916). 'Some Character Types met with in Psychoanalytic Work,' SE 14., pp. 313, 318.
98 Ibid., p. 319; GW 10, p. 373.
99 Ibid., p. 318.
100 Lacan, J. (1954–1955). *The Seminar of Jacques Lacan Book 2: The Ego in Freud's Theory and in the Technique of Psychoanalysis*, trans. S. Tomaselli, p. 142.
101 Freud, S. (1916). 'Psychopathic Characters on the Stage,' SE 7, p. 306.
102 Miller, J.-A. (1998–1999). *L'experience du réel e dans la cure analytique*. Op. cit., lesson of 10 February, 1999.
103 Freud, S. (1912). 'The Dynamics of Transference,' SE 12, p. 99; GW 8, p. 364.
104 Ibid. p. 100.
105 Freud, S. (1912). 'The Dynamics of Transference,' SE 12, p. 99.
106 Freud, S. (1914). 'On Narcissism: An Introduction,' SE 14, p. 21.
107 Freud, S. (1912). 'The Dynamics of Transference' SE 12, p. 99.
108 Freud, S. (1923). *The Ego and the Id*, SE 19, p. 38; GW 13, pp. 266–267.
109 Lacan, J. (1961–1962). *The Seminar of Jacques Lacan Book 9: Identification*, trans. C. Gallagher from unedited typescripts, lesson of 13.12.1961, www.lacaninireland.com
110 Freud, S. (1921). *Group Psychology and the Analysis of the Ego*, SE 18, p. 105; GW 13, p. 116.
111 Freud, S. (1923). *The Ego and the Id*, SE 19, p. 29; GW 13, p. 257.
112 Ibid., p. 28; GW 13, p. 257.
113 Freud, S. (1921). *Group Psychology and the Analysis of the Ego*, SE 18., p. 107; GW 13, p. 84.
114 Ibid., p. 109; GW 13, p. 117.
115 Lacan, J. (1960–1961). *The Seminar of Jacques Lacan Book 8: Transference*, trans. B. Fink, Cambridge, Polity, 2015, pp. 355–356.
116 It is perhaps not incidental that in Hebrew, the same word, 'ראוי,' /raui/, designates at once one's being seen and one's being worthy or deserving.
117 Lacan, J. (1960–1961). *Seminar 8: Transference*, Op. cit., p. 354.
118 See Lacan, J. (1960–1961). *Seminar 8: Transference*, Op. cit., pp. 355–356.
119 Lacan, J. (1968–1969). *The Seminar of Jacques Lacan Book 16: From the Other to the other*, trans. C. Gallagher from unedited typescripts, lesson of 22.1.1969, www.lacaninireland.com
120 Lacan, J. *The Seminar of Jacques Lacan Book 14: The Logic of the Phantasm*, trans. C. Gallagher from unedited typescripts, lesson of 23.11.1966, www.lacaninireland.com
121 Sherry, R. (1550). *Treatise of Schemes and Tropes*, ed. H.W. Hildebrant, Gainesville, FL, Scholars' Facsimilies and Reprints, 1961, p. 40, emphases mine.
122 Fraunce, A. (1588). *The Arcadian Rhetorike*, Oxford, Blackwell, 1950, p. 16, emphases mine.
123 Lacan, J. (1960–1961). *Seminar 8*, Op. cit., p. 356, emphases mine.
124 Fraunce, A. (1588). *The Arcadian Rhetorike*, Op. cit., p. 3.
125 Peacham, H. (1593). *The Garden of Eloquence*, Gainesville, FL, Scholars' Facsimiles and Reprints, 1983, p. 40, emphases mine.
126 Ibid., emphasis mine.

127 Sherry, R. (1550). *A Treatise of Schemes and Tropes*, Op. cit. p. 25; Fraunce, A. (1588) *Arcadian Rhetorike*, Op. cit., p. 24.
128 On the theoretical consequences of the programmatic distinction between trope and figure in the history of rhetoric see also S. Zisser (2001), *The Risks of Simile in Renaissance Rhetoric*.
129 Fraunce, A. (1588). *The Arcadian Rhetorique*, Op. cit., p. 51.
130 Sherry, R. (1550). *A Treatise of Schemes and Tropes*, Op. cit., p. 33.
131 Lacan, J. (1975). 'Geneva Lecture on the Symptom,' trans. R. Grigg, Op. cit. p.17.
132 Lacan, J. (1960–1961). *Seminar 8: Transference*, Op. cit., p. 355.
133 Lacan, J. (1975). 'Geneva Lecture on the Symptom,' Op. cit., p. 16, my emphasis.
134 Ibid., p. 17.
135 Erasmus, D. (1513). *On Copia of Words and Ideas*, trans. D. B. King and H.B. Rix, Milwaukee, WI, Marquette University Press, 1999.
136 See Cave, T. (1985). *The Cornucopian Text: Problems of Writing in the French Renaissance*, Oxford, Oxford University Press; Parker, P. *Literary Fat Ladies: Rhetoric, Gender, Property*, London, Methuen, 1998.
137 Lacan, J. (1975). 'Geneva Lecture on the Symptom,' Op. cit., p. 23.
138 Lacan, J. (1958) 'The Youth of Gide, or the Letter and Desire,' *Écrits*, Op. cit., p. 636.
139 Ibid.
140 Freud, S. (1901). 'Fragment of an Analysis of a Case of Hysteria,' SE 7, pp. 56–47; Freud, S. (1921) *Group Psychology and the Analysis of the Ego*, SE 18, p. 106–107.
141 Lacan, J. (1975). 'Geneva Lecture on the Symptom,' Op. cit., p. 23.
142 Lacan, J. (1958). 'The Youth of Gide,' *Écrits*, Op. cit., p. 636.
143 Lacan, J. (1961–1962), *The Seminar of Jacques Lacan Book 9: Identification*, trans. C. Gallagher from unedited typescripts, lesson of 6 December, 1961. www.lacaninireland.com
144 Lacan, J. (1954–1955). *Seminar 2: The Ego in Freud's Theory and the Technique of Psychoanalysis*, Op. cit., New York, Norton, 1991, p. 142.
145 Lacan, J. (1975). 'Geneva Lecture on the Symptom,' Op. cit., p. 2.
146 Lacan, J. (1961–1962). *Seminar 9*, Op. cit., lesson of 20 December, 1961, www.Lacan, J.inireland.com
147 Lacan, J. (1956). 'The Situation of Psychoanalysis and the Training of Analysts in 1956,' *Écrits*, Op. cit., p. 391.
148 Lacan, J. (1953) 'The Instance of the Letter in the Unconscious,' *Écrits*, Op. cit., 419.
149 Ibid.
150 Miller, J.-A. (1999b). 'Interpretation in Reverse,' *Psychoanalytical Notebooks of the London Circle*, 2, p. 11.
151 Derrida, J. (1972). 'Différance,' *Margins of Philosophy*, trans. A. Bass, Chicago, University of Chicago Press, 1982, pp. 5–6.
152 Lacan, J. *Seminar 11: The Four Fundamental Concepts of Psychoanalysis*, Op. cit., p. 249.
153 Lacan, J. (1953). 'The Instance of the Letter in the Unconscious,' *Écrits*, Op. cit., p. 419.
154 Lacan, J., 'The Youth of Gide,' *Écrits*, Op. cit., p. 636.
155 Lacan, J. (1976–1977). *The Seminar of Jacques Lacan Book 24: L'insu que sait de l'une-bevue s'aile a mourre*, trans. C. Gallagher from unedited French typescripts, lesson of 19 April, 1977, www.lacaninireland.com
156 Miller, J.-A. 'Interpretation in Reverse.' Op. cit., p. 13.

157 Derrida, J. (1967a). *Of Grammatology*, trans. G. C. Spivak. Baltimore, The Johns Hopkins University Press, 1974, p. 4 and *passim*.
158 Lacan, J. (1975). 'Geneva Lecture on the Symptom,' Op. cit., p. 23.
159 Lacan, J. (1968–1969). *The Seminar of Jacques Lacan Book 16: From an Other to the Other*, trans. C. Gallagher from unedited typescripts, lesson of 22 January 1969, www.lacaninireland.com
160 Lacan, J. (1970–1971). *'Lituraterre,' The Seminar of Jacques Lacan Book 18: On a Discourse that Might Not Be a Semblance*, trans. C. Gallagher from unedited typescripts, lesson of 12 May, 1971, www.lacaninireland.com
161 Miller, J.-A. (1995–1996). *La fuite du sens*, Course in the Department of Psychoanalysis, University of Paris 8, lesson of 2 December, 1998. http://jona-thanleroy.be/2016/02/orientation-lacanienne-jacques-alain-miller/
162 See, for instance, Lacan, J. (1955–1956). *The Seminar of Jacques Lacan Book 3: The Psychoses*, trans. R. Grigg, New York, Norton, 1993, pp. 238–240.
163 Miller, J.-A. (1995–1996). *La fuite du sens*, Op. cit., lesson of 17 January, 1996.
164 Lacan, J. (1956–1957). *Le Seminaire de Jacques Lacan Livre 4: La relation d'objet*, Paris, Seuil, 1998, p. 128.
165 Plato, *Phaedrus*, trans. C.E. Jones and W. Preddy, Cambridge, MA, Harvard University Press, 2019, 274d–e.
166 Derrida, J. (1969). 'Plato's Pharmacy,' *Dissemination*, trans. B. Johnson, Chicago. University of Chicago Press, 1983, p. 73.
167 Ibid., p. 68.
168 Plato, *Phaedrus*, Op. cit., 275a.
169 Derrida, J. (1969). 'Plato's Pharmacy,' *Dissemination*, Op. cit., p. 91.
170 Ibid., p. 110.
171 Ibid., p, 109.
172 Ibid., p. 111.
173 Cicero, M.T. *De Oratore*, trans. H. Rackham, Cambridge, MA, Harvard University Press, 1948, 2.351.
174 Plato, *Protagoras*, trans. W.M. Lamb, Cambridge, MA, Harvard University Press, 1924, 316d.
175 Cicero, M.T. *De Oratore*, Op. cit., 2.351–353.
176 Ibid., 2.352.
177 Wilson, T. (1553), *The Arte of Rhetorique*, ed. P.E. Medine, Philadelphia, PA, Pennsylvania State University Press, 1993, p. 75.
178 Lacan, J. (1959–1960). *Seminar 7: The Ethics of Psychoanalysis*, Op. cit., p. 279.
179 Lacan, J. (1958–1959). *The Seminar of Jacques Lacan Book 6: Desire and its Interpretation*, trans. B. Fink, Cambridge, Polity, 2019, p. 235.
180 Lacan, J. (1959–1960). *Seminar 7: The Ethics of Psychoanalysis*, Op. cit., p. 279.
181 Cicero, M.T. *De Oratore*, Op. cit., 2.351
182 Lacan, J. (1972–1973). *The Seminar of Jacques Lacan Book 20: Encore*, trans. B. Fink, New York, Norton, 1998, p. 116.
183 Shakespeare, W. (1609). *Hamlet*, ed. H. Jenkins, London, Arden, 1982, 5.2.382–391.
184 Wilson, T. (1553). *Arte of Rhetorique*, Op. cit., p. 75.
185 Lacan, J. (1956–1957). *Séminaire 4: La relation d'objet*, Op. cit., p. 384.
186 Lacan, J. (1964). *The Seminar of Jacques Lacan Book 11: The Four Fundamental Concepts of Psychoanalysis*, trans. A. Sheridan, New York, Norton, 1999, p. 6.
187 Lacan, J. (1977–1978). *The Seminar of Jacques Lacan Book 25: The Moment to Conclude*, trans. C. Gallagher from unedited typescripts, lesson of 15 November, 1977, www.lacaninireland.com
188 Cicero, M.T. *De Oratore*, Op. cit. 2.3.351.
189 Plato, *Theaetetus*, trans. H.N. Fowler, Cambridge, MA, Harvard University Press, 1921, 191cd.

190 Aristotle, *On Memory and Reminiscence*, trans. J.I. Beare, Adelaide, The University of Adelaide Press, 2005, 449b32.
191 See also Yates, F. (1956). *The Art of Memory*, New York, Random House, pp. 41–73.
192 Quintilian, *Institutio Oratoria*, trans. H.E. Butler, Cambridge, MA, Harvard University Press, 11.2.4.
193 Wilson, T. (1553). *Arte of Rhetorique*, Op. cit., p. 76.
194 Cappella, M. *De nuptiis Philologiae et Mercurii*, ed. A Dick, Leipzig, 1925, pp. 268–270.
195 Cited in Yates, F. (1956). *The Art of Memory*, Op. cit., p. 243.
196 Freud, S. (1925). 'A Note on the Mystic Writing Pad,' SE 19, p. 229.
197 Freud, S. (1925). 'Negation,' SE 19, p. 238.
198 Lacan, J. (1956). 'Seminar on "The Purloined Letter,"' *Écrits: The First Complete Edition in English*, trans. B. Fink et al., New York: Norton, 2002, p. 13.
199 Lacan, J. (1964). *Seminar 11: The Four Fundamental Concepts of Psychoanalysis*, Op. cit., p. 257.
200 Lacan, J. (1954–1955). *Seminar 2: The Ego in Freud's Theory and in the Technique of Psychoanalysis*, Op. cit., p. 42.
201 Freud, S. (1925). 'A Note on the Mystic Writing Pad' SE 19, p. 228; GW 14, p. 4.
202 Ibid.
203 Ibid., p. 225; GW 14, p. 4.
204 Ibid., pp. 227–228.
205 Ibid., p. 228.
206 Freud, S. (1896). Letter 52 to Wilhelm Fliess,' Op. cit., p. 233; *Briefe an Wilhelm Fliess*, Op. cit., p.151.
207 Ibid., p. 234; Ibid.
208 Derrida, J. (1967b). 'Freud, S. and the Scene of Writing,' *Writing and Difference*, trans. A. Bass, Chicago, Chicago University Press, 1983, p. 213.
209 Ibid., p. 200.
210 Ibid., p. 209.
211 Ibid., p. 230.
212 Ibid.
213 Freud, S. (1925). 'A Note on the Mystic Writing Pad', SE 19, p. 229.
214 Lacan, J. (1964). *Seminar 11: The Four Fundamental Concepts of Psychoanalysis*, Op. cit., p 257.
215 Jakobson, R. (1949). 'The Phonemic and Grammatical Aspects of Language in their Interrelations,' *Word and Language: Selected Writings*. Berlin: Walter de Gruyter, 1971, p. 103.
216 Freud, S. (1895). *Project for a Scientific Psychology*, SE 1, pp. 295–298.
217 Ibid.; GW 18S, p. 391.
218 de Saussure, F. (1916). *Course in General Linguistics*, trans. W. Baskin, New York, Columbia University Press, 2011, pp. 68–69.
219 Jung, C.G. (1921). *Psychological Types, Collected Works*, trans. R.F.C. Hull, Princeton, NJ, Princeton University Press, Vol. 6, p. 817.
220 Jakobson, R. (1949). 'The Phonemic and Grammatical Aspects of Language in their Interrelations,' Op. cit., p.103.
221 Ibid.
222 Lacan, J. (1972–1973). *Seminar 20: Encore*, Op. cit., p. 126.
223 Lacan, J. (1957). 'The Instance of the Letter in the Unconscious,' *Écrits*, Op. cit., p. 424.
224 Lacan, J. (1953). 'The Function and Field of Speech and Language in Psychoanalysis,' *Écrits*, Op. cit., p. 225.
225 Leenhardt, M. (1947). *Do Kamo: Person and Myth in the Melanesian World*, trans. B.M. Gulati, Chicago, University of Chicago Press, 1979, p. 129.

226 Lacan, J. (1953). 'The Function and Field of Speech and Language,' Op. cit., p. 225.
227 Ibid.
228 de Saussure, F. (1916). *Course in General Linguistics*, Op. cit., pp. 111–112.
229 Ibid, p. 113.
230 Freud, S. (1895). *Project for a Scientific Psychology*, SE 1, p. 295; GW 18S, p. 387–388.
231 Jakobson, R. (1949). 'The Phonemic and Grammatical Aspects of Language in their Interrelations,' Op. cit., p.103.
232 de Saussure, F. (1916). *Course in General Linguistics*. Op. cit., p. 112, my emphasis.
233 Ibid., p. 102.
234 Ibid., pp. 23–24.
235 Derrida, J. *Of Grammatology*, Op. cit., pp. 13–44.
236 de Saussure, F. (1916). *Course in General Linguistics*, Op. cit., p. 110.
237 Ibid., p. 10.
238 Lacan, J. (1964). *Seminar 11: The Four Fundamental Concepts of Psychoanalysis*, Op. cit., p. 156.
239 Freud, S. (1895). *Project for a Scientific Psychology*, SE 1, p. 364.
240 Lacan, J. (1959–1960). *Seminar 7: The Ethics of Psychoanalysis*, Op. cit., p. 32.
241 de Saussure, F. (1916). *Course in General Linguistics*, Op. cit., p. 7.
242 Derrida, J. (1967a). *Of Grammatology*, Op. cit., p. 23.
243 Ibid., p. 29.
244 Ibid., p. 71.
245 Derrida, J. (1967b). 'Freud and the Scene of Writing,' *Writing and Difference*, trans. A. Bass, Chicago, University of Chicago Press, 1980, p. 220.
246 Ibid., p. 229.
247 Ibid., pp. 276, 288–289.
248 Ibid., p. 289.
249 Lacan, J. (1957). 'The Instance of the Letter in the Unconscious,' *Écrits*, Op. cit., p. 520.
250 Freud, S. (1895). *Project for a Scientific Psychology*, SE 1, p. 296
251 Aristotle, *On Memory and Reminiscence*, Op. cit., 450 b1–6.
252 Freud, S. (1895). *Project for a Scientific Psychology*, SE 1, p. 299.
253 Ibid., p. 314.
254 Ibid., p. 389.
255 Derrida, J. (1967b). 'Freud and the Scene of Writing,' Op. cit., p. 201.
256 Ibid., p. 214.
257 Freud, S. (1895). *Project for a Scientific Psychology*, SE 1, p. 301; GW18S, p. 393.
258 Freud, S. (1925). 'A Note Upon the Mystic Writing Pad,' SE 19, p. 229; GW 14, p. 5.
259 Freud, S. (1895). *Project for a Scientific Psychology*, SE 1, p. 296; GW18S, p. 389.
260 Freud, S. (1915) 'The Unconscious,' SE 14, p.199; GW 10, p. 297. Strachey's translation of '*Triebregung*,' literally 'motion of the drive,' as 'instinctual impulse' somewhat obscures the kinetic inflection of Freud's term.
261 Cited in Yates, F. (1956). *Art of Memory*, Op. cit., p. 235.
262 See Miller, J.-A. (1999a). 'Six Paradigms of Jouissance,' trans. J. Jauregui, *Lacanian Ink* 17, 2000, pp. 8–47.
263 Lacan, J. (1968–1969). *The Seminar of Jacques Lacan Book 14: The Logic of the Phantasm*, trans. C. Gallagher from unedited typescripts, lesson of 10 May, 1969, www.lacaninireland.com
264 Ibid.
265 Ibid.

266 Ibid. See also the analysis of the bloody scrap as constituent of the signifier in Chapter 1 of this book.

267 Ibid.

268 Lacan, J. (1948). 'The Mirror Stage as Formative of the 'I' Function as Revealed in Psychoanalytic Experience,' *Écrits*, Op. cit., p. 76.

269 Gault, J.-L. (2017). '*Le symptôme et la langue chinoise*,' seminar given before the GIEP-NLS (The Israeli Society of the New Lacanian School, Tel Aviv May 2017, my translation.

270 Gault, J.-L. (2017). '*La conception lacanienne de la langue et de l'écriture*,' seminar given before the GIEP-NLS (The Israeli Society of the New Lacanian School, Tel Aviv, May 2017, my translation.

271 Ibid.

272 Ibid.

273 Lacan, J. (1953). 'The Function and Field of Speech and Language in Psychoanalysis,' *Écrits*, Op. cit., p. 215.

274 Freud, S. (1895). *Studies on Hysteria*, SE 2, 48–49; GW 1, 99–00.

275 Ibid., p. 79.

276 Ibid., p. 56.

277 Ibid., p. 86.

278 Derrida, J. (1967b). 'Freud and the Scene of Writing,' Op. cit. p. 226.

279 Lacan, J. (1971). '*Lituraterre*,' Op. cit.

280 Ibid.

281 Ibid.

282 Lacan, J. *Seminar 14*, Op. cit., lesson of 10 May, 1967.

283 Gault, J.-L. '*La conception lacanienne de la langue et de l'écriture*,' Op. cit.

284 Lacan, J. (1964). *Seminar 11: The Four Fundamental Concepts of Psychoanalysis*, Op. cit., p. 169.

285 Ibid., p. 164.

286 Ibid., p. 180.

287 Ibid., p. 181.

288 Lacan, J. (1953). 'The Function and Field of Speech and Language in Psychoanalysis,' *Écrits*, Op. cit., p. 228.

289 Freud, S. (1895). *Project for a Scientific Psychology*, SE 1, p. 322; GW 18S, p. 415.

290 Ibid.

291 Freud, S. (1915). 'Instincts and their Vicissitudes,' SE 14, p. 122. See also Lacan's remarks on this connection between quantum and *Drang* in *Seminar 11: The Four Fundamental Concepts of Psychoanalysis*, Op. cit., p. 163.

292 Lacan, J. (1964). *Seminar 11: The Four Fundamental Concepts of psychoanalysis*, Op. cit., p. 208.

293 Montrelay, M. (1977). *L'ombre et le nom: sur la féminité*,' Paris, Minuit, p. 39.

294 Lacan, J. (1953). 'The Function and Field of Speech and Language in Psychoanalysis,' *Écrits*, Op. cit., p. 281.

295 Freud, S. (1895) *Studies on Hysteria*. SE 2, p. 181.

296 Freud, S. (1895). *Project for a Scientific Psychology*, SE 1, p. 297.

297 Freud, S. (1938). *An Outline of Psychoanalysis*, SE 23, p. 159

298 Freud, S. (1914). *On Narcissism: An Introduction*, SE 14, p. 74.

299 Freud, S. (1895). *Project for a Scientific Psychology*, SE 1, p. 297.

300 Freud, S. (1920). *Beyond the Pleasure Principle*, SE 18, p. 38.

301 The following comments on the relation of narcissism and the unconscious signifier are indebted to the brilliant work of Tamar Gerstenhaber, 'The Shadow of a White Rose in a Mirror of Silver': The Vicissitudes of the Fetish in the Writings of Oscar Wilde PhD Dissertation, Tel Aviv University), 2021.

302 Freud, S. (1895). *Project for a Scientific Psychology*, SE 1, p. 298.
303 Ibid., p. 299. See also previous chapter in of this section.
304 See previous of this chapter in this section.
305 Freud, S. (1895). *Project for a Scientific Psychology*, SE 1 p. 304.
306 Ibid., p. 315.
307 Lacan, J. (1975). 'Geneva Lecture on the Symptom,' Op. cit., p. 23. See also previous chapter of this section.
308 Freud, S. (1895). *Project for a Scientific Psychology*, SE 1, pp. 296–297.
309 Lacan, J. (1949). 'The Mirror Stage as formative of the *I* Function,' *Écrits*, Op. cit., p. 78.
310 Lacan, J. (1960–1961). *The Seminar of Jacques Lacan Book 8: Transference*, Op. cit., p. 334
311 Lacan, J. (1948). 'Aggressiveness in Psychonalysis,' *Écrits*, Op. cit., p. 51.
312 Lacan, J. (1960–1961). *Seminar 8: Transference*, Op. cit., pp. 340–341.
313 Ibid., pp. 383, 376.
314 Ibid., p. 339, my emphasis.
315 Freud, S. (1912). 'The Dynamics of Transference,' SE 12, p. 99.
316 Freud, S. (1917). 'The Paths to the Formation of Symptoms,' *Introductory Lectures on Psychoanalysis*, Lecture 23, SE 10, p. 361.
317 Freud, S. (1914). *On Narcissism: An Introduction*, SE 14, p, 78.
318 Freud, S. (1921). *Group Psychology and the Analysis of the Ego*, SE 17, p. 105.
319 Lacan, J. (1960–1961). *Seminar 8: Transference*, Op. cit., p. 377.
320 Ibid., p. 122.
321 Lacan, J. (1955). 'The Freudian Thing, or the Meaning of the Return to Freud in Psychoanalysis,' *Écrits*, Op. cit., p. 360.
322 Miller, J.-A. (2005) 'A Fantasy', *Lacanian Praxis, International Quarterly of Applied Psychoanalysis*, 1, pp. 6–17.
323 Lacan, J. (1960–1961). *Seminar 8: Transference*, Op. cit., pp. 265–279.
324 Ibid., pp. 27, 279.
325 Lacan, J. (1958–1959). *Seminar 6: Desire and its Interpretation*, Op. cit., p. 92.
326 Freud, S. (1896). Letter 52 to Wilhelm Fliess, SE 1, p. 173.
327 Freud, S. *Project for a Scientific*, SE 1, pp. 365–366.

Chapter 3

Speaking the written

A Introduction: From writing in the flesh to speech under transference

As deducible from Freud's *Project for a Scientific Psychology* and subsequent developments of the psychic scene of writing in the works of Freud and Lacan, the substrate of the unconscious signifier is neuronic substrate that is furrowed by a quantum that irritates while facilitating it, that is, hollows it out. It is protoplasm in a state of perpetual excitation, a writ(h) ing shaped by the void it wraps but does not include. Palpitating grave or breathing cenotaph, symbolic urn for what would otherwise be nothing but the real experience of pain or its affective correlate in unbearable anxiety, the foundation of the unconscious signifier is an inscription in flesh. It is the conceptual heir of the fibres of the central nervous system such as the young Freud learnt to make appear in portions of neuronal tissue as 'pink, deep purple, blue or even black' 'stains' against the backdrop of the 'grey substance,'[1] a writ(h)ing to be read. For it is Freud's presence as a doctor and his actions in the laboratory, specifically the concoction of the appropriate solution to be applied to nervous tissue, that functions as the condition of possibility for the emergence of coloured stains, readable in their different colouring. Freud's conceptualization in the *Project* of the differentiation of organic tissue into writ(h)ings that become unconscious signifiers has at its backdrop a pre-psychoanalytic differentiation of nervous tissue into colours that can be read as indicators of pathologies or other organic conditions.

What interests the young Freud is a way of making differentiation in organic tissue appear as readable, that is to say, as written. A few years later, Freud's wager on histology as a way of recasting live tissue as a writ(h)ing to be read had been replaced by a consent to be taught by the hysteric's deciphering of this writ(h)ing under transference. Freud had exchanged a histological for a hysterological procedure, making psychic writ(h)ings emerge not in organic matter placed between glass slabs but in signifiers auditivated under transference. It was at this point in the history of psychoanalysis that symptoms began to be read not through the doctor's application of a chemical solution to nervous tissue but through his listening to the analysand's

DOI: 10.4324/9781003037958-4

speech under transference – and his act. From that point on, nothing in analysis could be conceived, Lacan says in the inaugural seminar of his return to Freud, 'without the intervention ... of the speech of the subject'[2] – and the analyst's acts on this speech: the punctuations, scansions, citations and cuts, themselves 'techniques of speech,'[3] that have incidence on the symptom and that, returning the subject's speech to him in inverted form, have the potential to transform the subject. In effect, on occasion it is the analyst's techniques of speech that transform segments of the analysand's speech from what Lacan in his early teaching calls 'empty speech,' conscious speech in which the subject is divorced from his unconscious desire,[4] to full speech in which the subject is confronted with what is strangest yet most intimate to him, the truth of his unconscious desire.[5] The desire that inhabits and enlivens the subject, unconscious desire, 'always becomes manifest at the joint of [true] speech, where it makes its appearance, its sudden emergence, its surge forwards.'[6] This is why Lacan insists in his early teaching that in the analytic situation, 'what is at issue is the value of speech,'[7] and, he adds emphatically at the end of one of the lessons of the second seminar, 'there is no before.'[8]

Yet in what sense is there 'no before' to true speech? To be sure, analysis is the only form of a social link which effectuates the encounters of subjects with master signifiers that had presided over their destiny without their knowing anything about this only to the extent that it has no other medium than the analysand's speech. This does not mean, however, that these signifiers emerge *ex-nihilo*. While Lacan is careful to remind us in *The Four Fundamental Concepts of Psychoanalysis* that the unconscious is not ontic but ethical,[9] that is to say, made to emerge in syncopating pulsations only thanks to the analytic act, this does not mean that true speech has no substance that logically and temporally precedes it. This is why the non-ontic nature of the unconscious is, in the very same seminar, qualified by Lacan as 'neither being nor non-being, but the unrealized.'[10] What is unrealized, perhaps even better not yet realized, both in the sense of not yet auditivated by the subject under transference and not yet recognized by the subject as an extimate alterity, is, I claim, what Lacan in *Encore* denominates 'what does not stop being written.'[11] And does not the 'what does not stop being written' of Lacan's late teaching resonate the *Weiderschrift*, the repeated, incessant writing of memory traces in the psychic apparatus that Freud theorizes in his Letter 52 to Fliess[12] and that in the *Project* he clarifies as a writ(h)ing, an inscription in the flesh?

Clinically, this is perhaps nowhere more apparent than in the formation of the unconscious that is the lapsus or slip of the tongue, where an unconscious signifier, written in the sand of the flesh, leaps out of the flesh of the buccal orifice as auditivated but without the deciphering, the secondary elaboration which unconscious signifiers undergo in other formations of the unconscious, most notably the dream. The lapsus, Colette Soler writes, focusing on Lacan's late teaching, specifically *Seminar 24*, whose title, a multilingual equivoque, equates the unconscious [German *Unbewusste*] with the lapsus [French *une bévue*],[13] unlike the dream, 'is not lucubrated... [but] makes an unexpected sign emerge in speech.'[14] This emergence, wherein a word 'imposes itself' on the subject, has its source in the '*motérialite*,'[15] the materiality of unconscious signifiers, which, as I have argued, is the materiality of irritation in the flesh before it is the phonic materiality Saussure speaks of to the exclusion of writing. And while the lapsus is a phenomenon of speech which is outside sense, pure manifestation, Soler writes, of the real unconscious,[16] pure block of the real[17] encountered in the beyond of the transferential unconscious which does not cease to decipher, the entirety of the subject's speech under transference, in which the subject always 'says more than he means to, always more than he thinks he says,'[18] is emitted 'through the ... body.'[19] What is spoken through the flesh, and as Lacan puts it in *Encore*, in the flesh of the 'speaking body,'[20] can only be what was first written in the flesh, by way of addition, by way of subtraction that is nevertheless never without a surplus jouissance, never without a trace of the real that is the kernel of every subject. The two sections that follow delineate first the motion of retranscription in which signifiers written in the sand of the flesh turn speech, and then various forms in which the real residues of the written manifest themselves as forms of speech in various clinical structures.

B The signifier in motion

a Introduction: Freud with Aristotle

Language moves. Its rhetorical usage, Cicero proclaims, aims to create 'impetus' and 'perturbation,' [*impetu ... et perturbatione*],[21] e(a)ffects whose implication in the category of motion is indicated not only by their derivation from what rushes and turns,[22] but by the very denomination of the aim itself: '*movere*.'[23] What had been an aim for the ancient rhetorician remains so for the contemporary psychoanalyst, of whom the rhetorician, Lacan writes, is the predecessor, no less preoccupied with the question of the subject's relation to the signifier.[24]

In the terms of Lacanian psychoanalysis, affect such as can arise from rhetorical argumentation or analytic intervention is a signal of an operation Jacques-Alain Miller has called '*corporisation*': the transformation of a unit of language into a body event.[25] Hence Lacan's comment at the beginning of the seminar on *Anxiety* that it is not incidental that it is in a work on language, the *Rhetoric*, that Aristotle discusses affect.[26] The *Rhetoric*'s structure – a 'net' of linguistic references in which affect is caught up – resonates the structural place of affect as quantum moored in the net of unconscious signifiers.[27] That language moves is thus a consequence of the relation between affect and the signifier such as founding Freudian metapsychology and the praxis it enchains.

This praxis merits the name, Lacan continues, of an 'erotology,'[28] a term anagrammatically indexing the rhetoricity in which this praxis is anchored. In a later seminar, Lacan qualifies analytic praxis as that of a rhetorician. This is not only because analytic praxis involves an operation on the real by means of the symbolic, on what is impossible in a subject's life by means of language. The praxis of analysis qua erotology is rhetorical primarily because the act on which it is predicated is a 'rectification" of the subject with the impasses of which he complains; real points of a psychic reality.[29] Rectification within the practice of an erotology seeking to move (effect a subjective transformation) precisely at an excruciating point in subjective life – 'cutting edge' point of anxiety[30] – such is the ethical orientation, confirmed by anagram and equivoque through which an unconscious knowledge speaks, of psychoanalysis qua rhetorical, a practice utilizing language to transitively move.

But is it possible to think language also as what moves intransitively? Is language psychoanalytically conceivable, that is, not only as a static synchronic system in whose throes the enjoying substance of the speaking being is caught up but as enjoying substance altering configurations? As the previous chapters have shown, the work of Freud and Lacan suggests as much, suggests, that is, that the unconscious signifier is, in Lacan's words, written in the sand of the flesh, not as pure form emptied of real substance but as writ(h) ing flesh. So, albeit differently, do Aristotle's works on language – the *Rhetoric*, the *Poetics*, and the *Sophistical Refutations* – in their unfolding of the rhetorical category of scheme, a signifier whose polyvalence, in Aristotle and beyond, gives pause to an analytic ear. In what follows, I consider Freud and Lacan's treatments of various intersections of language and movement, articulating these treatments with a psychoanalytic reading of the category of scheme in Aristotle's works on language. The result, I propose, may teach us something more about the relation between pulsating organic matter upon the qualitative and quantitative changes it undergoes, and the rhetorical, the theory of language whose forms, Lacan suggests, are also the forms of modulation of unconscious signifiers.[31] More importantly for the concerns of this book, the articulation of the psychoanalytic conceptualization of the unconscious signifier as writ(h)ing, outlined in the previous section of this book, may help precise the way in which the movement of unconscious signifiers topologically turns from a writ(h)ing in the flesh to spoken articulation through the flesh.

b Bewegung: The motions of psychic writ(h)ing

Indeed, in Freud's metapsychological work from its inception in the *Project* of 1895, language not only writ(h)es but moves. For the components of the psychic apparatus Freud postulates there in order to account for the clinical phenomena of the neuroses, components dubbed '*Vorstellungen*' [representations], and hence signalled as partaking of the order of semiosis, are, Freud writes, derivatives of a 'quantity in a state of flow [*fließender*]' which is 'subject to the general laws of *motion* [*Bewegungsgeset*].'[32] This quantity passes through the organic matter of the nervous system, characterized by the 'irritability [*Reizbarkeit*] of protoplasm' of which it is the inheritor.[33] Where this matter is not only irritable but also resistant, a quality Freud attributes to a category of neurons he names 'ψ,' its irritation by the quantity that passes through it alters it [*verändert*], leaves behind a trace that is the substrate of what Freud defines as memory.[34] The memory trace that Freud would later specify as unconscious, then, is nothing but the 'representation [*Darstellung*] of all the influences which ψ has experienced from the external world,'[35] that is to say, the product of the alteration of irritable organic matter by what flows through it, made possible by the matter's resistance. It is, as argued in the previous section of this book, an instance of writing whose resisting substrate is protoplasmic, made of flesh.

In the 1915 essay on 'The Unconscious' Freud specifies the nature of what writes in this substrate. First defined as a 'flow' subject to 'the laws of motion,' what leaves a trace behind in the psychic apparatus, makes it writhe, is now precised as a particular motion, the '*Triebregung*' or motion of the drive.[36] What is written in the unconscious stems from motion and hence points to it. It is because of the ostentive function of the unconscious trace that Freud renames it, specifying it as neither *Darstellung* nor *Vorstellung* but *Vorstellungsrepräsentanz*[37] what is of the order not of representation but of representativeness.

As representative of representation, the *Vorstellungsrepräsentanz* is at once symbolic and indexical. It is, Lacan emphasizes, 'strictly equivalent to the notion of the signifier,'[38] a unit of language subject to the conventions of a combinatory. At the same time, the *Vorstellungsrepräsentanz* is 'an isolated fragment' of an order 'neither conscious nor unconscious,' which has 'its own active impact.'[39] This order is nothing but the circuiting of the drive from one point of an erogenous zone to another, whose impact is real. The components of the unconscious, that is, as Lacan's critique of Saussure examined in the first chapter of this book makes very clear, are not only symbolic. They are ex-static fragments of a real whose reality is that of constant motion of which they are also the product. As Michèle Montrelay puts it, they are fragments of jouissance from which the subject may nevertheless separate.[40] Unconscious signifiers move. They do not cease to manifest the pulsating irritation of resistant organic tissue of which they are the precipitate, even as they sublate it, perform what Freud adequately names a '*Reizaufhebung*.'[41]

And yet this movement is precisely what seems alien to the psychic apparatus as Freud discovers it. The processes (conversions, substitutions, over-excitations) logically deduced from neurotic phenomena which are these apparatus's indices can only be explained, Freud writes, by its being governed by 'the principle of inertia'[42]: the tendency of components to 'divest themselves' of protoplasmic irritation,[43] be its origin in the 'external world,' understood in terms of physics as 'powerful masses which are in violent *motion* [*heftig bewegten Massen*]' and which transmit their *motion* [*Bewegung fortpflanzen*],'[44] or in what Freud calls the urgent needs of life. Neurotic phenomena, more often than not manifest in movement or its disturbance – the hysteric's facial tics, convulsions, or astasia-abasia, the obsessional's incessant motions in space to the benefit of a seemingly superfluous action of which the Ratman's series of stunted train journeys are a signal example, the force stronger than the phobic's conscious volition that propels him away from an object or site saturated with enjoyment – all these are but products (and hence indices) of the tendency towards the undoing of the motion of irritated protoplasm Freud finds at the logical foundation of unconscious representation, a tendency whose mode of implementation he names '*Abfuhr*' [discharge].[45]

Nor is the motile profile of neurotic symptoms *Abfuhr's* only outcome in the sphere of motion. Implicating muscular tissue, the aberrant and aborted motion typifying neurotic symptomatology seems but a variation on the 'motor excitation' carried out by the 'apparatus of motility' on behalf of the 'trend to discharge.'[46] So is the specific action, the 'alteration in the external world' carried out to appease the urgent needs of life.[47] Specific action, Lacan says in his reading of Freud's *Project* in the *Ethics* seminar, is 'not distinguishable from what takes place when a motor reaction occurs.'[48] Yet the movement of limbs to the benefit of the preservation of life is '*fremde*' [strange]. Movement is strange to the being affected by the signifier whose intricacies Freud begins to unfold in the *Project*.[49] Manifest at the foundation of the unconscious signifier as protoplasmic irritation, movement emerges in the musculature in various forms, all seeking movement's own extinction.

c Towards speech: From floating to syncopation and ex-pulsion

But there are various intensities to movement as what protoplasmic irritation conditions so as to consume, that of the muscular or motor apparatus by no means the highest of them. That Freud should, in the opening paragraphs of the *Project*, refer to this apparatus as a '*Muskelmaschine*' [muscle machine][50] points to what will be the text's very last pronouncement: the qualification of the motions of this apparatus as mechanical, 'monotonous'.[51] That this should be so has to do with a qualitative difference nevertheless distinguishing pure motor action from the motions supporting specific action and the motor phenomena of the neuroses, only seemingly its derivatives. For while neurotic symptoms involving motion are the products and indices of unconscious representations, kinetic monuments to memory traces inscribed in resistant organic matter (the ψ neurons) to which too much unpleasure is attached, and while specific action, Freud says, gives rise in ψ to a '*Bewegungsbild*,'[52] unconscious representation of a motion that brought about an experience of satisfaction,[53] other motions of the musculature, Freud says towards the end of the *Project*, are not associated with word-presentations at all.[54] They are a manifestation of discharge that is indifferent to language because what triggers it is a change in a substrate that does not resist that Freud names 'ϕ neurones.' Permeable to the flow of quantity through them, ϕ neurones are affected by it in a way related to but not identical with irritation. Their quasi-stimulation, moreover, 'does not persist for long and disappears towards the motor side,'[55] leaving not a trace behind as the substrate's lack of resistance does not allow it to become a writing. It is the relation of the motion involved in neurotic symptoms and in specific action to writing, unconscious inscription resulting from the irritation of a protoplasmic substrate that resists, then, that accounts for the relatively higher intensity of these symptoms with respect to motor discharge that is without reference to representation. Such motor discharge, Lacan says, has a 'diminished character'[56] with respect to the motion that takes place within the psychic apparatus.

What is the nature of the relation between psychic writing and motion? Both Lacan's reading of Freud's *Project* in the *Ethics* Seminar and Michèle Montrelay's account of the different statuses of the unconscious in '*Aux frontièrs de l'inconscient freudien*' and '*Le double statut, flottant et fragmentaire, de l'inconscient*,' make it possible to propose an answer. In the case of the motor phenomena of the neuroses, the panoply of motion aborted or in disarray paraded daily in the analytic clinic, what is at stake is the relation Freud names 'repression': the substitution of symptomatic motion for an inscription whose translation into conscious thought would entail too unbearable a unpleasure. As for specific action, the relation between unconscious inscription and movement has to do with the inherent difference between the action's inaugural and subsequent instances. For once an inaugural specific action treats the emergency of the human subject's native *Hilflosigkeit* [helplessness],[57] giving rise to an experience of satisfaction memorialized as an unconscious inscription of movement, an inherent gap, Lacan points out, opens up in human experience.[58] The Freudian unconscious, Montrelay too writes, is 'disjunction in action.'[59] An unbridgeable distance emerges between the inaugural inscription of movement that stopped upon a satisfaction and the memory traces left behind by any attempt to repeat this movement, themselves seized in a movement Montrelay characterizes as 'horizontal,'[60] or 'floating.'[61] This distance is a cause of discontent, as are the symptomatic motions precipitated by repression. But it is precisely this discontent that generates another kind of movement in the psychic apparatus: the vertical or 'centripetal' movement 'toward speech.'[62]

Were it not for the discontent, intense to the point of pain, born of motor symptoms or of the constitutive distance between desire and satisfaction, the conscious subject would know nothing, Lacan writes in his rereading of Freud's *Project*, 'of the movements that belong to the unconscious.'[63] In Freudian terms, these are nothing but the movement of units of irritated organic matter re-presenting motion excluded from conscious representation and of their collisions, coalitions and conjoinings. Only a 'dim perception' of the specifics of this movement would be possible, Lacan says, limited at the most to 'opposing [moments of] mobility and immobility' were it not for 'something in the sensory-motor circuit' – the discontent, intense to the point of pain, born of the dehiscence founding the unconscious, the split between the inaugural inscription of satisfaction and the memory traces of the inevitably failed attempts to repeat it – that 'manages to interest the ψ system at a certain level.'[64]

Between a motor phenomenon that is unpleasant or falls short of satisfaction and what it manages to interest – the irritated protoplasm that is the unconscious inscription – between movement and movement, another movement is generated whose product, 'perceived retroactively,' is 'the articulated movements of words' in the plastic medium of speech.[65] The precondition for the 'movement of speech'[66] as Freud theorizes it in the *Project* is the linking of unconscious signifiers (inscribed ψ neurones) with sound presentations [*Klangvorstellungen*], a process he denominates 'speech association' [*Sprachbildern*].[67] This process, the terminal point of the unconscious' folding inside-out Lacan would denominate its syncopating pulsation,[68] lends unconscious signifiers which might have otherwise remained obscure 'presence [and] structure.'[69] which is none other than the presence and structure of speech. This movement is the folding inside-out Lacan denominates the syncopating pulsation of the unconscious,[70] ending in the ejection in speech of unconscious signifiers which might have otherwise remained obscure. In Freudian terms, the archaic prototype of this ejection is the subject's scream[71] at a moment of helplessness that is nevertheless posterior to primary narcissism in which all libido is invested in the psychic apparatus, for in the moment of the scream the libido tied to unconscious inscriptions so that the store of libido would never run dry is finally mobilized in an appeal to the Other. The subtension of the ejection of speech by the ejection of a scream signalling a demand that is always ultimately a demand for love renders the movement of speech, Lacan says, 'strange' to the speaking subject.[72] For the speech in which the subject screams defamiliarizes the relative monotony, at once of motor action and of the motion of unconscious signifiers towards it, synecdochizing the intensity of irritated protoplasm, of the unpleasant memory traces it both shapes and recognizes.

In these moments in which signifiers of the subject's unconscious reach the peak of their intensity, 'everything happens,' Montrelay writes, 'as if elements [of the subject's] personal or familial history' that collide and coalesce in the unconscious in its configuration as a floating field come together to form a fragment that, given the process of speech association, is pushed out as a fragment of speech.[73] Whether precipitated contingently by the motion of the unconscious 'from *Vorstellung* to *Vorstellung*, from representation to representation,'[74] a moment of *tyché* in the subject's quotidian life which overlaps too precisely with an archaic erotic constellation,[75] or by an analytic intervention under transference, the syncopation of the unconscious whose terminal point is a speech association results in the ex-pulsion, a pushing out that is inseparable from the motion of the drive, the *Triebregung* Freud points to, of a condensation of unconscious signifiers[76] written in the flesh as a fragment of speech, an expulsion whose intensity is manifest in the trains of anxiety and strains of desire it leaves behind.[77]

The fragment of unconscious material inscribed in the flesh and ex-spelled, both ejected and spelled out in auditive form, Montrelay writes, is 'a precipitate of life,' of our life become Other.[78] Under transference, it can become an instance of what Lacan calls 'se savoir exister' [knowing one exists].[79] Knowing one exists, Lacan says in his rereading of Freud's case of Little

Hans in the fourth seminar, gives movement a 'special value.'[80] For the minimum of detachment from life involved in knowing one exists means, Lacan says, one may be 'seized by a movement without being totally implicated in it.'[81] The emergence of speech is simultaneous with language's rising to a second power, seizing itself in an apperception of itself – and since, as Freud indicates in the *Project*, language at once indexes, manifests and gives rise to motion – of itself as a movement synecdochizing life itself.

d Anxiety and the topology of speech

The movement of speech condensing life in its fullest intensity stands in stark contrast to the relatively monotonous movements of which the musculature is capable. It is the opposite, Lacan says, of what Aristotle defines as 'linear movement'[82] – the constant rotational movement Aristotle defines as fundamental, the condition for the perception of any finite locomotion from 'a point from which that which is in motion can be said to start and a point at which it can be said to finish its course.'[83]

Unlike in rectilinear motion, Aristotle writes, 'in circular motion there are no … definite points: for why should any one point on the line be a limit rather than any other?'[84] Rotational motion as fundamental is 'the only motion whose course is naturally such that it has no starting-point or finishing-point in itself.'[85] Rotational motion is infinite, an attribute Lacan in his later teaching would associate with an Other jouissance foreign to the moderating effects of the symbolic and situated as real.[86] Rotational motion as Aristotle theorizes it has 'the continuity of the real,' Lacan says even much earlier, alien to the 'discontinuities of the symbolic.'[87] And yet as we have seen, this movement, motion at the peak of its intensity, is endemic to the signifier, fundamental component of the symbolic. Manifest already in the writ(h)ing of unconscious signifiers written in the sand of the flesh, rotational movement can be said to be the most salient characteristic of those signifiers when they are joined with what Freud calls 'speech presentations' and ejected from the mouth qua erotogenic organ as speech, which in this case is the precipitate of the motion of the drive. Is not the intrication of rotational movement as an instance of infinite jouissance in the symbol as its limit that allows Montrelay to theorize the signifier ejected from the unconscious as speech as carrying not only symbolic but also real value? The unconscious signifier ejected in speech, she writes, is a 'fragment of jouissance' which it puts into play so as to limit it.[88] In this movement of expulsion in speech, Montrelay writes, 'the infinity [of life] is condensed into a fragment,' which, she reminds us, is historically and etymologically a symbol.[89]

In more modern terms, the infinite continuity of what Aristotle describes as rotational motion and which, I have argued, is endemic to speech auditivating an unconscious writ(h)ing as end point of the syncopation of the unconscious, is nothing but 'acceleration.'[90] Though rimmed by the symbolic, this acceleration is not without subjective perils. The growing velocity of a thing in motion, even if ejected from the orifices of the speaking being (his mouth, his syncopating unconscious), confronts the subject with a real, whose affective corollary is anxiety. Freud's case of Little Hans, as reread by Lacan in his fourth seminar, is a signal example.[91] Nothing causes Hans greater anxiety [*größere Angst*], Hans's father reports to Freud, than horses when they 'start moving' [*Pferde sich in Bewegung setzen*].[92] Something else starts moving for Hans without his consciously willing anything about this: his penis, whose erections baffle him. The acceleration that begins when the horses start moving is the surge of life he feels in his involuntary erections, displaced onto a phobic signifier of an animal in motion he articulates in the movement of his speech. More than a phenomenon of infantile sexuality, however, the great anxiety Hans articulates by means of his horse phobia is the corollary of knowing one exists, of the apperception of the movements of the unconscious. That this phenomenon is manifest, as the case of Hans demonstrates, as Lacan argues in the wake of Freud's *Project*, only thanks to the movement of speech, means that anxiety is the price also of the unconscious' folding inside out, pulsating to eject the suffering ecstasy of the subject's scream, language made plastic as it is brought to the second power and manifesting movement in the psychic apparatus at its most intense.

What this also means is that the phenomenon of speech, vehicle of the talking cure, is never completely sedative, nor should it be, for anxiety, just like love, can function as a median accessing the subject's desire[93] and serves as a compass in the clinic. That one speaks and hears one's self speak, perhaps especially in the resonance chamber that is the analytic cabinet, renders the realm of speech in its entirety what Montrelay calls a 'phobic space,' one in which 'one circulates without great difficulty, except that all of a sudden the ground drops from under one's feet.'[94] At the moment of full speech such as the analyst listens for, when buccal orifice and the orifice that is the unconscious open to eject a fragment whose foundation is a scream that gives shape to the unpleasure of protoplasmic irritation at the point of the urgent needs of life, 'psyche is extended, knows nothing about this,' as Freud writes in one of his very last notes.[95] In other words, Freud's case of Little Hans and Montrelay's rereading of this case history shore up one of Freud's very last articulations, namely, that space may be the projection of the extension of the psychical apparatus.[96] At the moment of the ejection of a morsel of the unconscious, the psychic apparatus folds inside out, projecting itself as space whose centre is a rotating vortex, a hole in motion generating anxiety. Lacan gives this hole the logical consistency of what he calls the object a. The chains of unconscious signifiers tangled around this object-hole, manifest in Hans's phobia in imaginary form as the 'holes' and 'behind-holes' ['*Loch*,' '*Podlloch*'] of the horses' sheds,[97] are spatialized as intersecting routes in which circulation is possible 'on condition the hole remains'[98] swirling vortex in which one knows one is always already about to be lost. The spatialization of the psychic apparatus Freud wrote about, then, in particular as it occurs under transference, then, is coeval with the emergence of anxiety. In this sense, the phobic space that unfolds in the Hans case is an extreme case of the corollary of any ejection of unconscious material in speech.

In the face of *größere Angst* attendant upon being seized in the movement of speech without the privilege of knowing nothing about this, what subjective recourse? Hans is calmer when the cart the horses draw 'stands still' [*steht*]; also if he stops [*Bleibt*] in the street.[99] In the face of the gaping hole at the center of phobic space, Montrelay writes, 'all one can do is freeze, no longer move.[100] Phobic symptoms, then, are nothing but attempts to bring to a halt the acceleration of jouissance whose vector is infinite and whose most intense manifestation, Lacan suggests, is the movement of speech. Conscious strategies will never appease anxiety, for in order for a subject to tolerate his existence which is caught up in movement, Lacan says, it is not enough that he 'perceive the acceleration that carries and transports him.' It is also necessary that there be an arrest.[101] The metapsychological name of this arrest, which the phobic symptom attempts to mimic at considerable cost to the subject, is the consent to register castration which amounts to a partial 'annihilation of jouissance.'[102] The corollary of this consent is the phallic value of speech. In the fourth seminar, Lacan casts the emergence of speech which has phallic value as 'the transformation which translates movement into substitution, the continuity of the real into the discontinuity of the symbolic.'[103]

As we shall see in the following section, however, this transformation is never without residue, for something of rotational movement remains, a segment of the real within the symbolic, at times a piece of the real carved out and sublated to the dignity of a signifier, in any ejection of speech as a result of the syncopation in which the psyche encounters itself as an extension in space. The psychic writ(h)ing in the sand of the flesh upon its two modes delineated in the second chapter of this book, itself in motion, accrues to a sound presentation and is ejected in a movement of speech whose intensity outdoes that of any muscular kinesis into a space that is nothing but the externalization of the psychic apparatus, a holed space in which spoken words embodying something of a jouissant real percolate. What makes this percolation possible without it shattering the subject whose unconscious inscriptions, sedimentations of jouissance etched into his flesh, are returned to him with the syncopation of the unconscious as kinetic and audal objects in the space which, like the insides of a Klein bottle, has suddenly turned from an 'inside' to an 'outside'? In the following section I shall propose one answer to this question, one that passes not through Aristotle's *Physics* but through his works on language.

e Scheme: The choreography of speech

In terms of Aristotelian physics, the moment of transformation Lacan speaks of in the fourth seminar when jouissance is annihilated for the subject would be the transition of rotational into rectilinear motion, made possible by a boundary which contains.[104] But it is Aristotle's works not on physics but on language that teach much more about the transformation of motion that can arrest jouissance and hence render existence more tolerable for the being that speaks as it moves and moves as it speaks. Specifically, it is Aristotle's treatment of the category of scheme that profiles a locus in language where the enjoyed corporeal movement involved in speech, trace of the irritated protoplasm that is the memory trace, is transformed from potentially infinite acceleration into acceleration that is crafted and punctuated. This locus, increasingly refined in the transference, is the analysand's *bien dire*.

What in Aristotle's *Physics* is denominated rotational motion whose vector is infinite has an isomorph in the treatment and topology of the category of σχῆμα [*skhēma*, scheme] in his works on language. In the *Poetics* and *Rhetoric*, σχῆμα is a general term for the components of λέξις [*lexis*] or style.[105] In the *Sophistical Refutations* it denominates sophisms in their entirety.[106] In the *Sophistical Refutations*, however, σχῆμα also designates a particular subdivision of sophisms, those based on the 'σχῆμα τῆς λέξεως' [*skhēma tēs lexeōs*, form of expression].[107] Appearing on two levels of elocutionary taxonomy, the treatment of scheme in the *Sophistical Refutations* is thus a Moebian instance where two levels become a continuous surface, where Aristotle's linguistic theory faces its own *mise en abŷme*, its own hole.

The Moebian structure of Aristotle's treatment of scheme in the *Sophistical Refutations* is precisely part of what makes it, for him, a point of unpleasure in the theory of language. Designating at once an elocutionary category and its subdivision, Aristotle's scheme is at odds with what to him is the principle of principles: there being one and only one word, with one and only one sense for a given thing. For a word not to have one sense, Aristotle states in the *Metaphysics*, is tantamount to its having no sense at all: 'το γαρ μη εν σημαινειν ουθεν σημαινειν εστιν' [*to gar mē sēmainein outhen sēmainein estin*].[108] The multiplication of sense, the polysemic potential of language that the unconscious exploits and that is retraced in the analyses of neurotics is thus, for Aristotle, not a resource of the cure it would be for Freud and Lacan, but 'ουκ αν ειη λογος' [*ouk an eiē logos*], what heralds the possible destruction of λογος [*logos*, speech] itself.[109] Scheme as positioned in Aristotle's *Rhetoric* creates a hole in the univocity of sense, effects what Lacan in Seminar 24, and speaking of poetry, calls 'hole effect' [*effet de trou*],[110] opens up within semanticity an abyss where different senses swirl, undercutting diachrony to the benefit not of the stasis of synchrony but of vorticiality, the infinite motion that Aristotle in the *Physics* calls rotational. In Aristotle's theory of language, such vortical polysemic motion at odds with the principle of non-contradiction is denominated 'εξεστηκεν ... λογος' [*exestēken logos*][111] speech which ex-sists, subsists in the ex-static locus where Lacan in *Encore* situates the a certain real of jouissance.[112] Permissible in poetry, it is marked out for expulsion from apodeictics, from logical and philosophical litigation with whose demonstrative thrust it is seldom 'ἁρμόττει' [*harmottei*, harmonic].

The truth of what is at stake in this expulsion emerges not in the *Rhetoric* or the *Poetics* but in the *Sophistical Refutations*, where the exemplifications of σχῆμα at the Moebian point where it is a category at once general and particular include the articulation of 'ὅιον το αρρεν θηλυ η το θηλυ αρρεν' [*hoion to arren thēlu hē to thēlu arren*, masculine by feminine or feminine by masculine].[113] Beyond its Moebian topology, *skhēma* in the *Sophistical Refutations* shores up what is at stake, for Aristotle, in the *troumatism* or horror of the *trou* [French = hole] in sense, the {rik} ריק [Hebrew = void] of rheto-ric qua re-turn to and around the void in language that opens up when a word is unmoored from a single sense: the erasure of a foundational difference which makes signification possible in the first place, the difference between masculine and feminine, sexual difference.

That for Aristotle the ultimate danger in the field of language is the danger of sexual equality is evinced also in the fourth rule for speech he lays down in the *Rhetoric*: to keep the 'αρρενα και θηλεα' [*arrena kai thēlea*, masculine and feminine] in words διηρει [*diērei*, distinct].[114] In Lacanian terms, this is the danger of the scotomization of the signifier functioning as the watershed of the formulae of sexuation – the phallic signifier, signifier of castration. This is the point of transsexual jouissance and the push to the woman Lacan speaks of in relation to the clinic of the psychoses.[115] It is also, differently, the point of the feminine jouissance that 'with respect to everything that can be used in the function ϕx [the phallic function], is in the realm of the infinite.'[116]

One of the manifestations of feminine jouissance as infinite as Lacan theorizes it in *Encore* is the 'pleasure of speaking,'[117] using language as pure jouissance value. 'λόγου χάριν λέγουσι' [*logou kharin legousī*] speaking in order to speak rather than in order to apodictically convey sense is Aristotle's description of this phenomenon.[118] He finds it in the *skhēmata* of the sophists – anadiploses, epanalepses, apostrophes, parisons, antitheses, isocolons, alliterations – favouring the free play of signifiers capitalizing on the equivocation effected by sound, accent, prosody and ambiguous grammaticality over the univocity of signification upholding the principle of non-contradiction.[119] These are forms that make sense vacillate, either because of ambiguity of grammatical construction or because what is at stake in them is no longer grammar but the foundational unit of the 'φωνὴ ἄσημος' [*phōnē asēmos*], the sound which does not in itself mean.[120] Destabilizing sense at the expense of the principle of non-contradiction, *skhēmata* as Aristotle theorizes them make language 'ξενικὸν' [xenikon], Other to itself.[121] This xenification which aligns the *skhēmata* with the radical alterity with which a jouissance without limits confronts the subject is precisely what justifies the necessity, for Aristotle, of admitting them into his logical-philosophical edifice only in stealth and on condition of an operation of subtraction.[122]

For Aristotle, then, the *skhēmata* of rhetoric are a perilous 'περίεργα' [*perierga*] – what is περί, in the direction of, but still auxiliary to the univocally sense-making εργα or work of language.[123] In the *Poetics*, the excessive use of elocutionary schemes that do not mean is likened to an artistic act lacking the virtue of 'λευκογραφήσας εἰκόνα' [*leukographēsas eikona*], drawings of black on white.[124] The leukographic operation of the drawing of outlines indeed plays a structuring role in Aristotle's enterprise. Synecdochized in Aristotle's recommendation to adhere to a 'παρατείνο' [*parateino*, outline] of plot in drama,[125] it features also in the programmatic statement of the *Poetics*' project of tracing the 'περὶ ποιητικῆς' [*peri poiētikēs*, circumference of the poetic], itself exemplifying the nomothetic thrust of the Aristotelian project in its entirety.[126]

Interfering with the leukographics of Aristotle's nomothetic project, the use of sophistical schemes in apodeictics and even the excessive use of schemes in poetry is nevertheless said to endow speech with a 'λαμπρὰ' [*lampra*, brilliance],[127] and to render it 'θαυμαστόν' [*thaumaston*, effecting wonder][128]: seductive by virtue of its very insertion of a radical alterity into the 'κυρίων' [*kuriōn*, common language].[129] It is likened to the covering of a surface with 'καλλίστοις φαρμάκοις' [*kallistois pharmakois*, beautiful colours].[130] Scheme in Aristotle's works on language thus partakes of the paradoxical logic of the *pharmakos/pharmakon*, the remedy-poison-colour-scapegoat whose polyvalent vicissitudes in the Platonic text of the *Phaedrus* have been famously traced by Derrida.[131] A perilous element marked out for expulsion (the Platonic *pharmakon*) on account of its destabilizing the univocity of signification, it is at the same time designated a colour [*pharmakos*] whose effects of beauty are recognized as responsible for the aesthetic pleasure proffered by the poetic text.

What renders the category of scheme, whose constitutive semantic polyvalence and Moebian positioning in the Aristotelian text make it, for Aristotle, a juncture of a jouissance supplementary to sense vortically swirling in the hole it opens up in the univocity of language Aristotle holds dear nevertheless worthy of aesthetic praise? Several references to scheme in Aritotle's works on language suggest an answer, and this answer has to do with the metapsychology of motion with respect to language. Not least of these references is the inaugural treatment of scheme in what was to become Aristotle's most canonized work in aesthetic theory, the *Poetics*. Aristotle locates the elocutionary as part of a broad diapason of the arts which includes the playing of musical instruments, visual art, whose medium is the chromatic, and the art of the 'ὀρχηστῶν' [*orkheston*, dancers], whose medium, Aristotle writes, is 'σχηματιζομένων ῥυθμῶν' [*skhēmatizomenōn rhuthmōn*, rhythmic gestures].[132] For Aristotle, then, the schematic is not only the elocutionary at the point at which it becomes vortical, point of an infinite swirling of sense, but also the choreographic. It is motion which, diverging from the algorithms of specific action to the profit of aesthetic pleasure, follows the logic of erogenization as Freud unfolds it in the *Three Essays on the Theory of Sexuality*,[133] on condition that it be part of a composition, that is, that it be not only erogenized but contrived, made part of a combinatory that proffers pleasure.

Not limited to Aristotle's unfolding of the panoply of arts in the *Poetics*, the choreographic erogenization of scheme implicitly reappears in the opening sentence of the *Rhetoric*. 'Rhetoric,' Aristotle writes there, is the 'ἀντίστροφος' [antistrophe] of dialectics.[134] Inaugurating the theorization of rhetoric with a term denoting the ode lines chanted by the chorus in the theatre as it moves across the stage in response to the στροφος or strophe, lines chanted in the opening move, Aristotle intricates rhetoric from the outset with a motor action that is not specific but contrived. As a component of rhetoric, scheme in its elocutionary inflection partakes of this intrication, is hence at once elocutionary form and gesture. This intrication reverberates in the rhetorical tradition. Scheme, writes Richard Sherry, author of the first English rhetorical treatise in the vernacular, the *Treatise of Schemes and Tropes* of 1550, 'is a Greek word which signifies properly the gestures that dancers use to make.'[135]

What reveals the truth of this intrication, of the function of the schematic as crafted speech that is also crafted motion, is Aristotle's treatment of a rhetorical category on whose unprecedented elaboration he prides himself: 'ὑπόκρισις' [hupokrisis].[136] Denoting archaic poets' practice of enacting the text of the tragedies they scripted, ὑπόκρισις is an art of corporization: the intaking of a chain of signifiers and its metabolization into speech and movement. 'Delivery' is the name later rhetorical treatises would give this practice, dividing it into 'pronunciation' and 'gesture,' in Freudian terms, speech and symptomatic motor action as two forms in which the irritated protoplasm at the foundation of the unconscious signifier might emerge at moments of syncopation in which the unconscious opens up. In his sixth seminar, while discussing a text whose corporization was to become the apex of an English acting career, Shakespeare's *Hamlet*, Lacan points out that such corporization in effect takes place in the life of any neurotic subject with respect to the scripted scenarios of the unconscious phantasm, which the subject enacts with his organs: 'the actor lends his members and his presence, not simply as a puppet, but with an unconscious that is truly real – namely the relationship of his members to his own history.'[137] In psychoanalytic terms, ὑπόκρισις is thus another name for phantasmatic jouissance such as saturates the speech of the neurotic subject and, at a lesser intensity, determines the symptomatic motions of his limbs.

Yet ὑπόκρισις is not only on the side of a phantasmatic jouissance imbuing speech and symptom. Etymologically indicating what is beneath [ὑπό-], operates as a preliminary condition for, the act of judgment or discernment [κρισις] rhetoric strives to effect, ὑπόκρισις in ancient Greek carries a diversified genealogy, from 'to separate' to 'to answer' to 'to answer a fellow actor on stage' to 'to play a part,'[138] a genealogy in which corporization does not exclude separation. In the ancient Greek theatre, the separation preliminary to the corporization of a dramatic text, the separation between an actor and the part he plays, involved an instrument that elides as it makes distinct: the mask, which in the *Rhetoric* is alluded to as, once again, σχῆμα, scheme. Rhetoric, Aristotle writes in the first book of the *Rhetoric*, 'ὑποδύεται ὑπὸ τὸ σχῆμα τὸ τῆς πολιτικῆς' [hupoduetai hupo to skhēma to tēs politikēs].[139] Rhetoric is 'ὑποδύεται' [hupodeutai], what slips under the political from which it derives so that the political becomes its σχῆμα, scheme or mask: the form by means of which it appears but from which it remains dissonant and by which it is hidden.

σχῆμα as mask is, in the *Rhetoric*, the instrument for ὑπόκρισις as corporization. The inflection of ὑπόκρισις in the *Poetics*, however, suggests that for Aristotle, this corporization is not limited to the use of the invocatory object (the voice) and the organs of the body, both susceptible, as Freud and Lacan teach, of being caught up in an acceleration that is nothing but the derivative of the movement of irritated protoplasm, that unpleasurable writ(h)ing that is the basis of unconscious representation and that can find some appeasement in motor action but even more so in ejection in speech. In the *Poetics*, what is said to be 'ὑποκριτικῆς' [*hupokritikēs*, an attribute of the art of ὑπόκρισις or a person skilled in this art] is the 'σχήματα τῆς λέξεως' [*skhēmata tēs lexeōs*] – the σχήματα of speech and style.[140] σχήματα as instruments of ὑπόκρισις are thus not only the masks of the theatrical arena but also the forms of elocution.

Rhetorical art as ὑπόκρισις, then, involves a process of corporization wherein signifierness affects zooic matter, and its instrument is the σχῆμα or scheme. σχῆμα is thus the Aristotelian name for what makes separation within the process of corporization possible, what guarantees that the signifierness that affects zooic matter stop short of the madness of total identification. σχῆμα is thus of the order of the limit to the illimited jouissance language can effect on zooic matter, whose analogue in Aristotelian physics is the infinity of rotational motion Lacan translates as acceleration, the limit Lacan in Seminar 20 teaches is phallic. σχῆμα in Aristotle's work on language is a site of phallic limitation no less than of a jouissance beyond the phallus, of arrest no less than of acceleration. While its tendency to make sense vacillate generates vorticial holes in the univocal fabric of language Aristotle is keen to maintain, it at the same time arrests the potentially infinite movement of polysemia within these vorticial holes by virtue of the very fact of its being contrived, stylized speech. σχῆμα as contrived speech, σχῆμα as stylized choreographic motion, σχῆμα as theatrical mask guaranteeing a minimal distance between actor and dramatic role – such are the points of arrest that Aristotle teaches us to recognize within his treatment of scheme, otherwise aligning this category with vorticial motion not only because of the semantic polyvalence it can generate but because of its Moebian structure which causes the hypotaxis of Aristotle's theory of language to fold in on itself.

The function of scheme in Aristotle's work on language to arrest the potentially infinite acceleration of speech and movement in which the subject is caught not only explains Aristotle's granting it an agalmatic status. It teaches the analyst that these elocutionary schemes, at work, Lacan says, in the rhetoric of the discourse the analysand actually utters are significant not only because, as Lacan affirms in 'The Instance of the Letter in the Unconscious,' they are not the veil but the actual manifestation of unconscious mechanisms,[141] but also because they serve the subject as condensators of an excess jouissance that troubles his limbs.

The metapsychological lesson of Aristotle's treatment of scheme in his works on language, then, is that beyond granting the subject's scream, plastic manifestation of the movement of irritated protoplasm phonic form that can be ejected from the unconscious, the category of scheme can function as a means of arresting this movement, otherwise potentially non-signifying and infinite. If signifiers ejected from the unconscious in the course of the analysand's speech under transference are charged with movement in the psychic apparatus at its most intense, scheme as theorized in Aristotle's works on language is at once situated as what manifests this potentially infinite movement and signalled as what might attenuate this movement, substitute the discontinuity not of the signifier but of stylized form for the continuity of the real as masses in motion. Operating as limit, scheme in its Aristotelian declension is a congealing that creates a rim in what would otherwise be a swirling vortex of enjoyment in language and/as body. It is where the staged movements of a choreography attain the status of a *bien dire* and where the *bien dire* of an analysand reveals itself as what moves to organ-ize a jouissance in excess. Perhaps especially at the *ultima thule* of analysis: the unprecedented choreography of an exit.

C Of signifiers spoken in the real

a Introduction

The syncopating emergence from the unconscious of psychic writ(h)ing in projectiles whose phenomenal form is phonic may be a choreography of speech, an elocutionary composition of schemes (and tropes)[142] in which jouissance is attenuated up to a terminal point which is the subject's singular version of what Freud called the '*Ablehnung der Weiblichkeit*' [repudiation of femininity, literally the refusal to lean on it][143] – the limitation of a ravaging Other jouissance which may also be the terminal point of analysis. And yet both in the course of an analytic cure and in its wake some of the signifiers irrupting from the unconscious are of a kinetic and economic intensity that makes them unpleasurable enough to be intolerable for the subject. The route of these portions of the psychic writ(h)ing apparatus inscribed in the sand of the flesh to their emergence in speech through fleshly limbs such as the vocal cords and lips, even under transference, does not void them of cathexis to a degree sufficient to make them bearable.

Michèle Montrelay provides a signal example of such a signifier in her return to Freud's case of the Wolfman. It is the signifier 'wolf' in the analysand's account of the dream that begins with an opening up of his eyes, of the window, and ultimately, Montrelay says, of his own unconscious which orificializes under the pressure of too much knowledge. Montrelay speaks of this signifier as charged with real value which is precisely what makes it less mortified, more alive. This signifier, Montrelay writes in *L'Ombre et le nom*, is 'a part of life, that exists in the real.'[144] Within such a signifier, which Montrelay names a '*rejeton*,'[145] what is (r)ejected from the unconscious whose libidinal economy it destabilizes, a part of life that for the subject is real, too unbearable to be known, glides into the signifier.

The real at stake in the *rejeton*, Montrelay writes, nevertheless partakes of language and its materiality.[146] The materiality of the *rejeton*, that is, is what Lacan in his later teaching called a *moteriality* [*motérialité*], the materiality of a word [*mot*].[147] Colette Soler describes *motérialité* as a 'fragmentation, trituration … [involving] a play between sonority and written form.'[148] The written form at stake, I suggest, is that of the psychic writing Freud delineates in such texts as Letter 52 to Fliess and the *Project*, the registering of unconscious memory traces as irritations in the body's entrails, and the sonority – that of the *Klangvorstellungen* coalescing with the unconscious memory traces that makes speech possible. And yet more than an exteriorized writing that wounds and is a wound, and a speech rooted in a scream signaling helplessness, the *rejeton* as Montrelay theorizes it is what these forms of language *en-corps* enables to appear phenomenally: a *plus de jouir* that plagues the subject, a real of too much life, too much movement, too much knowledge pushed out into the world as a 'projectile' in the plastic form of speech in a pulsation of the real unconscious qua orifice, source of the drive.[149]

The vicissitudes of the drive, as Freud has taught, are various.[150] They also vary across clinical structures. In the case of neurosis, the expulsion in speech under transference of a projectile of too much life and too much motion signals urgency and distress but subsequently enables, Montrelay writes, not only homeostasis in the economy of the psychic apparatus to be temporarily restored but also a topological transformation in the psychic apparatus, whose beneficial clinical effects retroactively reveal themselves, to take place.[151] But in the case of psychosis, the drive does not loop the Other to return to its source. If the vortex(t) of speech opens up at all, it is coextensive with the hole of foreclosure whose contours Lacan sketches in 'A Question Preliminary to Any Possible Treatment of Psychosis.'[152] Within this vortex(t), what Lacan calls signifiers in the real[153] swirl without having traversed the Other, that is to say, registered as unconscious signifiers in the sand of the flesh. They vehicle an acceleration without limit whose affective charge, destructive of any trace of desire, crushes the subject. It is to the metapsychological specifications of the various forms of signifiers in the real, across clinical structures, that I now turn.

b Psychosis: The unconscious phrase that enunciates itself

I Introduction

Economically speaking, what confers real value on psychotic speech is its narcissistic quality. It is the psychoses, primarily schizophrenia, that teach

Freud much about the possibility of psychic energy (libido) not being used even for the purpose for which it might have come to be in the first place, namely summoning the help of an extraneous agent simply in order to stay alive. The primary narcissism Freud discovers is the investment of libido not in the external world but in the organism itself.[154] This investment is crucial for binding libido, ensuring that the store of libido needed to summon help does not run dry. As an investment, it heightens the level of unpleasure in a system seeking homeostasis (the lowering of excitations) if not the complete stasis Freud would associate with the death drive.[155] The investment of libido in the organism itself is thus painful no less than it is vital, hence the close proximity between primary narcissism and what Freud would later theorize as 'primal masochism.'[156] It is the turning of libido towards the external world, if initially only by the uncoordinated signals of a motion or a scream, that indicates what might be an easing of unpleasure, an exit from the pain, essentially masochistic, of primary narcissism.

But catatonic states and experiences of the 'end of the world' [*Weltunterganges*, literally the going under or drowning of the world][157] in the fields of the schizophrenias and paranoias reveal to Freud that an invest-ment in the external world to which a subject's very existence is a testament can be impermanent, retreated from. In such states, the psychic apparatus as embodied, more than analogous to the corporeality [*Körper*] of a protoplas-mic micro-organism [*Protoplasmatierchens*] because made of the same bio-logical substance, is once again invested at the expense of objects, the result being a state of auto-cathexis so intense it can make existence itself intolerable.[158]

The introversion of libido in acute psychotic states, Montrelay suggests in her own essay on narcissism, finds its structural correlate in a psychotic dis-course, which 'folds into itself,' detached from any seeming interlocutor.[159] The psychotic's withdrawal of libido from objects into the psychic apparatus which spells a hypercathexis of unconscious signifiers stunts the voiding of libido in the process of retranscription across the registers of the psychic apparatus as Freud describes it in Letter 52. The result is words that, although emitted audibly, display the heightened cathexis of unconscious signifiers not subjected to palimpsestic restranscriptions. This is why Lacan would say that the psychotic's unconscious is under an open sky, brought out into the open[160]: when articulated audibly, its signifiers are neither veiled nor voided of libidinal investment. The psychotic's spoken words in their mate-rial phenomenality – in their form, their sonority, their gliding – *are*, Montrelay writes, the psychotic's unconscious: an unconscious speech-jouis-sance, outside sense.[161] The affect accompanying the psychotic's speech-jou-issance – its unwavering, absolute certainty – is nothing but the deontic manifestation of a libidinal investment whose voiding has encountered the blockage of a primary narcissism that insists. As Montrelay puts it, 'the psy-chotic is the phrase that enunciates itself'[162] – but in ways that admit of dif-ferences and specifications.

2 The schizophrenic's organ speech

It was Freud who first isolated and theorized the peculiarities of psychotic speech, specifically in the field of the schizophrenias. Schizophrenic 'word formation,' Freud explains, involves instances wherein a 'single word,' often pertaining to a subject's unconscious relation to a 'bodily organ,' and ultimately itself nothing if not a 'bodily innervation' [*körperliche Innervation*] 'arrogates' to itself 'the representation of a whole train of [unconscious] thought.'[163] Always already an innervation, the unconscious signifier representing a subject's relation to an organ thus becomes even more cathected, is hypercathected. It is as such that for the schizophrenic subject, the unconscious representation acquires the value of a thing,[164] what Freud had, as early as the *Project*, qualified as what is residual to the operation of the pleasure principle as a principle of judgment determining accessibility to unconscious representation. The hypercathected unconscious representation becomes economically equivalent to what is residual to the unconscious because of its unbearability for the subject, what in Lacanian terms is real. For the schizophrenic subject, Jacques-Alain Miller indeed writes in 'Ironic Clinic,' all of the symbolic, register of unconscious representations, is real.[165] It is as bodily innervation hyper-cathected to the point of acquiring real value for the subject that the schizophrenic's unconscious representation of a relation to an organ reaches the conscious register of word-presentations; and it is as such, in terms of Freud's argument in the *Project*, that it coalesces with a sound presentation, precipitate of a primordial scream as signal of helplessness, and is emitted audibly: 'the schizophrenic utterance [*Rede*, also speech],' Freud famously writes, 'has become "organ-speech."'[166] This characterization of schizophrenic speech, Colette Soler underscores in her commentary on Freud's text, corroborates Lacan's emphasis, in his later work, on a signifier reduced to the status of a thing, of sonorous or visual material.'[167]

3 Hallucination: The unspeakable object as heard word

And is not the psychotic's hallucination another phenomenon wherein the psychotic subject reveals itself as a phrase enunciating itself with the full centripetal intensity of a primary narcissism, exposed without veils under an open sky? Not because it is always in the invocatory field that the psychotic experiences hallucination. As Lacan explains in 'On a Question Prior to Any Possible Treatment of Psychosis,' it is 'theoretically conceivable that [the psychotic's hallucination] not be auditory at all (in the case of a deaf-mute, for example, or of some non-auditory register of hallucinatory spelling out of words).'[168] This is because hallucination is not, as classic psychiatry would have it, a '*perceptum* without an object,'[169] a phenomenon encountered though never empirically registered. Hallucination is an occurrence not empirical but subjective. It is at the same time, and not obviously, linguistic. Hallucination 'imposes itself' on the subject, Lacan writes; and it does so as signifying chain or a part thereof. [170]

Hallucination, then, is of the order of a signifier; but it is not a signifier in the chain constituting the subject's unconscious and structured like a language. What this means is that the signifier that appears in hallucination is one which, if initially registered as unconscious, that is, as an excitation that irritates the flesh, has not been preserved under the veil of repression. What is clinically known as 'repression' [*Verdragung*] Freud writes to Fliess in Letter 52, is nothing but 'a failure of translation' from unconscious inscription (which in terms of the *Project* is protoplasmic irritation) to the register of conscious word presentations, some of the cathexis invested in the unconscious representations being voided in the process. Years later, in *The History of an Infantile Neurosis*, Freud would use a different signifier [*Verwerfung*] to designate the radical refusal not of the possibility of translating an unconscious inscription into a conscious word presentation but of preserving an experience as unconscious. The Wolfman, Freud writes, did not want to know anything about his encounters with castration, even in the sense of repression.[171] Castration, that is, is in this case not repressed but radically rejected or foreclosed; it has undergone a *Verwerfung*, and '*Eine Verdrängung ist etwas anderes als eine Verwerfung*' [a repression is something different from a foreclosure].[172] *Verwerfung*, foreclosure as an operation of the pleasure principle as an agency of judgment seeking to maintain libido at a tolerable level appears in the case of the Wolfman not at the limit between the unconscious and the conscious but between the unconscious and what is rejected from it, that psychic realm of residues-things that Lacan would call real. And when it is at this point in the apparatus that the pleasure principle as an instance of judgment functions, what is subjected to its radical rejection, what is 'placed outside the symbolization structuring the subject,' returns not as the repressed returns, in symptoms and other formations of the unconscious, but 'from without'[173] the unconscious, from the real, in various elementary phenomena, of which hallucination is perhaps the best known.

In the case of the Wolfman, not a florid delusional psychosis such as Schreber's but an ordinary psychosis whose more acute outbreak was to occur years later,[174] the hallucination appears to the subject in the scopic field. His memory is of a scene that had taken place when he was five years old, playing in the garden near his nurse and carving with his pocket-knife in the bark of a walnut tree and then suddenly noticing that he had cut through the little finger of his hand, so that it was only hanging by its skin. He recalls his great anxiety ['*große Angst*'], so great that he finds himself uncapable ['*unfähig*'] of casting another glance ['*Blick*'] at his finger. When he at last calms down he casts ['*faßte*,' literally 'fastens' or 'grips') his eye ['*Auge*'] on his finger and sees it is entirely uninjured.[175]

The first reported memory in this scene is sufficiently emptied out of unpleasure to be written in the sand of a portion of flesh that resists by an operation of furrowing which subtracts and to then be retranscribed into a conscious word presentation. It is indeed a signifier ('carving') commonly designating a writing by way of subtraction that the Wolfman reportedly uses to refer to this memory trace. Such psychic writing by way of subtraction, we have seen, is always economically perilous for the subject because it is ultimately also a protoplasmic irritation [*Reizbarkeit*] raising levels of unpleasure.

In this instance, however, the psychic writing in question is more than perilous. The Wolfman with his pocket-knife does not only create furrows within the bark of the walnut tree at the very same time he registers the memory of this furrowing within that part of his *bios* rendered sufficiently resistant to be furrowed so as to bind libido. The German verb used to report his memory ['*schnitzelte*'], like its equivalent in the *Standard Edition* ('carving'), indicates not only a sculpting or writing *per via di levare*, one that involves a hollowing out, but also an operation carried out on meat: not a cutting in or on a piece of meat but a cutting or slicing *of* it. Appearing in an image of an almost severed organ, this cutting off is evidently of import to the castration complex with which the Wolfman grapples at the time of the reported memory.

The castration complex as Freud theorizes it is indeed a complex psychotextual and psycho-pictorial mechanism that emerges at the point of exit from a primary narcissism wherein, as Montrelay puts it, 'each organ enjoys itself for itself, independently of others.'[176] Without one of the formations of secondary narcissism, the ideal ego as orthopaedic totality of the specular image, body parts traversed by needs and drives, invested with libido not yet paid out in object cathexes,[177] are experienced in isolation, in fragments and morsels.[178] At the same time, as Lacan points out in the eighth seminar while alluding to an article by Karl Abraham, one of these body parts, the genital, is invested more than others. As Freud puts it in 'Some Psychical Consequences of the Anatomical Distinction between the Sexes,' for the male child the penis is the site of an 'extraordinarily high narcissistic cathexis,'[179] that in the earlier 'Infantile Genital Organization' he attributes to its anatomical, physiological, and neurological qualities: its being 'easily excitable, prone to changes and so rich in sensations.'[180]

This surplus excitation has psychic consequences. The penis, Montrelay writes, 'makes life mount towards [the little boy], organizing it as an intense and precise pleasure' and as such 'pulls him out of a fragmented, diffuse narcissism.'[181] It is thus not only that, as Lacan points out in the eighth seminar while alluding to an article by Karl Abraham, the (male) genital is invested more than other body parts. Its function of pulling the subject out of the shadow of primary narcissism and towards life entails an assumption [*vorauszusetzen*] that is the castration complex's primary text or *ursprüng*, situated in the imaginary that is the symbolic's shadow: the presupposition that all beings, animate and inanimate, and above all the mother, are equipped with this body part. This presupposition, for its part, arrogates the excess excitation in the penis to itself. The castration complex's *ursprüng*, then, is a primordial imaginary picture-text charged with surplus jouissance, a writ(h)ing close indeed to the thing. It is part of the primary imaginary Montrelay writes of in *L'Ombre et le nom*, 'which is not without relation to feminine jouissance,'[182] the jouissance without phallic limit that would allow it to be articulated in signifiers and, concomitantly, located in a single body part that Lacan formalizes in *Encore*.

The intensity of this jouissance can be intolerable. Nevertheless, the subject clings to the primary picture-text of sexual equality, jouissante and imaginary, with an extraordinary tenacity that is a manifestation of its clinging to life just as he clings to the over-excitation of the genitals, witness Lacan's comment in *Seminar 8*, following Abraham, that even when libido is paid out in the form of object cathexis, in the subject the genitals remain cathected.[183] The investment in the male genital as site of 'vital flow'[184] and in the *ursprüng* that is the precipitate of this investment persists even in the face of encounters in the visual field, confrontations with sexual difference, which puncture this primary picture-text, for these initially give rise only to a 'glossing over' ['*beschönigen*,' literally colouring or whitewashing],[185] to efforts to patch up the punctures with micro-narratives of which Little Hans's '"when she grows up it'll get bigger all right."'[186] is a signal example.

What eventually puts an end to the revisionary efforts to paradoxically preserve a primary psychic picture-text of a maternal body equipped with a penis is a consequence of the 'accidental' sight of the female genitalia that punctures this *ursprüng* in unprecedented fashion, leading to its shattering. The primary, hyper-invested picture-text in which the mother has a penis is destroyed and replaced by one in which the object that had rendered her complete had been cut off, leaving a wound in its wake.[187] If the subject is neurotic, this shattering is followed by '*acceptance* of the possibility of castration,' that is to say, a moment of subjective consent to register the *Kastrationsmöglichkeit* as an unconscious *Eindrück*, a furrowing in the flesh.[188] The primary picture-text of the castration complex then becomes not *ursprüng* but ur-*sprüng*,[189] primordial crack that is the crack in the flesh as unconscious signifier.

But in the case of the Wolfman, this *ur-sprüng* which takes the form of an imprint is precisely what the subject radically refuses to register as unconscious. What the Wolfman had encountered in the primal scene Freud reconstructs even before the Wolfman first heard of it from his Nanya or seen his father beat a snake into pieces progressively shatter the primary *ursprüng*, but this highly-cathected picture-text is not replaced by the unconscious *Eindrück* of castration, certainly not with its sequel, the assembling of the phallus as 'logical instrument.'[190] The phallus, Lacan says, is an instrument which is '*amovible*,' which can be dismantled and reassembled.[191] The material from which it is assembled is the shattered fragments of the hypercathected *ursprüng* of the castration complex, the primal, delusional arche-text of all beings equipped with a penis, whose core is the image of the mother without genital wound.

In the Wolfman's case, instead of paving the way to the assembling of the phallus, the encounter with castration becomes '*schnitzelte*.' Cut off from registration in the unconscious which is a furrowing in a portion of flesh, the image of the mother's penis as a piece of meat whose severance tore open a wound remains in the Wolfman's psychic apparatus *as* a portion of flesh, his flesh. This portion of flesh returns from without as severed, but not completely: 'it is hanging on by its skin' ['*an der Haut hing*'].[192] What is even more significant metapsychologically, its severance is not registered even as a mark, such as the scar of circumcision marking man's covenant with the word.[193] It is precisely as such – an almost severed piece of his own flesh never written as lost – that a portion of the Wolfman's own flesh appears to him, charged with a *große Angst* that between the moment of the blink and the instant of the gripping of the eye, immobilizes his field of vision.

What the reported scene of the Wolfman's visual hallucination teaches metapsychologically, then, is not only that '*Eine Verdrängung ist etwas anderes als eine Verwerfung,*' but that the *Verwerfung* at stake in this case is not just a radical exclusion from the possibility of psychic inscription in the unconscious, which according to Freud's theorization in the *Project* has the form of a carving, *per via di levare*, in a portion of subsequently irritated flesh. As such exclusion, *Verwerfung* takes on for the subject the form of a cutting, perhaps even more precisely an almost cutting *of* (and *off*) such a portion of flesh, which is never quite completed and never at all made a writ(h)ing. Such cutting is coeval with what Montrelay theorizes not as repression, which to her is an operation of structuring, but as what she differentiates from repression as a 'censoring' that leaves psychic material in the soma as a thing cut off from representation.[194] Hence the clinical phenomenology of attempts at amputation, self-mutilation, the carving [*schnitzelte*] of parts that seem to the subject to protrude (that is, to be stuck or hung on) that characterize passages to the act in the field of the psychoses, the castrations in the real of which Van Gogh's cutting off his ear is a signal example, preluded by his famous *impasto* style, preluding his suicide.

The imaginary dimension of psychotic phenomena, too, not incidentally often champions a portion or portions of flesh charged with an intolerable affectivity and cut off or almost so, witness the Wolfman's own hallucination, replete with a great anxiety which immobilizes vision, of his almost cut off finger, the delusions of a body without organs of subjects with Cotard's syndrome, or the delusion of Lacan's paranoid interviewee, cited both in the seminar on the psychoses and in the 'Question Prior to Any Possible Treatment of Psychosis,' whose certainty (and perplexity) pertain to the delusionally purported plan of her husband and in-laws to 'slice her up'[195] or 'carve her up piece by piece.'[196]

Whether appearing in oral declension as a 'quartered pig'[197] or in the visual field as a finger almost sliced off, the object of hallucination in the case of the Wolfman and in the case of Lacan's interviewee is cast in the imaginary as a portion of flesh such as Shakespeare's Shylock insists on. What the reading of Freud's text on the Wolfman suggests is that this is so not only because of the severe disturbances in the imaginary that characterize the clinical picture in the psychoses, the psychotic's always already being, as Lacan puts it, 'disjointed, a fragmented body, *membra disjecta,*'[198] but principally and structurally because, as the case of the Wolfman's hallucination demonstrates,

Verwerfung, the psychotic's structuring way of not knowing about castration, is a cutting off in the second power.

Foreclosure is a cutting off from inscription in the flesh of the encounter with the mother's penis that was never there as a portion cut off from the subject's own flesh. Its clinical manifestations appear mainly in forms of an imaginary invested with jouissance (as images of organs missing, cut up, or almost cut off, such as manifest in the cases of the Wolfman and of Lacan's interviewee) or as real (passages to the act involving an attempt to cut off portions of an over-invested organism, from clusters of hair to pieces of flesh). What Lacan emphasizes in 'On a Question Prior to Any Possible Treatment of Psychosis' and what is most pertinent to the concerns of unconscious grammatology, the cutting off that is foreclosure's structural substrate can appear in the symbolic when it assumes the form of a signifier cut off from a chain, an isomorph of the cut off piece of flesh sometimes precipitated by the failure to register castration.

In the example Lacan cites in his major writings on psychosis what realizes (also in the sense of rendering real) the subject's 'rejecting intention,' that is to say, the operation of foreclosure, is neither a self-mutilatory attempt at castration in the real such as sometimes appears in the clinic of autism and schizophrenia, nor its imagistic index as a cut off piece of flesh. Instead, it is in discourse, within speech as a manifestation of the symbolic, that the operation of foreclosure appears.

Like the interrupted sentences Schreber reports about in his *Memoirs*, the fragment of discourse of Lacan's interviewee includes two parts, strophe and anti-strophe, separated by a pause that transcribes as a dash. The strophe, 'I've just been to the butcher's,' is the sentence which Lacan's interviewee admits to have uttered just before she heard the hallucination which triggered her psychotic outbreak (the word 'Sow!' experienced as invective). This strophe is laden with perplexity, an oscillation as to which of the three people involved in the situation (the woman, her mother, their neighbour) the shifter initiating the sentence ('I') alludes to. Lacan, who follows the subjective logic of the interviewee's discourse, recognizes that it involves an exclusion of the symbolic axis, orbiting between two poles of the imaginary, the ego and its double (a-a').[199] Without the cut (*sprüng*) of symbolic castration, the circuit of the interviewee's discourse 'closes on the ... puppets before her who are the other, who speaks, and in which her own message resonates, and herself, who, as an ego, is always an other and speaks by allusion.'[200]

In other words, the two segments of discourse, the one whose attribution is uncertain and the one experienced with certainty as an insult, are instances not of a dialogue but of a circuitous chain whose components are not isochronous (of equal length of pronunciation). Instead, these components constitute strophe and antistrophe, postulation and reply, of what is in effect a single sentence, whose 'disparaging antistrophe' ('Sow!') restores to the patient, previously perplexed and oscillating as to who is speaking, the index of the 'I.'[201] What has just been to the butcher's is the I-Sow, the subject as

about to be cut up; but the signifiers 'I' and 'Sow,' while syntactically appo-
site, are economically and affectively disparate – which is why Lacan designates them as strophe and antistrophe in the interviewee's spoken statement.
In this statement, what separates strophe from antistrophe, the pause in
speech whose transcription is the dash, is occasioned not by simple interrup-
tion but by an affective shift from oscillation or perplexity to certainty. The
sentence thus becomes divided not between signifiers emanating from two
different speakers, but between signifiers sufficiently voided of cathexis to be
strung into a chain and a signifier so cathected that its value becomes real and
its function is that of an invective directed at the subject.

This signifier, Lacan writes, appears in the place that 'has no name,' the
place opened up by the operation of foreclosure, where an object too unpleasurable to be granted access to the symbolic as a registering in the unconscious that is a furrowing in the flesh, and articulated in speech which is the
unconscious's folding inside out to eject an auditivated fragment – in this
case – the subject's sense of herself as a piece of meat about to be cut up –
nevertheless appears as a word in speech. But the operation of foreclosure
being what Freud's case of the *Wolfman* suggests it is, namely a cutting off
from unconscious registration as a cutting of and off (rather than in) the
flesh, the word that in the imaginary terms of the subject's delusion designates the piece of meat that she is and is about to be apportioned appears in
the symbolic in spoken form as a portion of discourse, antistrophe, cut off
from the strophe that precedes it.

Like the image of the almost cut off finger in the Wolfman's hallucination,
the word 'Sow' that in the hallucination of Lacan's interviewee not only
appears as isomorphically almost cut off, the dash or pause designating the
almost separation that in the Wolfman's hallucinated image appears as a
piece of skin is not an unconscious inscription, a furrowing in the flesh that
is ejected, coupled with a sound presentation, but an attempt at furrowing or
cutting-in whose excess cathexis turns it into an almost cutting off, coupled
with the subject's own voice as an object from which she had failed to separate[202] and appearing as invective which takes her as its object.

c Neurosis: The real forms of desiring speech

I Introduction

But it is by no means the clinic of the psychoses alone that exhibits the phenomenon of a signifier emitted from the unconscious in speech as real. As
Colette Soler has recently argued, such irruption characterizes the very structure of one of the formations of the unconscious that are the staple of the
neuroses: the lapsus or slip of the tongue. The lapsus, Soler writes, relying on
Lacan's opening statement in his 'Preface to the English-language Edition of
Seminar 11,' is a spoken 'word, an element of knowledge which has not only
emerged in spite of the subject … but which finally remains in its facticity, as

an isolated signifier.' This word that has emerged, turned speech, Soler continues, is 'outside sense but not outside jouissance, quasi-neological.' It 'carries the weight of an ineffable and personal jouissance.' As an isolated signifier that is also saturated with a particular jouissance, Soler concludes, 'the word of the lapsus can ultimately be said to be real' just like the signifier in the real first theorized by Lacan in relation to psychosis,[203] a theorization which, as argued above, has a precedent in the Freudian conceptualization of schizophrenic organ-speech.

If the psychotic, who in grappling with the castration complex, does not cease to invent narrative patches with which to stitch the holes torn open by in the primary and hyper-invested picture-text of a mother who is not penisless, for the subject who will be neurotic there comes a moment of a consent to cease the myriad visions and revisions of this picture-text. What is at stake in this ceasing is the consent to register the Other as incomplete not lexically and linguistically (for as Lacan points out in *Seminar 8*, a language by definition includes all the signifiers that can be articulated in it)[204] but subjectively. It is the recognition of the Other as lacking one signifier that will open the way towards the subject's desire. But as both Freud and Lacan teach, the hysteric and the obsessional have peculiar relations towards their desire, fraught with the obstacles of dissatisfaction and impossibility. And these obstacles, manifestations of the (real) object as '*ob*'[205] that disturb the banquet of the subject's desires just as symptoms do, emerge as signifiers in the real in speech in the analyses of the neuroses. It was already Freud who pointed out in 'The Dynamics of Transference' that there are moments in the cure when the analysand's free associations 'fail,' manifest a 'stoppage.' '*Stockung*,' a congestion or damming up, is the German noun Freud uses to indicate this stoppage to the speech of *Durcharbeitung* where unconscious desire glides; '*versagen*' [to refuse] is the verb with which he qualifies this stoppage, a cognate of the *Versagung* Lacan would speak of in the context of his analysis of the Coûfontaine trilogy in *Seminar 8* as implying 'the failure to keep a promise,' in this case, the promise implicit in the fundamental rule of free association.[206]

The speech of a neurotic subject under transference, then, includes not only the alternation between what Lacan in his early work calls 'empty' speech in which the subject seems to 'speak in vain about someone who ... will never join him in the assumption of his desire'[207] and the 'full speech' where unconscious signifiers vehicling desire are worked through in the transference, reordering 'past contingencies by conferring on them the sense of necessities to come.'[208] In addition, the neurotic's speech under transference includes points of stoppage to full speech as the speech where unconscious desire can emerge which is not the empty speech as Lacan speaks of it in 'Function and Field,' where desire becomes submerged in the imaginary monotony Heidegger would denominate the speech of the 'they.'[209] These moments of stoppage are close to empty speech as Lacan reformulates it in his late teaching, as speech emptied of the sense,[210] such as generated by the neurotic phantasm, manifesting a hole in sense coeval with the hole that is the object a, reducing speech to its material (vocal, phonic) phenomenality as envelope of this hole. What ob-jects to the neurotic analysand's speech that is not the empty speech as defined in the early teaching, as speaking in vain and without connection to desire,[211] is forms in which the real emerges in speech not, at least not only, as the silence indexing a piece of the transference Freud refers to[212] but as spoken signifiers whose weight and localization are not only symbolic.

Spoken signifiers in the real, projectiles of too much life and too much motion, then, appear not only in psychosis but also in the two major structures of neurosis: obsession and hysteria; and as in the case of the word that makes itself heard in the place of a foreclosed object in the case of paranoid hallucination detailed by Lacan, those projectiles can at times appear in the form of different slopes of the invective or insult, a signifier that hurts or wounds the flesh.

2 'Get thee to a nunnery!': The obsessional's sign(ifier)-invective

The psychotic crumbles under the weight of the foreclosed signifier cut off from unconscious inscription and hence appearing as an unbearable sight, sound, or smell whose linguistic correlate is an invective cut off from other signifiers in the chain by a pause or dash. The obsessional neurotic signals a proximity to psychosis not only in what Freud calls the 'deliria' interspersing his discourse[213] but also in its own particular version of invective. In the case of obsessional neurosis, the invective as an unconscious fragment ejected as projectile is not a portion of the discourse of the subject that, even if allusively attributable to an other is ultimately an (almost) cut off portion of his own flesh (for instance, the uncastrated object voice) that returns in real or imaginary form to crush him under the thin and only slightly mitigating guise of a signifier. In the case of obsessional neurosis too, a signifier carrying a jouissance that grants it real value can emanate in the subject's speech. In the case of obsessional neurosis as in the case of paranoid psychosis, such a signifier has the performative value of an invective. But while the paranoid experiences the invective as taking him as its object, the obsessional directs his invective towards the Other.

The obsessional, Lacan says, lives in the perpetual vertigo of the destruction 'not of the desire of the Other, but of its signs. ... Which determines the exceedingly odd impossibility that the obsess[ional]'s own desire ever manifest itself.'[214] Like the hysteric, the obsessional is a subject who has registered castration, that is to say, a subject of desire. But while having registered the Other as missing a signifier (the mother's penis, part of the *ursprüng*), the obsessional never completely comes to terms with what he has registered, and not only in the sense of being passive in relation to another man that Freud indicates towards the end of 'Analysis Terminable and Interminable.'[215] One of the manifestations of the obsessional's unease with the castration he has registered is his notorious rage, evident, in the case of Freud's Rat Man, in the hostility against his father. Freud explains that at around age three, the Rat Man 'hurled abuse at his father'[216] after the latter had uncharacteristically hit him following some 'sexual misdemeanour connected with masturbation,'[217] that is to say, with the physical manifestation of Oedipal phantasies in which the subject cannot cast himself as castrated in relation to his paternal rival. No doubt, as Freud explains to the Rat Man, his aggression followed 'the principle of the Adige at Verona,'[218] that is, was ultimately directed at himself, an instance of self-punishment against the Oedipal misdemeanour. Even so, underlying the exercise of this principle is the identification with the father as an agent of the law who can dispense or at least threaten to dispense castration. The Ratman's verbal abuse, that is, has at its root an offensive against an agent who embodies the threat of castration, in Lacanian parlance, against 'the Other in so far precisely as he may present himself as phallus.'[219] Rage in obsessional neurosis, Lacan goes on to say, is always present as directed at the phallus, signifier of castration and hence desire. The path it chooses is to 'strike the phallus in the Other, to strike it at the imaginary level, in order to heal symbolic castration.'[220]

A telling instance of an obsessional hitting out at the phallus on the imaginary plane occurs in the Shakespearean play which occasions Lacan's remarks cited above. 'Shall I strike at it with my partisan?'[221] is the jaculation of one of the guards of the citadel at Elsinore when confronted with the Ghost of Hamlet the Father, the play's dramatization of what is not there but bequeathes desire to the son as does the father of the Rat Man. While partisans may or may not have been drawn on the Shakespearean stage, what is drawn on the text are the signifiers ultimately marking an absence: "tis here … 'tis here …'tis gone.'[222] Words are what appear in the Shakespearean text to strike at the emergence of the signifier of castration and desire – in this early scene as in a later one where Ophelia ('O Phalos' as Lacan aptly reads her name), dramatization of the desire Hamlet will not let live.[223] 'Get thee to a nunnery, wilt thou be a breeder of sinners?' is Hamlet's lethal response to the words of a woman who implores him to mark, not strike at, her desire that fuels his. It is the obsessional's own desire that his attempt to cure symbolic castration puts at risk, and in the case of Hamlet as in that of the Rat Man, it is with words this attempt is made.

In the mouth of the obsessional, words are partisans with which to strike at the desire of the Other, ultimately the obsessional's own desire, but it is not their sense with which the obsessional seeks to adversely affect the Other. In the case of the Rat Man, Freud writes, the young child did not yet know any 'bad language' ['Schimpfworte'] and so resorted to the limited content of his conscious vocabulary: the names of common objects ['Gegenständen'] such as 'lamp,' 'towel,' 'plate.'[224] It is obviously not the common semantic sense of the words designating the commonest of objects that rendered his use of them an *'elementaren Ausbruch'* [elementary outbreak] of rage.[225]

The consent to confront the registration of the phallus in the Other which the hysteric keeps veiled so as to sustain her desire as unsatisfied leaves the obsessional face-to-face precisely with what in the phallus is intolerable to him: 'its being not simply a sign and a signifier, but the presence of desire.'[226] It is this intolerability that leads the Rat Man to invent the nocturnal phantasmatic scenario where he imagines his father resuscitated and knocking at the door only to insult him by masturbating before him.[227] This too, Lacan remarks, is 'an insult to real presence' (of desire).[228] But is not this staged insult to the real of desire a later version of the verbal insults hurled at the father much earlier in the Rat Man's life, when in dispensing the threat against masturbation rooted in Oedipal phantasies the father in effect points to his wife as the object cause of his desire, however fraught this desire may be by his unpaid symbolic debt to the woman he loved but did not marry?

In the mouth of the three-year-old Ratman, what is summoned against the real presence of the desire of his father as manifest in his interdictions on his son's masturbation are words turned instruments with which to hurt, implements of a sadistic jouissance. The commonest of words break out not only because they are part of a tantrum but because they break the signifying mould. They are signifiers the subject breaks out of the signifier-signified connection, utilizing them not for the oral satisfaction Lacan in *Encore* would associate with *lalangue*,[229] the pure jouissance of rolling words on the tongue, but for anal-sadistic enjoyment ultimately directed, as Lacan precises, beyond the signifier, at the rejection of the Other's signs.[230]

Alluding to an iconic action of another Shakespearean character, Lady Macbeth, Lacan explains that the obsessional's 'very particular way of dealing with the signifier 'is ... putting it in doubt, of knowing how to polish it, to efface it, to triturate it, to break it into pieces,' rediscovering under it 'the sign'[231] – what C.S. Pierce teaches 'stands to somebody for something,' but as an object, not woven into a linguistic system subtended by laws of combinatory.[232] Whether in his eternal doubt or his attempts to repair castration via invective – both lethal to his desire – the obsessional in his rage pushes words towards the real. Not because he makes of them material objects, or in Freudian parlance, 'things,' but because he reduces them to their use value, which is often of a variety that seeks to hurt the Other.

3 Somatic compliance: The word that slaps the hysteric

There is an inverse relation between signifiers turned projectile signs uttered by the obsessional in an effort to crush the desire of the Other and the effect of signifiers on the hysteric. If the obsessional can turn words into objects that hurt, signs cut off from sense, it is precisely sense that hurts the hysteric, a clinical fact well-known to Freud, stated, for instance, in his theorization of hysterical identification in *Group Psychology and the Analysis of the Ego*:

Supposing, for instance, that one of the girls in a boarding school has had a letter from someone with whom she is secretly in love which arouses her jealousy, and that she reacts to it with a fit of hysterics; then some of her friends who know about it will catch the fit, as we say, by mental infection. The mechanism is that of identification based upon the possibility or desire of putting oneself in the same situation.[233]

Freud's interest in this passage is the mechanism of identification at work in hysteria, as distinct from the two other forms of identification he mentions: the primordial identification with the father and the identification with the unary trait. The supposed (and clinically common) example for this identification, however, has to do with the hysteric's relation to the letter in the sense of a missive made of words: it can arouse her jealousy, cause a reaction of a painful jouissance.

But Freud was of course familiar with the pain the word can cause the hysteric from the very beginning of his practice, as evident, for instance, in the *Studies on Hysteria*, in particular in the case of Frau Caecilie M., the woman Freud referred to as his 'teacher' ['*meine Lehrmeisterin*'], and as the 'most severe and instructive' case he had encountered till that time.[234] For over three decades, Caecilie turned to various doctors with a complaint concerning recurrent and prolonged attacks of facial neuralgia, pain in the upper two thirds of her cheekbones and in the middle of her forehead, which would become intensified while she was eating or when she felt offended – but not when she spoke. When Caecilie moved her lips not only for the purpose of autoerotic oral satisfaction but for an address to the Other, the pain would not intensify.

It is by inviting the subject to make use of the language registered in her flesh where it hurts less that Freud came upon the contingency that was registered as an insult and tied with the registration of excess excitation, that is to say, in terms of the *Project*, of pain that was already there in the flesh and thus became a necessity, *ananke* ['Aνάγκη] that did not cease to be written on her face. For three years, Caecilie would present the pain written on her face to the analyst who came for daily visits, not only as an aching body part but in speech. What Freud encountered in his daily visits, then, was, as he puts it, 'a series of pictures with explanatory texts' [*Bildern mit erläuterndem Texte*].[235] It was not the pictures (the attacks of facial neuralgia and other hysterical symptoms) but the explanatory texts (Caecilie's speech under transference, which tries to decipher these symptoms) that enabled Freud to unearth a primary text that affected the flesh, perhaps because, as Freud put it, 'it may be that [hysteria] does not take linguistic usage as its model at all, but that both hysteria and linguistic usage alike draw their material from a common source.'[236]

It is with these words that Freud concludes the chapter on Frau Elizabeth von R. in the *Studies on Hysteria*, refraining from commenting on what this 'common source' might be. As I have argued in the previous chapters, however, the common source of hysteria and linguistic usage might be the Freudian formulation of what Lacan in his fourteenth seminar indicates as the commonality of structure between the unconscious signifier and the *ragade* in the hysteric's body in its interaction with what Freud calls the 'clouding' [*Trübung*], which is nothing but the refusal to know about the jouissance of the flesh seized in suffering ecstasy.

In the case of Caecilie, and not only there, the source itself remains veiled. As Freud learned from another hysteric, to whom he referred as 'Emma,' the moment of origin or source, the primordial and fateful instance when jouissance hits flesh still too close to primal helplessness does not emerge into consciousness. It is accessible as a construction alone and this too by means of a second moment that joins it as a mask because the first moment fits it as a face of the same features. What Freud theorizes as trauma is the wound created in the unbearable connection between the two moments, the moment when the mask touches the face. What results is a masking wound, a wounded mask that Freud calls a 'picture' [*Bild*], copies of which do not cease to be multiplied as the attacks of pain on Caecilie's face.

But if Caecilie does not remember the moment jouissance hit the flesh, she does remember the masking moment, when pain emerged. Years earlier, when she was a 15-year-old girl, her stern grandmother looked at her with a 'penetrating' gaze, following which she felt a sharp pain between her eyes that went on for weeks. A gaze penetrated and wounded the flesh where it encountered the registration of a painful moment that did not manage to become a past nor a conscious memory, but that proved fateful, for since then, for three decades, it returned on Caecilie's face as a wounding mask. Returned in her love life as well.

Thus, for instance, in the course of a conversation with Caecilie's husband, he said something to her which she felt as a '*schwere Kränkung,*' a serious insult, and she felt pain in her cheek. When she tells Freud about this, she says: 'it was like a slap in the face.'[237] It is within the realm of Eros, then, that the early painful encounter struck again as a *ragade*, a painful irritation in the body. And this is no surprise, for it was Freud who, in his article on 'The Dynamics of Transference,' itself, as he observes, a form of love,[238] wrote that a subject's erotic style is a stereotype plate, a '*Klichee,*' made from sedimentations [*Neiderchlag*] operating by way of addition,[239] left behind by painful encounters in the life of the drives, whether these originate in what is of the order of *tyché*, a contingent encounter at the beginning of the subject's life, or of the order of *daimon*, what had once been a contingent encounter in the subject's ancestral chain[240] and became a trait that the subject, who had never ceased eating his dead, appropriated by way of identification[241] that according to Freud in 'Group Psychology' is a way of swallowing.[242] In other words, it is from Caecilie that Freud learnt that the vicissitudes, not of the drives but of love life, are daemonic too, in the sense that love life is a site where an archaic pain that determined a destiny hurts again – not in itself but as a response to a signifier that masks it.

Unlike the signifier-hallucination that crushes the psychotic, the mask of an archaic moment of pain that offends or hurts the hysteric – in Caecilie's case, literally so – is not a signifier rendered real. But its power to hurt derives from its masking an archaic moment of pain such as Freud describes in the *Project*, when all screens against *Qn* break down.[243] If the obsessional pulverizes the signifier to the point of its becoming an anal-sadistic instrument that can hurt an other, the hysteric, manifesting a jouissance of a more primal, masochistic slant, is a subject who can experience the signifier as a mask of what Lacan in *Seminar 17* calls the primal mark, primal instance of a flagellation of jouissance.[244] In psychosis, for its part, the signifier can appear to the subject almost without symbolic mask, pure real cut off from the signifying chain, not only hurting but shattering, and not an other but the subject himself. In all three cases, proximity of the spoken signifier to the real is revealed to be at the root of the sadistic and masochistic faces of that form of spoken language whose performativity is characterized as insult or invective.

4 The hysteric's enunciation-thing

But it is of course not only as insult suffered or inflicted that the spoken signifier manifests as real. Montrelay delineates one other form of speech unfolding in the transference in which what originates in the unconscious representation as inscription in the flesh acquires the status of a thing outside sense whose value is real. In '*Parole de femme*,' [speech of a woman], an exemplary analysis of speech under transference in the transference neuroses, in particular hysteria, Montrelay notes that such speech manifests a particular overarching rhythm of flux and reflux, folding and unfolding. The first beat of this rhythm is those times in the cure of the hysteric in which the analysand is intensely engaged in what she knows how to do better than anyone else: to decipher the signifying chain constituting her unconscious, ever eager to unfold equivoques and exploit the polysemic potential of language while continuing not to know something about her *plus de jouir*, more often than not involving a satisfaction in dissatisfaction.

Montrelay's interest lies, however, more in the second beat of the rhythm characterizing the hysteric's speech under transference: those times in the cure when the signifying articulation of the hysteric 'resists any effort towards commentary or interpretation: it presents itself as residue of symbolic effects.'[245] At these points in the analytic cure, the signifiers articulated from the couch, though signifiers, have nothing to do with what is commonly known as the signifying articulation. Traversing the blind spots of the symbolic, Montrelay writes, these signifiers escape linguistic categorization, each one of them folding in upon itself as though frozen, as though separated by an abyss from the one that follows it. The analyst thus must consider these signifiers not as words whose sense might unfold but as 'material thing[s]' whose value is that of the object a, the object that falls as residue once the subject of the unconscious is formed.[246] Symbolic in appearance only, these signifiers are there in the session as real, emerging alongside weighty and vertiginous silences where the analysand's body exposes on the couch 'a real which it is impossible to eroticize.'[247] In effect, although the hysteric knows nothing about this, these signifiers are indistinguishable from her body, presentifying that part of her corporeality which Montrelay calls the infinite, nameless jouissance subtending the hysteric's femininity, and Lacan, who acknowledges a theoretical debt to Montrelay, would denominate the Other jouissance, beyond castration and hence beyond sense.[248]

The hysteric's speech under transference as Montrelay theorizes it, then, displays an iambic prosody which recurs, sequences of intense deciphering of the unconscious in which the subject lets herself be fascinated by the poetic power of her own words alternating with sequences where words fall from her lips as corporeal part objects. To the extent that the analyst resists the temptation to treat these objects as the signifiers they pretend to be, respecting them with the silence of the drive of which they partake, Montrelay teaches, they might acquire the function of an object cause, not only relaunching desire but relaunching it differently.[249]

But what are these objects masquerading as words if not instances where psychic writing as an irritation in the flesh turns inside out without cathexis being voided from what is emitted from it in the process of turning to speech? And is this not common to forms of speaking the written as real from the psychotic's organ-speech as described by Freud, the psychotic hallucination as described by Lacan, to the neurotic's slip of the tongue as instance of what Soler calls the real unconscious? Montrelay's theorization of the *rejeton* that closely follows the economic logic of Freudian metapsychology from the *Project* onwards suggests that in these instances the unconscious remains real, stops short of the voiding of cathexis that would enable it to emit signifiers spoken within a chain in whose links desire emerges.

And yet at least insofar as work in the field of the neuroses is concerned, what is elaborated in the sessions is a chain, perhaps more precisely a network or lattice, on which the analyst operates in his interventions, punctuations, or cuts. In other words, other than the signifiers of the real unconscious, isolated, outside a chain, drenched with anxiety and urgency, analytic work with neurosis involves traffic with unconscious signifiers voided of cathexis and susceptible of being linked or combined. It is as linked or combined that these signifiers appear in the speech of the analysand, and it is the forms of these articulated li(n)kings that teach Lacan about the linguistic structure of the unconscious.

What, in terms of the teachings of Freud and Lacan, makes it possible for the unconscious signifiers to be linked in ways that yield the formations of the unconscious – the dream, the parapraxis, the witticism, and above all, the symptom – the neurotic desciphers while traversing the transferential unconscious? What, in other words, are the metapsychological conditions of the copula that renders the unconscious an Other scene whose structure is rhetorical? These questions remain beyond the confines of this book, which has sought to delineate the specifics of an unconscious grammatology, the ways in which psychic writ(h)ings are formed in and emitted from the flesh, at times retaining the weight of the real, of a jouissance it is impossible to negativize or dialecticize. They remain the task of a metapsychological endeavour to come, the specification of the erotics of rhetorical linkings at once in the transferential unconscious and in the social bonds where it plays itself out, that I have called a psycho-rhetoric.

Notes

1   Freud, S. (1884). 'A new Histological Method for the Study of Nerve-Tracts in the Brain and Spinal Cord.' *Brain: A Journal of Neurology* 7, pp. 86–88.
2   Lacan, J. (1954–1955). *The Seminar of Jacques Lacan Book 2: The Ego in Freud's Theory and in the Technique of Psychoanalysis*, trans. S. Tomaselli, New York, Norton, 1988, p. 188.
3   Ibid., p. 261.
4   Lacan, J. (1953) 'The Function and Field of Speech and Language in Psychoanalysis,' *Écrits: The First Complete Edition in English*, trans. B. Fink et al., New York, Norton, 1988, p. 211.
5   Lacan, J. (1953–1954). *The Seminar of Jacques Lacan Book 1: Freud's Papers on Technique*, trans. J. Forrester, New York, Norton, 1991, p. 50.
6   Lacan, J. (1954–1955). *Seminar 2: The Ego in Freud's Theory and in the Technique of Psychoanalysis*, Op. cit., p. 241.
7   Ibid., p. 230.
8   Ibid., p. 160.
9   Lacan, J. (1964). *The Seminar of Jacques Lacan Book 11: The Four Fundamental Concepts of Psychoanalysis*, trans. A. Sheridan, New York, Norton, 1999, p. 34.
10 Ibid., p. 30.
11 Lacan, J. (1972–1973). *The Seminar of Jacques Lacan Book 20: Encore*, trans. B. Fink, New York, Norton, 1998, p. 59.
12 Freud, S. (1896). Letter 52 to Wilhelm Fliess, *The Standard Edition of the Complete Psychological Works of* Sigmund *Freud*, trans. J. Strachey et al., London, Vintage, 2001, 24 Vols., Vol. 1, p. 233, henceforth SE. Quotations in German are from the Gesammelte Werke, ed. A. Freud, Frankfurt, Fischer Verlag, 1999, 18 Vols., henceforth GW.
13 Lacan, J. (1976–1977). *The Seminar of Jacques Lacan Book 24: L'insu que sait de l'une-bévue s'aile à mourre*, trans. C. Gallagher from unedited typescripts, www.lacaninireland.com. The French title relies on the multilingual equivoque between '*l'insu que sait*' [French for 'the unknown that knows'] and '*unsuccess*' [failure], between '*une-bévue*' [French for 'blunder,' 'lapsus,' 'parapraxis,' and '*Unbewusste*' [German for unconscious], '*s'aile à mourre*' [French for 'flies to death'] and '*c'est l'amour,*' [French for 'is love']. The equivocal, multilingual title indexes Lacan's focus, during this period of his teaching, on the jouissance value of lalangue, and his interest in the lapsus as a phenomenon of the real unconscious.

14 Soler, C. (2009). *Lacan: The Uncoscious Reinvented*, trans. E. Faye and S. Schwartz, London, Karnac, 2014, p. 54.
15 Ibid., p. 40; Lacan makes use of this term, condensing '*mot*' [word] and 'material-ism' for the first time in the 'Geneva Lecture on the Symptom.' See Lacan, J. (1975). 'Geneva Lecture on the Symptom,' trans. R. Grigg, *Analysis* 1, 1989, p. 14.
16 Ibid., p. 44.
17 See Lacan, J. (1975–1976), *The Seminar of Jacques Lacan Book 23: The Sinthome*, trans. A.R. Price, Cambridge: Polity, 2016. In the second lesson of the seminar, which J.-A. Miller entitled 'On What Makes a Hole in the Real') (pp. 17–32), Lacan radically retheorizes the nature of the symbolic register. If in his early teaching, the symbolic is the unconscious chain of signifiers, and the real is what cannot be metabolized into an unconscious signifier because even its uncon-scious knowledge would be unbearable for the subject, in Seminar 23 the real is conceptualized as an opaque block from which the subject chisels his or her signifiers.
18 Lacan, J. (1953–1954). *Seminar 1: Freud's Papers on Technique*, Op. cit., p. 266.
19 Ibid.
20 Lacan, J. (1972–1973). *Seminar 20: Encore*, Op. cit., p. 131.
21 Cicero, M.T. *De Oratore*, trans. H. Rackham, Cambridge, MA, Harvard University Press, 1948, 2.42:179.
22 '*Impetu*' is a derivative of *petere* [to rush]; '*perturbatione*' is a derivative of *turba* or *turbo* [turmoil], whose etymological root is the Sanskrit *turāmi*, to hasten. See Charlton T. Lewis and Charles Short, A Latin Dictionary Oxford, Oxford University Press, 1879.
23 Cicero, M.T., Op. cit., 2.51:235.
24 Lacan, J. (1955–1956). *The Seminar of Jacques Lacan Book 3: The Psychoses*, trans. R. Grigg, New York, Norton, 1993, p. 219.
25 Miller, J.-A., '*Biologie lacanienne et évènement de corps*,' *La Cause freudienne* 44, 2000, pp. 5–45.
26 Lacan, J. (1962–1963). *The Seminar of Jacques Lacan Book 10: Anxiety*, trans. A.R. Price, Cambridge, Polity, p. 14.
27 Ibid.
28 Ibid., p. 15.
29 Lacan, J. (1977–1978). *The Seminar of Jacques Lacan Book 25: The Moment to Conclude*, trans. C. Gallagher from unedited typescripts, lesson of 15.11.1977, www.lacaninireland.com
30 Lacan, J. (1962–1963). *Seminar 10: Anxiety*, Op. cit., p. 15.
31 Lacan, J. (1953). 'The Function and Field of Speech and Language in Psychoanalysis,' *Écrits: The First Complete Edition in English*, trans. B. Fink et al., New York, Norton, 2002, p. 221.
32 Freud, S. (1895). *Project for a Scientific Psychology*, SE 1, p. 29, GW 18S, p. 387.
33 Ibid., GW 18S:389.
34 Ibid., pp. 299–300; GW 18S, pp. 391.
35 Ibid., p. 365; GW 18S, p. 456.
36 Freud, S. (1915). '*Das Unbewüsste*,' GW 10, p. 276. Strachey's translation of '*Triebregung*,' literally 'motion of the drive,' as 'instinctual impulse' SE 14, p.177, somewhat obscures the kinetic inflection of Freud's term.
37 Freud, S. (1915). '*Das Unbewüsste*,' GW 10, p. 276.
38 Lacan, J. *The Seminar of Jacques Lacan Book 6: Desire and its Interpretation*, trans. B. Fink, Cambridge, Polity, 2019, p. 49.
39 Ibid.

40 Montrelay, M. (1977). *L'Ombre et le nom: sur la féminité*, Paris, Minuit, my translation.
41 Freud, S. (1915). 'The Unconscious,' *SE 14*, p. 317, GW 18S, p. 411. Strachey's translation, 'removal of stimulus' misses the implication implicit in Freud's resorting to the term *'aufhebung'* upon its Hegelian connotations – that not all irritation occasioned by the *Not des Lebens* is ever removed by specific action.
42 Freud, S. (1895). *Project for a Scientific Psychology*, SE 1, pp. 295–296.
43 Ibid., p. 296.
44 Ibid., p. 305; GW 18S, p. 397, emphases mine. The German *'fortpflanzen'* has the sense not only of 'moving elsewhere' but also of 'propagating.' The masses Freud speaks of hence both move and in doing so perpetuate their motion.
45 Freud, S. (1895). *Project for a Scientific Psychology*, SE 1 pp. 297 ff., GW 18S, pp. 390 ff.
46 Freud, S. (1895). *Project for a Scientific Psychology*, SE 1, p. 318, GW 18S, p. 406.
47 Ibid.; GW 18S, p. 410.
48 Lacan, J. (1958–1959). *The Seminar of Jacques Lacan Book 7: The Ethics of Psychoanalysis*, trans. D. Porter, New York, Norton, 1997, p. 41.
49 Freud, S. (1895). *Project for a Scientific Psychology*, SE 1, p. 318; GW 18S, p. 410.
50 Strachey translates the term as 'muscular mechanisms,' see Freud (1895). *Project for a Scientific Psychology*, SE 1, p. 296, GW 18S, p. 389.
51 Ibid., p. 389; GW 18S, p. 477.
52 Ibid., p. 318; GW 18S, p. 411.
53 Ibid., p. 317; GW 18S, p. 410.
54 Ibid., p. 387.
55 Ibid., p. 314.
56 Lacan, J. (1958–1959). *Seminar 7: The Ethics of Psychoanalysis*, Op. cit., p. 42.
57 Freud, S. (1895). *Project for a Scientific Psychology*, SE 1, p. 318, GW 18S, p. 411.
58 Lacan, J. (1958–1959), *Seminar 7: The Ethics of Psychoanalysis*, Op. cit., p. 41.
59 Montrelay, M. (1981). *'Aux frontièrs de l'inconscient freudien,' Cahiers confrontation* 6, p. 27, my translation.
60 Ibid., p. 30, my translation.
61 Montrelay, M. (1982). *'Le double statut, flottant et fragmentaire, de l'inconscient,' Sciences et symbols*, ed. M. Cazenave, Paris, Albin Michel, p. 96, my translation.
62 Lacan, J. (1958–1959), *Seminar 7: The Ethics of Psychoanalysis*, Op. cit., p. 41.
63 Ibid., p. 32.
64 Ibid., pp. 32, 49.
65 Ibid., p. 49.
66 Lacan, J. (1958–1959), *Seminar 7: The Ethics of Psychoanalysis*, Op. cit., p. 48.
67 Freud, S. (1895). *Project for a Scientific Psychology*, SE 1, p. 364; GW 18S, p. 455.
68 Lacan, J. (1964). *Seminar 11: The Four Fundamental Concepts of Psychoanalysis* Op. cit., p. 156.
69 Lacan, J. (1958–1959). *Seminar 7: The Ethics of Psychoanalysis*, Op. cit., p. 32.
70 Lacan, J. (1964). *Seminar 11: The Four Fundamental Concepts of Psychoanalysis*, Op. cit., p. 156.
71 Freud, S. (1895). *Project for a Scientific Psychology*, Op. cit., SE 1, p. 366.

72 Lacan, J. (1958–1959). *Seminar 7: The Ethics of Psychoanalysis*, Op. cit., p. 47.
73 Montrelay, M. (1982). '*Le double statut*,' Op. cit., p. 99, my translation.
74 Lacan, J. (1958–1959), *Seminar 7: The Ethics of Psychoanalysis*, Op. cit., p. 49.
75 Montrelay, M. (1982). '*Le double statut*,' Op. cit., p. 99, my translation.
76 Ibid., my translation.
77 Montrelay, M. (1981). '*Aux frontièrs de l'inconscient freudien*,' Op. cit., p. 28, my translation.
78 Ibid., p. 29, my translation.
79 Lacan, J. (1956–1957). *Le séminaire de Jacques Lacan, livre 4: la relation d'objet*, Paris, Seuil, 1998, p. 348, my translation.
80 Ibid., my translation.
81 Ibid., my translation.
82 Ibid., my translation.
83 Aristotle, *Physics*, trans. R.P. Hardie and R.K. Gaye, Princeton, Princeton University Press, 1984, 8.9.256b.
84 Ibid. 8.9.265.
85 Ibid.
86 Lacan, J. (1972–1973). *Seminar 20: Encore*, Op. cit., p. 103.
87 Lacan, J. (1956–1957). *Le séminaire, livre 4: la relation d'objet*, Op. cit., p. 348, my translation.
88 Montrelay, M. (1977). *L'ombre et le nom*, Op. cit., p. 39, my translation.
89 Monterlay, M. (1981). '*Aux frontièrs de l'inconscient freudien*,' Op. cit., p. 29, my translation. See also Chapter 2C of this book.
90 Lacan, J. (1956–1957). *Le séminaire, livre 4: la relation d'objet*, Op. cit., p. 348, my translation.
91 Freud, S. (1909). *Analysis of a Phobia in a Five-Year-Old Boy*, SE 10, p. 135.
92 Ibid., p. 46; GW 7, p. 280.
93 Lacan, J. (1962–1963). *Seminar 10; Anxiety*, Op. cit., p. 174.
94 Montrelay, M. (1977). *L'Ombre et le nom*, Op. cit., p. 123, my translation.
95 Freud, S. (1938). 'Findings, Ideas, Problems,' SE 23, p. 300.
96 Ibid.
97 Freud, S. (1909). *Analysis of a Phobia in a Five-Year-Old Boy*, Op. cit., SE 10, p. 96, GW 7, p. 331.
98 Montrelay, M. (1977). *L'Ombre et le nom*, Op. cit., p. 132, my translation.
99 Freud, S. (1909). *Analysis of a Phobia in a Five-Year-Old Boy*, Op. cit., SE 10, p. 47; GW 7, p. 281.
100 Montrelay, M. (1977). *L'Ombre et le nom*, Op. cit., p. 123, my translation.
101 Lacan, J. (1956–1957). *Le séminaire, livre 4: la relation d'objet*, Op. cit., p. 363, my translation.
102 Ibid., my translation.
103 Ibid., p. 349.
104 Aristotle, *Physics*, Op. cit., 4.212a.
105 Aristotle, *Poetics*, trans. W.H. Fyfe and D.C. Innes, Cambridge, MA, Harvard University Press, 1995, 1456b; *Rhetoric*, trans. J. Freese, Cambridge, MA, Harvard University Press, 1927, 3.8.1; *On Sophistical Refutations*, trans. E.S. Forster and D.J. Furle, Cambridge, MA, Harvard University Press, 1955, 177a 20–21.
106 Aristotle, *On Sophistical Refutations*, Op. cit.,177a 20–21.
107 Ibid., 166b10.
108 Aristotle, *Metaphysics*, trans. H. Tredennick, Cambridge, MA, Harvard University Press, 1933, 4.4.1006a–1006b.

109 Aristotle, *Metaphysics*, Op. cit., 4.4.1006b.10. See also the remarks on this passage in Cassin, B. (2013). *Jacques le Sophiste: Lacan, logos et psychanalyse*, Paris, Epel, pp. 117–121.

110 Lacan, J. (1976–1977). *The Seminar of Jacques Lacan Book 24: l'insu que sait de l'une-bévue s'aile à mourre*, trans. C. Gallagher from unedited typescripts, lesson of 4 November, 1975, www.lacaninireland.com

111 Aristotle, *Rhetoric*, Op. cit., 3.2.3.

112 Lacan, J. (1972–1973). *The Seminar of Jacques Lacan Book 20: Encore*, Op. cit., p. 22.

113 Aristotle, *Sophistical Refutations*, Op. cit., 169a30.

114 Aristotle, *Rhetoric*, Op. cit., 3.5.5.

115 Lacan, J. (1957–1958). 'On a Question Preliminary to Any Possible Treatment of Psychosis, *Écrits*, *Op. cit.* p. 474.

116 Lacan, J. (1972–1973). *The Seminar of Jacques Lacan Book 20: Encore*, Op. cit., p. 103.

117 Ibid., p. 79.

118 Aristotle, *Metaphysics*, Op. cit., 4.5.1009a.20–21.

119 Cassin, B. (2012). *Jacques le sophiste*, Op. cit., p. 127, my translation.

120 Aristotle, *Poetics*, Op. cit. 1456b.

121 Ibid., 1458a.

122 See Zisser, S. (2016) 'Calliope's Sc(D)ream: Feminine Jouissance in Aristotle's Works on Language,' *The Letter: Irish Journal of Lacanian Psychoanalysis* 62, pp. 37–64.

123 Aristotle, *Rhetoric*, Op. cit., 3.1.5.

124 Aristotle, *Poetics*, Op. cit., 1450b.

125 Ibid., 1451b.

126 Aristotle, *Poetics*, Op. cit., 1447a.

127 Ibid., 1460b.

128 Aristotle, *Rhetoric*, Op. cit., 3.2.3.

129 Aristotle, *Poetics*, Op. cit., 1458a.

130 Ibid., 1450b.

131 Derrida, J. (1973). 'Plato's Pharmacy,' *Dissemination*, trans. B. Johnson, Chicago, Chicago University Press, 1981, pp. 63–171.

132 Aristotle, *Poetics*, Op. cit., 1447a.

133 Freud, S. writes: 'To begin with, sexual activity attaches itself to one of the functions serving the purpose of self-preservation and does not become independent of them until later.' That is, erogenization is mothing but the annexation of an anatomic function to the profit of pleasure. Freud, S. (1905). *Three Essays on the Theory of Sexuality*, SE 7, p. 222.

134 Aristotle, *Rhetoric*, Op. cit., 1.1.1.

135 Sherry, R. (1555). *A Treatise of Schemes and Tropes*, ed. H.W. Hildebrandt, Gainesville, Fl., Scholars' Facsimiles and Reprints, 1961, p. 21.

136 Aristotle, *Rhetoric*, Op. cit., 3.1.3.

137 Lacan, J. (1958–1959). *The Seminar of Jacques Lacan Book 6: Desire and its Interpretation*, Op. cit., p. 276.

138 See Liddle et al., (1843). *A Greek-English Lexicon*.

139 Aristotle, *Rhetoric*, Op. cit., 1.2.7.

140 Aristotle, *Poetics*, Op. cit., 1456b.

141 Lacan, J. (1953). 'The Instance of the Letter in the Unconscious or Reason Since Freud,' *Écrits*, Op. cit., p. 433.

142 Lacan, J. in his early teaching often remarks that the subject's speech in analy-
     sis displays the entire array of the figures (or schemes) and tropes theorized in
     the antiquated tradition of rhetoric. See for, instance, his comment in 'The
     Function and Field of Speech and Language' on the narration of dreams in
     the transference: 'What is important is the version of the text, and that, Freud
     tells us, is given in the telling of the dream—that is, in its rhetoric. Ellipsis and
     pleonasm, hyperbaton or syllepsis, regression, repetition, apposition—these
     are the syntactical displacements; metaphor, catachresis, antonomasia, alle-
     gory, metonymy, and synecdoche—these are the semantic condensations;
     Freud teaches us to read in them the intentions—whether ostentatious or
     demonstrative, dissimulating or persuasive, retaliatory or seductive—with
     which the subject modulates his oneiric discourse.' Lacan, J. (1953). 'The
     Function and Field of Speech and Language in Psychoanalysis,' *Écrits: The
     First Complete Edition in English*, trans. B. Fink et al., New York, Norton,
     2012, pp. 221–222. Lacan's treatment of the place of rhetoric at once in the
     mechanisms of the unconscious and in speech under transference, what I call
     'psychorhetoric,' is crucial to my concerns, but will be treated in a separate
     book to which the present one is a prelude.
143 Freud, S. (1937). 'Analysis Terminable and Interminable.' SE 23, p. 250.
     Quotations in German are from the *Gesammelte Werke*, ed. A. Freud, Frankfurt,
     Fischer Verlag, 1999, 18 Vols. Vol. 16, p. 96., henceforth GW.
144 Montrelay, M. (1977). *L'Ombre et le nom: sur la féminité*, Paris, Minuit, p. 116,
     my translation.
145 Ibid.
146 Montrelay, M. (1981). '*Aux frontièrs de l'inconscient freudien,*' *Cahiers
     Confrontation* 6, p. 29, my translation.
147 Lacan, J. (1975). 'Geneva Lecture on the Symptom,' Op. cit., p. 14.
148 Soler, C. (2014). *Lacan: The Unconscious Reinvented*, trans. S. Schwartz and
     E. Faye, London, Karnac, p. 50.
149 Montrelay, M. (1977). *L'Ombre et le nom*, Op. cit., pp. 116-117; Montrelay, M.
     (1981). 'Aux *frontiérs de l'inconscient freudienne,*' Op. cit., pp. 27–29; (1982);
     Montrelay, M. (1982). '*Le double statut, flottant et* fragmentaire, de l'inconscient,'
     Op. cit., pp. 90-92, 96, my translations.
150 Freud, S. (1915). 'Instincts and their Vicissitudes,' SE 14, pp. 109-140.
151 Montrelay, M. *L'Ombre et le nom*, Op. cit., pp. 96, 104, 106, 108, 116. See also
     '*Aux frontièrs de l'inconscient freudienne,*' Op. cit., pp. 27–29; '*Le double statut,*'
     pp. 97–101, my translations.
152 Lacan, J. (1957–1958). 'On a Question Preliminary to Any Possible Treatment of
     Psychosis, *Écrits*, Op. cit., p. 476.
153 Lacan, J. (1955–1956). *Seminar 3: The Psychoses*, Op. cit., pp. 130–143.
154 Freud, S. (1914). 'On Narcissism,' SE 14, p. 75.
155 Freud, S. (1920). *Beyond the Pleasure Principle*. SE 18, pp. 1–64.
156 Freud, S. (1924). 'The Economic Problem of Masochism.' SE 19, p. 162.
157 Freud, S. (1911). *Psycho-Analytic Notes on an Autobiographical Account of a
     Case of Paranoia (Dementia Paranoides)*, SE 12, p. 68.
158 Freud, S. (1914). 'On Narcissism,' SE 14, p. 75; GW 10, p. 140.
159 Montrelay, M. (1977). *L'Ombre et le nom*, Op. cit., p. 47, my translation.
160 Lacan, J. (1955–1956). *Seminar 3: The Psychoses*, Op. cit., p. 59,
161 Montrelay, M. (1977). *L'Ombre et le nom*, Op. cit., p. 47., my translation
162 Ibid., my translation.

163 Freud, S. (1915). 'The Unconscious,' SE 14, p. 198; GW 10, p. 296.
164 Ibid., SE 14, p. 203; GW 10, p. 301.
165 Miller, J.-A. (1988). 'Ironic Clinic,' trans. V. Voruz and B. Wolf, *Psychoanalytical Notebooks* 7, 2000, pp. 9–26.
166 Freud, S. 'The Unconscious' SE 14, p. 198; GW 10, p. 296.
167 Soler, S. (2002). *L'inconscient à ciel ouvert de la psychose*, Op. cit., pp. 116–117, my translation.
168 Lacan, J. (1957–1958) 'On a Question Prior to Any Possible Treatment of Psychosis,' *Écrits*, Op. cit., p. 446.
169 Ibid.
170 Ibid., p. 447.
171 This is Lacan's translation. See Lacan, J. (1955–1956). *The Seminar of Jacques Lacan Book 3: The Psychoses*, Op. cit., p. 12.
172 Freud, S. (1918). *From the History of an Infantile Neurosis.* SE 17, p. 79; GW 12, p. 111. Strachey renders '*Verwerfung*,' as 'rejection.'
173 Lacan, J. (1955–1956). *The Seminar of Jacques Lacan Book 3: The Psychoses*, Op. cit., p. 47.
174 Mack Brunswick, R. (1928). 'A Supplement to Freud's *From the History of an Infantile Neurosis*,' in Gardiner, M. (ed.) *The Wolf-Man by The Wolf-Man*, New York: Basic Books, 1972, pp. 286–330. In 1926, six years after the termination of his analysis with Freud, the patient known as the Wolfman (Sergei Pankejeff) returned to Freud in a state of great distress. Freud referred him to Ruth Mack Brunswick, who was then undergoing analytic formation in Vienna. Mack Brunswick describes the analysand as suffering from a 'hypochonodriacal *idée fixe*,' of a hole in his face which he would incessantly try to cover with face powder, using a women's pocket mirror (p. 287). After recounting the analysand's history between the two analyses, and constructing her own treatment of the Wolfman, Mack Brunswick concludes: 'the diagnosis of paranoia seems to me to require little evidence than that supplied by the case itself. The picture is typical of those cases known as the hypochondriacal type of paranoia' (p. 321). In retrospect, that is, the case Freud had constructed as an obsessional neurosis was in effect a minor psychosis, a clinical structure that has become increasingly ubiquitous since the end of the 1990's and that J.-A. Miller christened 'ordinary psychosis.' On ordinary psychosis, see, e.g., Miller, J.-A. (2009), 'Ordinary Psychosis Revisited,' *Psychoanalytical Notebooks* 19, pp. 137–139. For an illuminating account of the Wolfman as a case of ordinary psychosis see Grigg (2013). 'Treating the Wolf Man as a Case of Ordinary Psychosis,' *Culture/Clinic 1*, pp. 86–98.
175 Freud, S. (1918). *From the History of an Infantile Neurosis*, SE 17, p. 117.
176 Montrelay, M. (1977). *L'Ombre et le nom*, Op. cit., p. 44, my translation.
177 In *Beyond the Pleasure Principle* Freud describes primary narcissism as the state of an individual 'who retains his libido in his ego and pays none of it out in object-cathexes. Object cathexis is thus in Freud's terms a payment or '*Verausgabt*,' literally a giving out, a primordial form of symbolic exchange. Freud, S. (1920). *Beyond the Pleasure Principle*, SE 18, p. 50; GW 13, p. 53.
178 Lacan, J. (1949). 'The Mirror Stage as Formative of the *I* Function as Revealed in Psychoanalytic Experience,' *Écrits*, Op. cit., pp. 76–78.
179 Freud, S. (1925). 'Some Psychical Consequences of the Anatomical Distinction between the Sexes,' SE 19, p. 257.
180 Freud, S. (1923). 'The Infantile Genital Organization,' SE 19, p. 142.

181 Montrelay, M. *L'Ombre et le nom*, Op. cit., p. 143, my translation.
182 Ibid., p. 156, my translation.
183 Lacan, J. (1960–1961). *The Seminar of Jacques Lacan Book 8: Transference*, trans. B. Fink, Cambridge, Polity, 2015, p. 382.
184 Lacan, J. (1958). 'The Signification of the Phallus,' *Écrits*, Op. cit., p. 581.
185 Freud, S. (1923). 'The Infantile Genital Organization,' SE 19, p. 143.
186 Freud, S. (1909). Analysis of a Phobia in a Five-Year-Old Boy,' SE 10, p. 11.
187 Freud, S. (1923). 'The Infantile Genital Organization,' SE 19, p. 144.
188 Freud, S. (1924). 'The Dissolution of the Oedipus Complex,' SE 19, pp. 176, 398, author's italics.
189 One of the significations of the German *'sprung'* is 'crack.'
190 Lacan, J. (1956–1957). *Le séminaire de Jacques Lacan livre 4: la relation d'objet*, Paris, Seuil, 1994. p. 266, my translation.
191 Ibid.
192 Freud, S. (1918). *From the History of an Infantile Neurosis*, Op. cit., SE 17, p. 85; GW 12, p. 117.
193 In his seminar on *Anxiety*, Lacan discusses ancient rituals of circumcision as founding 'a certain relation to the Other,' that is to say, of the symbolic, as hinging on the loss of an object cut off from the flesh, in this instance the foreskin. Lacan, J. (1962–1963). *The Seminar of Jacques Lacan Book 10: Anxiety*, trans. A. Price, Cambridge, Polity, 2014, pp. 206–213.
194 Montrelay, M. (1977). *L'Ombre et le nom*, Op. cit., p. 67, my translation.
195 Lacan, J. (1955–1956). *Seminar 3: The Psychoses*, Op. cit., p. 49.
196 Lacan, J. (1957–1958). 'On a question Prior to Any Possible Treatment of Psychosis,' *Écrits*, Op. cit., p. 448.
197 Lacan, J. (1955–1956). *Seminar 3: The Psychoses*, Op. cit., p. 52.
198 Ibid.
199 Lacan, J. (1955–1956). *Seminar 3: The Psychoses*, Op. cit., p. 52.
200 Ibid.
201 Lacan, J. 'On a Question Prior to Any Possible Treatment of Psychosis' *Écrits*, Op. cit., p. 448.
202 On the absence of invocatory castration as subtending autism, an acute structure at the limit of the psychoses see, Maleval, J.-C. (2009). *L'autiste et sa voix* Paris: Seuil.
203 Soler, C. (2014). *Lacan: The Unconscious Reinvented*, Op. cit., p. 44.
204 Lacan, J. (1960–1961). *Seminar 8: Transference*, Op. cit., p. 246.
205 One of the significations of the prefix 'ob-,' deriving fro the Proto Indo-European root *'epi,* 'near, against,' is 'in the way of.' See *Online Etymology Dictionary*, https://www.etymonline.com/
206 Freud, S. (1912) 'The Dynamics of Transference,' SE 12, 101 GW 8, 365.
207 Lacan, J. (1953). "The Function and Field of Speech and Language in Psychoanalysis,' *Écrits*, Op. cit., p. 211.
208 Ibid., p. 213.
209 Heidegger, M. (1927). *Being and Time*, trans. J. Macquarri and E. Robinson, London, MCM Press, 1962, pp. 113–149.
210 Lacan, J. (1976–1977). *The Seminar of Jacques Lacan Book 24: L'insu que sait de l'une-bévue s'aile à mourre*. trans. C. Gallagher from unpublished typescripts, lesson of 8 March, 1977, www.lacaninireland.com
211 Lacan, J. (1953). 'The Function and Field of Speech and Language in Psychoanalysis,' *Écrits*, Op. cit., p. 213.
212 Freud, S. (1912). 'The Dynamics of Transference,' SE 12, p. 101 GW 8, p. 365.

213 See Freud, S. (1909). 'Notes Upon a Case of Obsessional Neurosis,' SE 10, pp. 151–318. For instance, Freud defines deliria as 'hybrids' between 'reasonable considerations' and 'obsessional thoughts (p. 221). While Freud does not explicitly mention psychosis in this context, the quotation marks repeatedly used to frame the word 'deliria' are ostensibly designed to distinguish the phenomenon as it occurs in obsessional neurosis from the paranoid delusion of a Schreber where 'the delusional formation' is not such a hybrid but '*an attempt at recovery, a process of reconstruction*', a phenomenon on the side of an attempt to realign with the Other and not on the side of a pathology. See Freud, S. (1911), 'Psycho-Analytic Notes on an Autobiographical Account of a Case of Paranoia (*Dementia Paranoides*),' SE 12, p. 71, italics author's. Nevertheless, the use of the same term in the theorization of obsessional neurosis and paranoid psychosis indicates Freud's notion of an affinity between these two clinical structures.

214 Lacan, J. (1960–1961). *Seminar 8: Transference*, Op. cit., p. 246.

215 Freud, S. (1937). 'Analysis Terminable and Interminable,' SE 23, p. 250; GW 16, p. 96.

216 Freud, S. (1909). 'Notes Upon a Case of Obsessional Neurosis,' SE 10, p. 265.

217 Ibid., p. 205.

218 Ibid., p. 265.

219 Lacan, J. (1960–1961). *Seminar 8: Transference*, Op. cit., p. 246.

220 Ibid., pp. 246–247.

221 Shakespeare, W. (1603). *Hamlet*, ed. H. Jenkins, London, Arden, 1984, 1.1.143.

222 Ibid., 1.1.145–147.

223 Lacan, J. (1958–1959). *The Seminar of Jacques Lacan Book 6: Desire and its Intrepretation*, trans. B. Fink, Cambridge, Polity, 2019, p. 304.

224 Freud, S. (1909). 'Notes Upon a Case of Obsessional Neurosis,' SE 10, p. 205.

225 Ibid.; GW 7, p. 126.

226 Lacan, J. (1960–1961). *Seminar 8: Transference*, Op. cit., p. 246.

227 Freud, S. (1909). 'Notes Upon a Case of Obsessional Neurosis,' SE 10, pp. 204–205.

228 Lacan, J. (1960–1961). *Seminar 8: Transference*, Op. cit., p. 246.

229 Lacan, J. (1972–1973). *Seminar 20, Encorere*, Op. cit., p. 71.

230 Lacan, J. (1960–1961). *Seminar 8: Transference*, Op. cit., p. 247.

231 Lacan, J. (1962–1963). *Seminar 10: Anxiety*, Op. cit., p. 62.

232 Peirce, C.S. (1897). 'Logic as Semiotic: The Theory of Signs,' *Philosophical Writings of Peirce*, ed. J. Buchler, New York, Dover Publications, 2011, p. 99. Peirce's division of signs is into icon, index and symbol, the latter operative according to 'a law, or regularity of the indefinite future' (p. 112). I believe that Lacan's use of Peirce extends from the clarification of the notion that as distinct from the Peircean sign as representing something for someone, the signifier represents a subject to another signifier' (e.g. Lacan, J. [1964]. 'Position of the Unconscious,' *Écrits*, Op. cit., p. 708), to an unspoken reliance on the Peircean definition of the symbol in the theorization of the symbolic as a register of signifiers operating according to laws. See Lacan, J. (1953). 'The Function and Field of Speech and Language in Psychoanalysis,' *Écrits*, Op. cit., p. 225.

233 Freud, S. (1921). *Group Psychology and the Analysis of the Ego*, SE 18, p. 107.

234 Freud, S. (1893). *Studies on Hysteria*, Op. cit., SE 3, p. 175; GW 1, p. 244.

235 Ibid., SE 3, p. 177; GW 1, p. 245.

236 Ibid. SE 3, p. 181.

237 Freud, S. (1893). *Studies on Hysteria*, Op. cit., SE 2, p. 178.

238 Freud, S. (1915). 'Observations on Transference-Love,' SE 12, pp. 157–71.

239   See Chapter 2, Section 1, of this book.
240   Freud, S. (1912). 'The Dynamics of Transference,' SE 5, p. 99.
241   Lacan, J. (1960–1961), *Seminar 8: Transference*, Op. cit., p. 377.
242   Freud, S. (1921). *Group Psychology and the Analysis of the Ego*, SE 18, p. 115.
243   Freud, S. (1895). *Project for a Scientific Psychology*, SE 1, p. 320.
244   Lacan, J. (1969–1970). *The Seminar of Jacques Lacan Book 17: The Other Side of Psychoanalysis*, trans. R. Grigg, New York, Norton, 2006, p. 49.
245   Montrelay, M. (1977). *L'Ombre et le nom*, Op. cit., p. 27, my translation.
246   Ibid., pp. 29, 33, 36 my translation.
247   Ibid., p. 34, my translation.
248   Ibid., p. 35. Lacan, J. (1972–1973). *Seminar 20: Encore*, Op. cit., 73–77.
249   Montrelay, M. (1977). *L'Ombre et le nom*, Op. cit., p. 37.

Epilogue
Chiselled from the real – The feminine signifier

Flesh is cut from the body. In Hungarian director Ildikó Enyedi's 2017 film, *Body and Soul* ['*Testről és lélekről*'], cows are cut in a slaughterhouse. Their heads are chopped off. A knife cuts through their moving flesh, parsing them into slices that later in the film, appear as objects that might have appeased: steaks offered the police officer as bribe, thin segments of salami in which the film's male protagonist fails to find comfort in the solitude of one who had shut the door on what had almost been for him love. The film's female protagonist, Maria, herself sliced from the love that almost was, chooses a pop song to give words and melody to the hurt she cannot speak but that she silently cuts into her flesh.

Flesh is cut from the body. So too in Israeli artist Michal Na'aman's version of Michelangelo's 'Creation of Adam' fresco (1508–1512), 'Goulash' (2005).

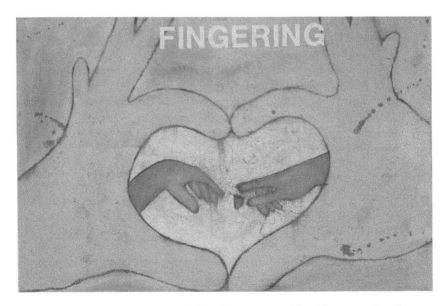

Figure 4.1 Michal Na'aman, *Goulash*, 2005. Oil on canvas, 30 x 40 cm, artist's collection.
Source: Reproduced courtesy of the artist.

DOI: 10.4324/9781003037958-5

If in the Renaissance painting the index finger at the left of the composition, almost touching the human index finger to the right, is nothing less than 'the finger of God,' originally a Biblical phrase denoting the supernatural source of an event (specifically, the punishment of lice inflicted on the ancient Egyptians),[1] in Na'aman's work, a bleeding piece of flesh falls from it. In the country whose unparalleled trochaic language Ildikó Enyedi's film speaks is a language of the flesh, it is from such pieces of flesh that the stew indicated by Na'aman's title is made.

Psychoanalysis, most of whose first principles were formulated not in the land of speaking flesh and fleshly speech that is the setting of Ildikó Enyedi's film, but in Vienna, has its own versions of flesh cut in and from the organism of the *parlêtre*, which this book has sought to delineate. For a while, Freud's formulations of these first principles ran parallel to the development, in Hungary, of a psychoanalytical '*wissenschaft*' [knowledge] which Freud characterizes as '*entfremdete*' [foreign, alien] to his own, despite geographical proximity.[2] The work in question is especially that of Sándor Ferenczi, born in Miskolc, Hungary, land of green plains, hot springs and thermal baths that Freud predicted could have become 'the analytic capital of Europe, had not political catastrophes and personal tragedy put a merciless end to these fair hopes.'[3]

The particular flavour of Hungarian psychoanalysis Freud encouraged while pointing out its strangeness with the same signifier ['*fremde*'] he had used in the *Project* to characterize the foreignness of *das Ding* to representation[4] is not the inspiration Ferenczi's idea of mutual analysis gave to theories of intersubjectivity. If at the conclusion of his letter of congratulations to Ferenczi on his fiftieth birthday, Freud states that Ferenczi 'has held back even more than he has been able to make up his mind to communicate,'[5] hinting that his most important work was still in the making, a decade later, in the obituary written following Ferenczi's premature death, he points out that project, a short book whose title, *Thalassa*, is the name of an ancient goddess of the sea, as Ferenczi's 'most brilliant and most fertile achievement' as well as 'perhaps the boldest application of psycho-analysis that was ever attempted.'[6] Freud is succinct in pointing out what he regards as the essence of the short book he characterizes as the 'summit of [Ferenczi's] achievement'[7]: the thesis according to which 'the characteristics of what is psychical preserve traces of primaeval changes in bodily substance.'[8] Freud adds: '[i]t is probable that some time in the future there will really be a "bio-analysis", as Ferenczi has prophesied,' and it will have to mark its origin in Ferenczi's book.[9]

The Hungarian title of Ferenczi's book, first published in German, is not the name of a goddess but a signifier for disaster: '*Katasztrófák a nemi müködés fejlôdésében*,' [catastrophes in the development of the genital function]. The catastrophe in question is the primeval drying up of the oceans, for our forefathers, Ferenczi writes, were nought but fish in an oceanic world where satisfaction was complete, and when the seas ran dry their organs could not breathe.

What Freud in the *Project* calls the native '*hilflosigkeit*' [helplessness] of the human being who is at first unable to satisfy his '*Not das Lebens*,' [the exigencies of life][10] is experienced, Lacan says in his return to the *Project* in *Seminar 7*, as a 'pressure, urgency... the state of emergency in life.'[11] What Lacan in 'The Mirror Stage' describes as the human being's natal 'anatomical incompleteness of the pyramidal tracts' typifying veritable specific prematurity of birth [12] are nothing but the presentification in the flesh of a moment of an archaic catastrophe of having been suddenly ejected from the comfort of piscinal existence,[13] or, as Ferenczi puts it in the Hungarian version, '*h a l i d ő k b ő l*' [existence in the days of the fish].[14] And as far as Ferenczi is concerned, it is not a specular image that would allay the distress of those who underwent the catastrophe of the drying of the oceans nor any specific action of an Other such as Freud in the *Project* points to as transforming the needs of life into an experience of satisfaction – unless this specific action be specified as genital copulation. Within psyche and soma (but in Ferenczi's own terms, as well as those of Freud, may we conceive them as distinct?), Ferenczi writes, there are preserved whole portions of buried and otherwise inaccessible history – 'much in the manner of hieroglyphic inscriptions from out of the prehistoric past.'[15] Male genitalia and its secretions are such 'portions' – living remnants in an organism that, once the complete satisfaction of oceanic existence had been lost, was forced to take on the misery of existence on land. And the insides of a woman's genitalia – are these not also such a remnant, is not their smell the smell of fish, of herring? Even physiologists, Ferenczi writes, confirm that the origin of this smell is a chemical compound (trimethylamine) produced in the decomposition of fish.[16]

Trimethylamine is the same chemical substance whose formula appears at the end of Freud's dream of Irma's injection, the inaugural dream Freud recounts and analyzes in *The Interpretation of Dreams*.[17] 'Discourse as such, independently of its meaning, since it is a senseless discourse,' Lacan says of this formula in his reading of the dream of Irma's injection in his second seminar,[18] a formula designating for Lacan, at that early phase of his teaching, the very structure of the word 'in an eminently symbolic form.'[19] But for Ferenczi, trimethylamine is not a signifier, not a component of the symbolic, not a symbol in the Peircean sense of a component of a semiotic system given as such to laws of combinatory, but an index, a sign whose materiality is identical to the materiality of what it points to.[20] In terms of Derrida's reading of the myth of the creation of writing in Plato's *Phaedrus*, trimethylamine as it features in the Ferenczian text is not hypomnestic but mnemic.[21] Not the foundation for the unconscious signifier as a mnemic trace particular to a subject but a portion of living memory that does not cease to pulsate in the body of a woman.

What this means is that the hieroglyphic writing as Ferenczi speaks of it in *Thalassa* is not at all equivalent to hieroglyphic writing as theorized by Freud, for instance in the *Interpretation of Dreams*. For Freud, the hieroglyphic writing that is the manifest thoughts of the dream is susceptible of being 'translated' in reverse into the unconscious signifiers whose rhetorical conjunction had produced them.[22] For Ferenczi, the hieroglyphic writing that manifests itself at a moment of copulation for the man who swims in the body of a woman is a 'historical monument'[23] to a satisfying piscial or piscinic existence that the catastrophe of the drying up of the oceans excised from the world.[24] What enables the moment of copulation to function as a historic monument is its being a remnant, what was once at one with what it represents.[25] The Freudian hieroglyphic is a substitutive formation resulting from processes of retranscription, condensation, displacement and other rhetorical operations.[26] The Ferenczian hieroglyphic is the smell of *h a l i d ő k b ol* as the smell of life in the body of a woman, and the male genital as a portion of flesh folded into the orifices or body of a sexual partner.[27] The topological structure of the Ferenczian hieroglyphic is identical to that of *tepertő*, the quintessential Hungarian appetizer made of a portion of chicken or duck skin folded many times into itself and fried until crisp enough to crack in the buccal orifice beyond its rim of flesh. In Ferenczi's terms, what grants an object the dignity of a hieroglyphic is not its being, like the oneiric signifier for Freud, a substitutive formation. It is its being a fragment or synecdoche, an index of sorts. As such, it has no sense and is not susceptible to operations of deciphering. Its entire essence and purpose is to embody within a body part the jouissance of the organism in its entirety in a primeval oceanic state long lost.

As we have seen throughout this book, it is not the case that for Freud, or for Lacan who reads the Freudian text *à la lettre*, unconscious representation is not intricated with the flesh. Indeed, as Freud puts it in the *Project*, unconscious representation is a consequence of the 'general irritability of the protoplasm,'[28] a procedure in which protoplasm is hollowed out and yet plagued by an excess quantum.[29] But in Freudian terms, the price of irritated, wounded or hollowed out protoplasm being metabolized into an unconscious memory trace (in Lacan's terms, a signifier) is another subtraction; the pushing out of the unconscious (but of course not out of the psychic apparatus itself) as a net of portions of resistant protoplasm altered by the passage of excitations of one such portion: the one altered by an experience of satisfaction.[30] The condition for the subsistence of psychic reality, Freud writes in 'Negation,' is that 'things should have been lost that once brought real satisfaction.'[31] Unconscious representation, that is, is predicated upon loss, and no one dramatizes this better than the hysteric, who knows how to parade the irritated and ailing portion of her organism, attesting to the portion of hollowed out protoplasm that is at its origin, and knows even better how to subtract her body *in toto* from the scene once a sexual encounter becomes imminent. As we have seen, the production of the unconscious signifier is a consequence of multiple subtractions in and from the flesh, on the micro-level of unconscious signifiers and on the macro-level of hysterical symptoms that are generated after their prototype, on condition that subtraction or discharge is not complete and a sufficient store of libido remains in the psychic apparatus so as to be able to turn to the Other in a demand for specific action.[32]

To learn more of the subtraction of a portion of flesh as a condition for the constitution of the unconscious signifier Lacan, in his tenth seminar, turns not to the hysteric but to the ancient ritual of circumcision that is the Jewish male's covenant with the word.[33] For at the moment of circumcision, the prepuce, the portion or fold of flesh cut off from the penis, is an object (phenomenal veil of the object a) given to the Other in an operation of *sym-ballain*, a throwing together resulting in the institution of a symbolic pact.[34]

Yet Ferenczi, born in Miskolc into one of the most prosperous Jewish communities that once were in the land Freud phantasized in vain would become the capital of psychoanalysis, writes of the symbol as a conjunction (indicated by the Greek prefix '*sym*' or '*syn*') that is not one that generates a social covenant, the covenant with the word that involves a subtraction of jouissance, theorized by Freud also in *Civilization and its Discontents* and *Totem and Taboo*.[35] The conjunction Ferenczi calls 'symbol' in *Thalassa* is in effect no symbol at all but a synecdoche, a conjunction that involves a reception (from Greek '*dekhestai*,' to receive) of something from a place already there. The symbol, Ferenczi writes in *Thalassa*, 'has the value of a historic monument'; it is a 'remnant of memory' to which the subject does not cease to return as *parlêtre*, speaking body.[36]

As for the prepuce, in Ferenczi's text it appears as a portion of flesh that is not lost in the institution of the covenant with the word but that when enfolded in another portion of flesh achieves the status of a remnant of the existence of an object enveloped in folds whose topological structure is precisely that underlying the Hungarian cuisine whose dishes include, aside from the folds within folds of the *tepertő*, *töltött káposzta* (ground meat enfolded in cabbage leaves), *Szilvásgombóc* (cooked fruit enfolded within cheese dumplings), *palacsinta* (large thin panckaes rolled and filled with strawberry jam or sweetened cheese). For Ferenczi, the prepuce lost after the seven days preceding circumcision in the Jewish tradition is at the same time the remnant in the body of the satisfaction that was there then, before the pools and oceans ran dry. And the folds within folds of Hungarian dishes, are they not oral objects structured to synecdochize the same piscine satisfaction?

For Ferenczi, Freud writes in his obituary for his Hungarian disciple, 'the characteristics of psychic life preserve traces of archaic alterations in physical substance.'[37] Conversely, as Nicolas Abraham puts it in the Preface to the French edition of *Thalassa*, for Ferenczi the entire organism is a language developed in the course of philogenesis. The infection of a bodily tissue or the functioning of the cardiac muscle are organic semantemes, bodily parts that bespeak ancient catastrophes of the species. Ancient catastrophes synecdochically preserved in organs and their functioning, not traces of contingent encounters that remain etched in the flesh as unconscious signifiers, nor symptomatic substitutes for such traces. For Ferenczi the organic symbol is a remnant of a catastrophic jouissance that does not cease to speak across the ages. In his obituary for Ferenczi, Freud writes that for Ferenczi symbols are witnesses ['*Zeugen*'] of what had once 'hung together,' [*Zusammenhänge*],[38] or perhaps better, been enfolded together: jouissant flesh and what envelops it. The psychic as such, Freud adds, is for Ferenczi nought but traces [*Spuren*] of an organic substance that once was.[39]

As we have seen, though, for Freud the unconscious representation is there in the first place so that the appeal to the Other to relieve the exigencies of life might be possible.[40] The appeal to the Other which is at the foundation of love and the foundation of the social bond is what makes it possible for representation to emerge out of primary narcissism, possible for the dream to emerge from the shadow. In other words, for Freud, the unconscious representation whose substrate is protoplasmic irritation is an instrument at the service of Eros, an instrument without which not only transference but existence as such would not be tolerable. For Ferenczi, representation, which is always *en-corps*, is a remnant of archaic jouissance and the catastrophe of its loss.

The *entfremdete*, the radical otherness between the Freudian and the Ferenczian theory of the symbol is thus not at all a dispute as to whether or not language is a language of the flesh, but a fundamental difference as to the function of language qua language of the flesh in its relation to the Other. Theorizing the language of the flesh as what ensures the subsistence of a store of libido which might make an appeal to the Other possible is something entirely different from theorizing the language of the flesh as a compendium of remnants of a philogenetic catastrophe supplemented by single remnants (the male organ in the act of copulation, the odour of the insides of the vagina) of the jouissance the catastrophe had cut short. Such is also the Otherness between a myth (*Totem and Taboo*) whose response to the impossible question of the origin of the human is caught up in the categories of guilt and the law, of the symbolic operation, and a myth whose informing principle, so Freud writes of *Thalassa*, is the drives upon their 'conservative'[41] nature – the tendency to conserve not the inanimate state Freud references in *Beyond the Pleasure Principle*[42] but an archaic state in which nothing operated as a limit to the drive. The Otherness, the structural difference between a myth foregrounding the birth of the symbolic out of jouissance and a myth insisting on the tendency to return to the satisfaction intrinsic to an archaic drive – is this not the difference between a myth subtending neurosis and one subtending perversion? Is it not, at the same time, the difference between a libidinal economy grounded in castration and one that gestures to castration's beyond, a psychic zone Lacan in *Encore* would name that of supplementary, feminine jouissance? Might Ferenczi's contributions to psychoanalysis, in other words, make it possible to theorize a distinctive feminine covenant with the word? A covenant coeval with what Lacan in *Seminar 20* theorizes as a woman's not-All, the singular limit she forges to the Other jouissance, proximate to primary narcissism, which ravages her, a singular limit that is thus also, in terms of *Seminar 23*, sinthomatic.

Ferenczi's Thallasal theorizations may be read as granting mythic form to the two economies Montrelay posits as at once incompatible and structuring of the feminine unconscious.[43] Montrelay speaks of a phallocentric economy, the economy of castration, that is operative in a woman's unconscious alongside a 'concentric' economy based on archaic schemas of drives that do not push forward but absorb.[44] Montrelay's work on the structure of the feminine unconscious, to which Ferenczi's formulations grant mythic resonance, alongside the late work of Lacan, suggests a possible orientation for the theorization of a woman's covenant with the word, one which it is incumbent on a woman to forge if she is to emerge from the pain of primary narcissism by something other than a scream, an appeal to the Other for succour.

In *L'ombre et le nom*, Montrelay writes of a form of cutting off from unconscious representation less absolute and irreversible than psychotic foreclosure, a form she denominates 'censorship' while distinguishing it from the censor Freud talks about in *The Interpretation of Dreams*.[45] According to Montrelay, what is censored is not what is represented as unconscious. Indeed, it is what partakes of the psychic domain peculiar to the feminine unconscious, a domain which is 'the ruin of representation,'[46] which remains 'exterritorial' to castration.[47] The phantasm having been traversed, the censored zone Montrelay speaks of is located within the desolation of the real, drenched in anxiety and a pain of existence relieved only by occasional wisps of desire that a woman proceeds to address the analyst – when she is able to speak at all. With what words? Certainly not the signifiers constituting symbolic debt, those that had emerged in the deconstructing traversal of the phantasm, along the years of the deciphering of the transferential unconscious. But the zone exterritorial to the language that is under the sway of castration, resting on a covenant with the word for which a morsel of flesh drenched in jouissance, closed off in its real satisfaction, is the stake that must be endlessly renewed, might be, for all its inexplorability noted already by Freud, the source of a singular covenant with the word which is also a singular, sintjomatic way of being woman.

The real, Lacan suggests in the 23rd seminar, on the basis of his analysis of the writing of James Joyce, is not impervious to the symbolic. An opaque block, it is nevertheless susceptible of being holed. The quotient of 'what makes a hole in the real,' in Lacan's terms, is 'the way in which language makes its purchase on the real.'[48] This is a symbolic hewn from the real, a writing different from the protoplasmic irritation indicated by Freud in the *Project* as the substrate of representation, which nevertheless makes possible for the subject the opening up of a space clear of the real that had afflicted the flesh, where the mitigating effects of desire might emerge.

Ildikó Enyedi's film suggests that something of Maria's sexuality is censored, cast as a frozen piece of meat such as those surrounding her in the slaughterhouse where she works. But this censored part is at the same time precisely what is not completely foreclosed, that is to say, in terms offered by

Freud's analysis of the Wolfman, cut from her flesh. In the film's penultimate scene, flesh is almost cut from Maria's own body, and the status of this flesh, so Laura Marling's song played in the background suggests, is the status of the 'tongue,' the organ making speech possible, the organ by means of which the subject situates himself in the field of the signifier and at the same time, the organ of osculation. For Maria, neither speech and language, nor the very possibility of being caught up in a social bond, nor the possibility of osculation, of love in body as soul for/with a man, props of a subject's existence in a social bond, can be taken for granted. She finds herself excluded from them, closer to the flesh of the cows she monitors in the slaughterhouse, or the flesh of the animals that appear in her dreams, identical to those of her fellow dreamer, flesh not seized by the signifier.

What, then, can be a woman's covenant with the word? In Ildikó Enyedi's film it is thanks to the decision to exchange self-mutilation of body/soul for love in soul/body that Maria gains a chance to live erotically, the pain of her existence as a piece of flesh mitigated by desire. This is because, neither repressing nor foreclosing, she is able, in the film's last scene, to hew from the censored territory of her psyche, from the bloc of the real, words that speak love. '*Szeretlek,*' ['I love you'] she says to Endre, the man in relation to whom she had almost failed to thaw, this failure propelling her to a passage to the act in which she cuts her flesh. Maria is metapsychologically right in turning to an operation of cutting. She is initially wrong in locating this cutting not in the silent, censored territory of her psyche but in the frozen flesh that is its manifestation. But when what is hewn from is not the frozen flesh but the censored zones of the speaking being of which sexual immobility was an effect, what emerges is a word, the Hungarian eros, that bespeaks connection. 'Eros assembles,' Montrelay writes.[49] It is the copulaic principle in human life, what brings unconscious signifiers and the bodies that carry them together. It is with words hewn from the real, the film's ending suggests, that Maria might construct a singular, sinthomatic limit that Freud, at the end of 'Analysis Terminable and Interminable,' calls the '*Ablehnung der Weibleichkeit*' [repudiation of femininity],[50] a limit to the intolerable pain of primary narcissism that is her version of what Lacan in Seminar 20 calls the not-All, singular limit to what had made her flesh frozen in a silent feminine jouissance. This subjective decision to hew in and from this silent territory that is the ruin of representation words different from those comprising the transferential unconscious, words that slash a hole in the Thing, opens up in the flesh of the soul a space, suggested by the last dream in the film, mutually dreamt by the fellow dreamers who, willing to risk, willing to pay, had become fellow lovers in flesh/soul, showing a forest clearing empty of the deer that had previously inhabited it. Such is a space in which words hewn from a psychic territory on which the phallus has no purchase might emerge and make use of the copulaic force of eros to construct an unprecedented form of love and life.

Notes

1 Exodus, 8.19.
2 Freud, S. (1914). 'On the History of the Psycho-Analytic Movement,' *The Standard Edition of the Complete Psychological Works of Sigmund Freud*, trans. J. Strachey et al., London, Vintage, 2001, 24 Vols, Vol. 14, p. 33, henceforth SE 14. Quotations in German are from the *Gesammelte Werke*, ed. A. Freud, Frankfurt, Fischer Verlag, 1999, 18 Vols. Vol. 10, p. 7, henceforth GW.
3 Freud, S. (1923). 'Dr. Sándor Ferencz'i (on his 50Th Birthday),' SE 19, p. 265.
4 Freud, S. (1895). *Project for a Scientific Psychology*, SE 1, p. 320; GW 18S, p. 414.
5 Freud, S. (1923). 'Dr. Sándor Ferenczi (on his 50th Birthday),' SE 19, p. 269.
6 Freud, S. (1933). 'Sándor Ferenczi,' SE 22, p. 228.
7 Ibid., p. 229.
8 Ibid., p. 228.
9 Ibid., pp. 228–229.
10 Freud, S. (1895). *Project for a Scientific Psychology*, SE 1, p. 321; GW 18S, p. 412.
11 Lacan, J. (1959-1960). *The Seminar of Jacques Lacan Book 7: The Ethics of Psychoanalysis*, trans. D. Porter, New York, Norton, 1997, p. 46.
12 Lacan, J. (1949). 'The Mirror Stage as Formative of the *I* Function as Revealed in Psychoanalytic Experience,' *Écrits: The First Complete Edition in English*, trans. B. Fink et al., New York, Norton, 2002, p. 78.
13 Ferenczi, S. (1924). *Thalassa: A Theory of Genitality*, trans. H.A. Bunker, London. Karnac, 1979, p. 45.
14 Ferenczi, S. (1928). *Katasztrófák a nemi működés fejlődésében*. Budapest, Filum, 1997, p. 65.
15 Ferenczi, S. (1924). *Thalassa*, Op. cit., p. 44.
16 Ibid., p. 57.
17 Freud, S. (1900). *The Interpretation of Dreams*, SE 4, p. 107.
18 Lacan, J. (1954–1955). *The Seminar of Jacques Lacan Book 2: The Ego in Freud's Theory and in the Technique of Psychoanalysis*, trans. S. Tomaselli, New York, Norton, 1988, p. 170. 'Discourse' at this period of Lacan's teaching designates the symbolic register in operation. The idea of 'discourse' as a social bond will be introduced only in Seminar 17 (1969-1970). Lacan too notes, however, with a possible echo of Ferenczi, that trimethylamine is a 'decomposition product ... of sexual substances,' *Seminar 2*, Op, cit., p. 156.
19 Ibid, p. 159.
20 Peirce, C.S. (1897). 'Logic as Semiotic: The Theory of Signs,' *Philosophical Writings of Pierce*, ed. J. Buchler, New York, Dover, 2011, pp. 102–103.
21 Derrida, J. (1969). 'Plato's Pharmacy,' *Dissemination*, trans. B. Johnson, Chicago, University of Chicago Press, 1983, p. 110. See also Section 2.1 of this book.
22 Freud, S. (1900). *The Interpretation of Dreams*, Op. cit., SE 4, p. 341.
23 Ferenczi, S. (1924). *Thalassa*, Op, cit., p. 43.
24 Ibid., p. 43.
25 Ibid., p. 22.
26 See Lacan's statement on the rhetoric of the dream work in 'The Function and Field of Speech and Language in Psychoanalysis.' After explaining that adults' dreams make use of 'the simultaneously phonetic and symbolic use of signifying elements found in the hieroglyphs of ancient Egypt and in the characters still used in China,' Lacan adds: 'What is important is the version of the text, and that, Freud tells us, is given in the telling of the dream—that is, in its rhetoric. Ellipsis and pleonasm, hyperbaton or syllepsis, regression, repetition, apposition—these are the syntactical displacements; metaphor, catachresis, antonomasia, allegory, metonymy, and synecdoche—these are the semantic condensations;

Freud teaches us to read in them the intentions—whether ostentatious or demonstrative, dissimulating or persuasive, retaliatory or seductive—with which the subject modulates his oneiric discourse.' Lacan, J. (1953) 'The Function and Field of Speech and Language in Psychoanalysis,' *Écrits*, Op, cit., p. 221–222. A discussion of rhetorical operations in the psychic apparatus and their functions, what has been called a 'psycho-rhetoric,' is beyond the scope of this book and remains a task for its sequel.

27 Ferenczi, S. (1924). *Thalassa, Op, cit., p. 28*.
28 Freud, S. (1895). *Project for a Scientific Psychology*, SE 1, p. 296.
29 See Chapter 2B of this book.
30 See Freud, S. (1895). *Project for a Scientific Psychology*, SE 1, pp. 318–319.
31 Freud, S. (1925). 'Negation,' SE 19, p. 238.
32 See Freud, S. (1895). *Project for a Scientific Psychology*, SE 1, p. 297, and Chapter 2B of this book.
33 The Hebrew signifier for circumcision, ברית מילה [*brith-mila*] also means 'a covenant with the word.'
34 See Lacan's discussion of circumcision in Lacan, J. (1962–1963). *The Seminar of Jacques Lacan Book 10: Anxiety*, trans. A. Price, Cambridge, Polity Press, 2014, pp. 206–220.
35 See Freud, S. (1913). *Totem and Taboo*, SE 13, pp. 1–161; Freud (1930). *Civilization and its Discontents*, SE 21, pp. 57–146.
36 See Lacan, J. (1972–1973). *The Seminar of Jacques Lacan Book 20: Encore*, trans. B. Fink, New York: Norton, 1998, p. 131.
37 Freud, S. (1933). 'Sándor Ferenczi,' SE 23, p. 228.
38 Ibid., p. 227; GW16, p. 268.
39 Ibid.
40 See Chapter 2D of this book.
41 Freud, S. (1933). 'Sándor Ferenczi,' SE 23, p. 228.
42 Freud, S. (1920). *Beyond the Pleasure Principle*, SE 18, pp. 38–40.
43 Montrelay, M. (1977). *L'ombre et le nom, sur la féminité*, Paris, Minuit, 1977, p. 61, my translation.
44 Ibid, p. 68, my translation.
45 Freud, S. (1900). *The Interpretation of Dreams*, SE 4, p. 506.
46 Montrelay, M. (1977). *L'Ombre et le nom*, Op. cit., p. 66, my translation.
47 Ibid., p. 72, my translation.
48 Lacan, J. (1975–1976). *The Seminar of Jacques Lacan Book 23: The Sinthome*, trans. A. Price, Cambridge, Polity, 2016, p. 21.
49 Montrelay, M. (1977). *L'Ombre et le nom*, Op. cit., p. 85, my translation.
50 Freud, S. (1937). 'Analysis Terminable and Interminable,' SE 23, p. 250; GW 16, p. 96.

Bibliography

Abraham, K. (1923). 'Contributions to the Theory of the Anal Character.' *International Journal of Psychoanalysis*, 4, pp. 400–418.

Alberti, L.B. (1464). *De statua*. Trans. J. Arkles. Raleigh, NC, Lulu.com

Aristotle, *On Memory and Reminiscence*. Trans. J.I. Beare. Adelaide, The University of Adelaide Press, 2005.

Aristotle, *Metaphysics*. Trans. Hugh Tredennick. Cambridge, MA, Harvard University Press, 1933.

Aristotle, *Physics*. Trans. R.P. Hardie and R.K. Gaye. Princeton, NJ, Princeton University Press, 1984.

Aristotle, *Poetics*. Trans. W.H. Fyfe and D.C. Innes. Cambridge, MA, Harvard University Press, 1995.

Aristotle. *Rhetoric*. Trans. J. Freese. Cambridge, MA, Harvard University Press, 1927.

Aristotle, *Sophistical Refutations*. Trans. E.S. Forster and D.J. Furle. Cambridge, MA, Harvard University Press, 1955.

Biberman, E. and Zisser, S. (2018). *Art, Death and Lacanian Psychoanalysis*. London, Routledge.

Biberman, E. (2021). *Weaving a Painting: Israeli Art and Lacan's Late Teaching*. Jerusalem, Magnes Press, forthcoming. In Hebrew.

Cappella, M. (410–439). *De nuptiis Philologiae et Mercurii*. Ed. A. Dick. Leipzig, 1925.

Cassin, B. (2013). *Jacques le Sophiste: Lacan, logos et psychanalyse*. Paris, Epel.

Cicero, M.T. *De Oratore*. Trans. H. Rackham. Cambridge, MA, 1948.

Cole, M. (2007). 'Bernini Struts.' *Projecting Identities: The Power of Material Culture*. Ed. J. Sofaer Derevenski. London, Blackwell, pp. 55–66.

da Vinci, L. (c. 1540). *A Treatise on Painting*. Trans. J.F. Rigaud. London, J. Taylor, 1802.

de Man, P. (1984). 'Autobiography as De-Facement.' *The Rhetoric of Romanticism*. New York, Columbia University Press, pp. 67–81.

de Saussure, F. (1916). *Course in General Linguistics*. Trans. W. Baskin. New York, Columbia University Press, 2011.

Derrida, J. (1967a). *Of Grammatology*. Trans. G.C. Spivak. Baltimore, The Johns Hopkins University Press, 1974.

Derrida, J. (1967b). 'Freud and the Scene of Writing.' In *Writing and Difference*. Trans. A. Bass. Chicago, Chicago University Press, 1983, pp. 196–231.

Derrida, J. (1969). 'Plato's Pharmacy.' *Dissemination*. Trans. B. Johnson. Chicago, University of Chicago Press, 1981, pp. 61–171.

Derrida, J. (1972). *Margins of Philosophy*. Trans. A. Bass. Chicago, University of Chicago Press, 1984.

Erasmus, D. (1513). *On Copia of Words and Ideas*. Trans. D.B. King and H.B. Rix. Milwaukee, WI, Marquette University Press, 1999.

Fenner, D. (1584). *The Arts of Logike and rhetorike*. Middleburgh (unpaginated).

Ferenczi, S. (1924). *Thalassa: A Theory of Genitality*. Trans. H.A. Bunker. London, Karnac, 1979.

Ferenczi, S. (1928). *Katasztrófák a nemi működés fejlődésében*. Budapest, Filum, 1997.

Fraunce, A. (1588). *The Arcadian Rhetorike*. Oxford, Blackwell, 1950.

Freud, S. (1962). *Briefe an Wilhelm Fliess, 1887u–1904*. Frankfurt, Fischer Verlag.

Freud, S. (2001). *The Standard Edition of the Complete Psychological Work of Sigmund Freud*. Trans. J. Strachey et al. London, Vintage, 24 Vols. Henceforth SE.

Freud, S. *Gesammelte Werke*. Ed. A. Freud. Frankfurt, Fischer Verlag, 1999, 18 Vols. Henceforth GW.

Freud, S. (1884). 'A New Histological Method for the Study of Nerve-Tracts in the Brain and Spinal Cord.' *Brain: A Journal of Neurology*. Vol. 7, pp. 86–88.

Freud, S. (1893). *Studies on Hysteria. SE* 3, 1–305.

Freud, S. (1895). *Project for a Scientific Psychology. SE* 1, pp. 281–391.

Freud, S. (1900). *The Interpretation of Dreams. SE* 4, pp. ix–627.

Freud, S. (1901). 'Fragment of an Analysis of a Case of Hysteria,' 7, pp. 1–122.

Freud, S. (1904). 'On Psychotherapy.' *SE* 7, pp. 255–268.

Freud, S. (1905). *Three Essays on the Theory of Sexuality. SE* 7, pp. 123–246.

Freud, S. (1908). 'Character and Anal Erotism.' *SE* 9, pp. 167–176.

Freud, S. (1909a). *Analysis of a Phobia in a Five-Year-Old Boy. SE* 10, pp. 1–150.

Freud, S. (1909b). *Notes Upon a Case of Obsessional Neurosis. SE* 10, pp. 151–318.

Freud, S. (1911). 'Psycho-Analytic Notes on an Autobiographical Account of a Case of Paranoia (*Dementia Paranoides*).' *SE* 12, pp. 1–82.

Freud, S. (1912). 'The Dynamics of Transference.' *SE* 12, pp. 97–108.

Freud, S. (1914a). 'On the History of the Psycho-Analytic Movement.' *SE* 14, pp. 1–66.

Freud, S. (1914b). 'On Narcissism: An Introduction.' *SE* 14, pp. 67–102.

Freud, S. (1915a). 'Instincts and their Vicissitudes.' *SE* 14, pp. 109–140.

Freud, S. (1915b). 'Observations on Transference-Love.' *SE* 12, pp. 157–171.

Freud, S. (1915c). 'The Unconscious.' *SE* 14, pp. 159–215.

Freud, S. (1916a). 'Some Character Types Met with in Psychoanalytic Work.' *SE* 14, pp. 309–333.

Freud, S. (1916b). 'Psychopathic Characters on the Stage.' *SE* 7, pp. 303–310.

Freud, S. (1917a). 'The Paths to the Formation of Symptoms.' *Introductory Lectures on Psychoanalysis*, Lecture 23, *SE* 16, pp. 358–371.

Freud, S. (1917b). 'On Transformations of Instinct as Exemplified in Anal Erotism.' *SE* 17, pp. 125–134.

Freud, S. (1918). *From the History of an Infantile Neurosis. SE* 17, pp. 1–124.

Freud, S. (1920). *Beyond the Pleasure Principle. SE* 18, pp. 1–64.

Freud, S. (1921). *Group Psychology and the Analysis of the Ego. SE* 18, pp. 65–144.

Freud, S. (1922). 'Medusa's Head.' *SE* 18, pp. 273–274.

Freud, S. (1923a). 'The Infantile Genital Organization (An Interpolation into the Theory of Sexuality).' *SE* 19, pp. 139–146.

Freud, S. (1923b). *The Ego and the Id. SE* 19, pp. 1–66.

Freud, S. (1924a). 'The Dissolution of the Oedipus Complex.' *SE* 19, pp. 171–180.

Freud, S. (1924b). 'The Economic Problem of Masochism.' *SE* 19, pp. 155–170.

Freud, S. (1925a). 'A Note Upon the Mystic Writing Pad.' *SE* 19, pp. 225–232.

Freud, S. (1923c). 'Dr. Sándor Ferenczi (on his 50th Birthday).' *SE* 19, pp. 265–270.

Freud, S. (1925b). 'Negation.' *SE* 19, pp. 233–240.

Freud, S. (1925c). 'Some Psychical Consequences of the Anatomical Distinction between the Sexes.' *SE* 19, pp. 241–258.

Freud, S. (1926). *Inhibitions, Symptoms and Anxiety*. SE 20, pp. 75–176.

Freud, S. (1931). 'Female Sexuality.' *SE* 21, pp. 221–244.

Freud, S. (1933a). 'Femininity.' *New Introductory Lectures in Psychoanalysis*, Lecture 33. SE 22, pp. 112–135.

Freud, S. (1933b). 'Sandor Ferenczi.' *SE* 22, pp. 225–230.

Freud, S. (1937). 'Analysis Terminable and Interminable.' *SE* 23, pp. 209–254.

Freud, S. (1938a). *An Outline of Psychoanalysis*. SE 23, pp. 139–208.

Freud, S. (1938b). 'Findings, Ideas, Problems.' *SE* 23, pp. 299–300.

Gerstenhaber, T. (2021). *'The Shadow of a White Rose in a Mirror of Silver': The Vicissitudes of the Fetish in the Writings of Oscar Wilde*. PhD Dissertation, Tel Aviv University.

Gault, J.-L. (2017a). *'Le symptôme et la langue chinoise,'* seminar given before the GIEP-NLS (The Israeli Society of the New Lacanian School, Tel Aviv May 2017.

Gault, J.-L. (2017b). *'La conception lacanienne de la langue et de l'écriture,'* seminar given before the GIEP-NLS (The Israeli Society of the New Lacanian School, Tel Aviv, May 2017.

Grigg, R. (2008). *Lacan, Language, and Philosophy*. Albany, NY, SUNY Press.

Grigg, R. (2013). 'Treating the Wolf Man as a Case of Ordinary Psychosis,' *Culture/Clinic* 1, pp. 86–98.

Heidegger, M. (1927). *Being and Time*. Trans. J. Macquarrie and E. Robinson. London, MCM Press, 1962.

Hegel, G.W.F. (1835). *Aesthetics: Lectures on Fine Art*. Trans. T.M. Knox. Oxford, Clarendon Press, 1988.

Hobbes, T. (1637). *The Art of Rhetorike, The Collected Works of Thomas Hobbes*, London, Delphi, 2019.

Jakobson, R. (1935). 'The Dominant,' *Language in Literature*. Ed. K. Pomorska and S. Rudy. Cambridge, MA, Belknap Press, 1987, pp. 41–44.

Jakobson, R. (1949). 'The Phonemic and Grammatical Aspects of Language in their Interrelations.' *Word and Language: Selected Writings*. Berlin: Walter de Gruyter, 1971, pp. 103–111.

Jones, E. (1918). 'Anal-Erotic Character Traits.' *Journal of Abnormal Psychology* 13, pp. 261–284.

Jung, C.G. (1921). *Psychological Types. Collected Works*. Trans. R.F.C. Hull. Princeton, NJ, Princeton University Press, Vol. 6.

Kant, E. (1790). *The Critique of Judgment*. Trans. J.H. Bernard. London, Macmillan, 1914.

Lacan, J. *Écrits: The First Complete Edition in English*. Trans. B. Fink et al. New York, Norton, 2002.

Lacan, J. (1948). 'Aggressiveness in Psychoanalysis.' In *Écrits: The First Complete Edition in English*. Trans. B. Fink et al. New York, Norton, 2002, pp. 82–101.

Lacan, J. (1949). 'The Mirror Stage as formative of the *I* Function.' In *Écrits: The First Complete Edition in English*. Trans. B. Fink et al. New York, Norton, 2002, pp. 75–81.

Lacan, J. (1953). 'The Function and Field of Speech and Language in Psychoanalysis.' In *Écrits: The First Complete Edition in English*. Trans. B. Fink et al. New York, Norton, 2002, pp. 197–268.

Lacan, J. (1953–1954). *The Seminar of Jacques Lacan Book 1: Freud's Papers on Technique*. Trans. J. Forrester. New York, Norton, 1991.

Lacan, J. (1954a). 'Introduction to Jean Hyppolite's Commentary on Freud's "*Verneinung*."' In *Écrits: The First Complete Edition in English*. Trans. B. Fink et al. New York, Norton, 2002, pp. 318–333.

Lacan, J. (1954b). 'Variations on the Standard Treatment.' In *Écrits: The First Complete Edition in English*. Trans. B. Fink et al. New York, Norton, 2002, pp. 269–302.

Lacan, J. (1954–1955). *The Seminar of Jacques Lacan Book 2: The Ego in Freud's Theory and in the Technique of Psychoanalysis*. Trans. S. Tomaselli. New York: Norton, 1988.

Lacan, J. (1955–1956). *The Seminar of Jacques Lacan Book 3: The Psychoses*. Trans. R. Grigg. New York, Norton, 1993.

Lacan, J. (1955a). 'Variations on the Standard Treatment.' In *Écrits: The First Complete Edition in English*. Trans. B. Fink et al. New York, Norton, 2002, pp. 269–302.

Lacan, J. (1955b). 'The Freudian Thing, or the Meaning of the Return to Freud in Psychoanalysis.' In *Écrits: The First Complete Edition in English*. Trans. B. Fink et al. New York, Norton, 2002, pp. 334–344.

Lacan, J. (1956a). 'Seminar on the Purloined Letter.' In *Écrits: The First Complete Edition in English*. Trans. B. Fink et al. New York, Norton, 2002, pp. 6–50.

Lacan, J. (1956b). 'The Situation of Psychoanalysis and the Training of Analysts in 1956.' In *Écrtts: The First Complete Edition in English*. Trans. B. Fink et al. New York, Norton, 2002, pp. 384–411.

Lacan, J. (1956–1957). *Le Séminaire de Jacques Lacan livre 4: La relation d'objet*. Paris, Seuil, 1994.

Lacan, J. (1957a). 'Psychoanalysis and its Teaching.' In *Écrits: The First Complete Edition in English*. Trans. B. Fink et al. New York, Norton, 2002, pp. 364–383.

Lacan, J. (1957b). 'The Instance of the Letter in the Unconscious or Reason Since Freud.' In *Écrits: The First Complete Edition in English*. Trans. B. Fink et al. New York, Norton, 2002, pp. 412–444.

Lacan, J. (1957–1958). *The Seminar of Jacques Lacan Book 5: The Formations of the Unconscious*. Trans. R. Grigg. Cambridge, Polity, 2017.

Lacan, J. (1958a). 'On a Question Preliminary to Any Possible Treatment of Psychosis.' In *Écrits: The First Complete Edition in English*. Trans. B. Fink et al. New York, Norton, 2002, pp. 455–488.

Lacan, J. (1958b). 'The Signification of the Phallus.' In *Écrits: The First Complete Edition in English*. Trans. B. Fink et al. New York, Norton, 2002, pp. 575–584.

Lacan, J. (1958c). 'The Youth of Gide or the Letter and Desire.' In *Écrits: The First Complete Edition in English*. Trans. B. Fink et al. New York, Norton, 2002, pp. 623–644.

Lacan, J. (1958d). 'The Direction of the Treatment and the Principles of its Power.' In *Écrits: The First Complete Edition in English*. Trans. B. Fink et al. New York, Norton, 2002, pp. 489–542.

Lacan, J. (1958–1959). *The Seminar of Jacques Lacan Book 6: Desire and its Interpretation*. Trans. B. Fink. Cambridge, Polity, 2019.

Lacan, J. (1959). 'In Memory of Ernest Jones: His Theory of Symbolism.' In *Écrits: The First Complete Edition in English*. Trans. B. Fink et al. New York, Norton, 2002, pp. 585–601.

Lacan, J. (1959–1960). *The Seminar of Jacques Lacan Book 7: The Ethics of Psychoanalysis*. Trans. D. Porter. New York, Norton, 1992.

Lacan, J. (1960). 'The Subversion of the Subject and the Dialectic of Desire in the Freudian Unconscious.' In *Écrits: The First Complete Edition in English*. Trans. B. Fink et al. New York, Norton, 2002, pp. 671–702.

Lacan, J. (1960–1961). *The Seminar of Jacques Lacan Book 8: Transference*. Trans. B. Fink. Cambridge, Polity, 2015.

Lacan, J. (1961–1962). *The Seminar of Jacques Lacan Book 9: Identification*. Trans. C. Gallagher from unedited typescripts. www.lacaninireland.com

Lacan, J. (1962–1963). *The Seminar of Jacques Lacan Book 10: Anxiety*. Trans. A.R. Price. Cambridge, Polity, 2014.

Lacan, J. (1964a). *The Seminar of Jacques Lacan. Book 11: The Four Fundamental Concepts of Psychoanalysis*. Trans. A. Sheridan. New York. Norton, 1999.

Lacan, J. (1964b). 'The Position of the Unconscious.' In *Écrits: The First Complete Edition in English*. Trans. B. Fink et al., New York, Norton, 2002, pp. 703–721.

Lacan, J. (1964–1965). *The Seminar of Jacques Lacan Book 12: Crucial Problems for Psychoanalysis*. Trans. C. Gallagher from unedited typescripts. www.lacaninireland.com

Lacan, J. (1966–1967). *The Seminar of Jacques Lacan Book 14: The Logic of Phantasy*. Trans. C. Gallagher from unedited typescripts. www.lacaninireland.com

Lacan, J. (1968–1969). *The Seminar of Jacques Lacan Book 16: From the Other to the other*. Trans. C. Gallagher from unedited typescripts. www.lacaninireland.com

Lacan, J. (1969–1970). *The Seminar of Jacques Lacan Book 17: The Other Side of Psychoanalysis*. Trans. R. Grigg. New York, Norton, 2007.

Lacan, J. (1970–1971). *The Seminar of Jacques Lacan Book 18: On a Discourse that Might not be a Semblance*. Trans. C. Gallagher from unedited typescripts. www.lacaninireland.com

Lacan, J. (1970–1971). '*Lituraterre.' The Seminar of Jacques Lacan Book 18: On a Discourse that might not be a Semblance*, Trans. C. Gallagher from unedited typescripts. www.lacaninireland.com, lesson of 12 May, 1971.

Lacan, J. (1971–1972). *Talking to Brick Walls: A Series of Presentations in the Chapel at Sainte-Anne Hospital*. Trans. A. R. Price. Cambridge, Polity, 2019.

Lacan, J. (1971–1972). *The Seminar of Jacques Lacan Book 19: ....Or Worse*. Trans. A. R. Price. Cambridge, Polity, 2018.

Lacan, J. (1972–1973). *The Seminar of Jacques Lacan Book 20: Encore*. Trans. B. Fink. New York, Norton, 1998.

Lacan, J. (1975a). 'Conférence à Genève sur le symptôme.' *La cause du désir* 95, 2007, pp. 7–24,

Lacan, J. (1975b). 'Geneva Lecture on the Symptom.' Trans. R. Grigg, *Analysis* 1, 1989, pp. 1–24.

Lacan, J. (1975–1976). *The Seminar of Jacques Lacan Book 23: The Sinthome*. Trans. A.R. Price. Cambridge, Polity, 2016.

Lacan, J. (1976–1977). *The Seminar of Jacques Lacan Book 24: l'insu que sait de l'une-bevue s'aile a mourre*. Trans. C. Gallagher from unedited typescripts.www.lacaninireland.com

Lacan, J. (1977–1978). *The Seminar of Jacques Lacan Book 25: The Moment to Conclude.* Trans. C. Gallagher from unedited typescripts. www.lacaninireland.com

Leenhardt, M. (1947). *Do Kamo: Person and Myth in the Melanesian World.* Trans. B.M. Gulati. Chicago, University of Chicago Press, 1979.

Lévi-Strauss, C. (1955). 'The Structural Study of Myth.' *The Journal of American Folklore*, 68.270, pp. 428–444.

Lewis, C.T. and Short, C. (1879). *A Latin Dictionary*, Oxford, Oxford University Press.

Liddell, G., Scott, R. and Jones, H.S. (1843). *A Greek-English Lexicon.* Oxford, Oxford University Press

Mack Brunswick, R. (1928). 'A Supplement to Freud's *From the History of an Infantile Neurosis*,' in *The Wolf-Man by The Wolf-Man*. Ed. M. Gardiner. New York, Basic Books, 1972, pp. 286–330.

Maleval, J.C. (2009). *L'autiste et sa voix*. Paris, Seuil.

Miller, J.-A. (1966). 'Suture: Elements of the Logic of the Signifier.' Trans. J. Rose. *Screen* 18, 1978, pp. 24–34.

Miller, J.-A. (1995–1996). *La fuite du sens*. Course in the Department of Psychoanalysis, University of Paris 8. http://jonathanleroy.be/2016/02/orientation-lacanienne-jacques-alain-miller/

Miller, J.-A. (1998–1999). *L'experience du reel dans la cure psychanalytique*. Course in the Department of Psychoanalysis, University of Paris 8. http://jonathanleroy.b.e/wp-content/uploads/2016/02/1998-1999-Le-reel-dans-l-experience-psycha-nalytique-JA-Miller.pdf

Miller, J.-A. (1988). 'Ironic Clinic.' Trans. V. Voruz and B. Wolf. *Psychoanalytical Notebooks* 7, 2000, pp. 9–26.

Miller, J.-A. (1995–1996). *La fuite du sens*, Course in the Department of Psychoanalysis, University of Paris 8. http://jonathanleroy.be/wp-content/uploads/2016/02/1995-1996-La-fuite-du-sens-JA-Miller.pdf

Miller, J.-A. (1999a). 'Six Paradigms of Jouissance.' Trans. J. Jauregui. *Lacanian Ink* 17, 2000, pp. 8–47.

Miller, J.-A. (1999b). 'Interpretation in Reverse.' Trans. V. Voruz and B. Wolf. *Psychoanalytical Notebooks* 2, pp. 9–16.

Miller, J.-A. (2000). '*Biologie lacanienne et évènement de corps*.' *La Cause freudienne* 44, pp. 5–45.

Miller, J.-A. (2004). 'A Fantasy.' Trans. R. Warshavsky. *Lacanian Praxis, International Quarterly of Applied Psychoanalysis*, 1, pp. 6–17.

Miller, J.-A. (2009). 'Ordinary Psychosis Revisited.' *Psychoanalytical Notebooks* 19, pp. 137–139.

Miller, J.-A. (2012). 'Reading a Symptom.' http://ampblog2006.blogspot.com/2011/06/nls-messager-24-20112012-towards-tel.html

Montrelay, M. (1977). *L'Ombre et le nom: sur la féminité*, Paris, Minuit.

Montrelay, M. (1981a). '*Aux frontièrs de l'inconscient freudienne*.' *Cahiers Confrontation* 6, pp. 23–32.

Montrelay, M. (1981b). '*L'appareillage*.' *Cahiers Confrontation* 6, pp. 33–43.

Montrelay, M. (1982). '*Le double statut, flottant et fragmentaire, de l'inconscient*,' *Sciences et symbols: Les voies de la connaissance*. Ed. M. Cazenave. Paris, Albin Michel, pp. 85–101.

Online Etymology Dictionary, n.d. https://www.etymonline.com/

Overbury, T. (1615). *Overburian Characters*. Ed. J. Hall. London, Routledge, 1924.

Parker, P. (1987). *Literary Fat Ladies: Rhetoric, Gender, Property*. London, Methuen.

Peacham, H. (1593). *The Garden of Eloquence*. Gainesville, FL, Scholars' Facsimiles and Reprints, 1983.

Peirce, C.S. (1897). 'Logic as Semiotic: The Theory of Signs.' *Philosophical Writings of Peirce*. Ed. J. Buchler. New York, Dover Publications, 2011, pp. 98–119.

Plato, *Phaedrus*. Trans. C.E. Jones and W. Preddy. Cambridge, MA, Harvard University Press, 2019.

Plato, *Protagoras*. Trans. W.R.M. Lamb. Cambridge, MA, Harvard University Press, 1924.

Plato, *Theaetetus*. Trans. H.N. Fowler. Cambridge, MA, Harvard University Press, 1921.

Quintilian, *Institutio Oratoria*. Trans. H.E. Butler. Cambridge, MA, Harvard University Press, 2002.

Reich, W. (1933). *Character Analysis*, Trans. V. Carfagno. New York, Farrar, Straus and Giroux, 1980.

Shakespeare, W. (c. 1592). *The Taming of the Shrew*. Ed. B. Hodgdon. London, Arden, 2010.

Shakespeare, W. (1593). *Richard III*. Ed. J. Semion. London, Arden, 2009.

Shakespeare, W. (1599a), *Henry V*. Ed. T.W. Craik. London, Arden, 1995.

Shakespeare, W. (1599b). *As You Like It*. Ed. Juliet Dunsiberre. London, Arden, 2006.

Shakespeare, W. (1600). *The Merchant of Venice*. Ed. J. Drakakis. London, Arden, 2001.

Shakespeare, W. (1601). *Hamlet*. Ed. H. Jenkins, London, Arden, 1982.

Shakespeare, W. (1605). *Timon of Athens*. Eds. A.B. Dawson and G.E. Minton, London, Arden, 2008.

Sherry, R. (1550). *Treatise of Schemes and Tropes*. Ed. H.W. Hildebrant. Gainesville, FL, Scholars' Facsimiles and Reprints, 1961.

Soler, C. (2002). *L'inconscient à ciel ouvert de la psychose*. Presses Universitaires de Mirail.

Soler, C. (2009). *Lacan: The Unconscious Reinvented*. Trans. E. Faye and S. Schwartz. London, Karnac, 2014,

Stoichita, V. (1997). *The Self-Aware Image: An Insight into Early Modern Painting*. Cambridge, Cambridge University Press.

Wilson, T. (1553), *The Arte of Rhetorique*. Ed. P.E. Medine. Philadelphia, PA, Pennsylvania State University Press, 1993.

Yates, F. (1956). *The Art of Memory*. New York, Random House.

Zisser, S. (2001). *The Risks of Simile in Renaissance Rhetoric*. New York, Lang, New Studies in Aesthetics.

Zisser, S. (2016) 'Calliope's Sc(D)ream: Feminine Jouissance in Aristotle's Works on Language.' *The Letter: Irish Journal of Lacanian Psychoanalysis*, 62, pp. 37–64.

Index